CAMPING guide to VICTORIA

Craig Lewis and Cathy Savage

BOILING BILLY
PUBLICATIONS

WOODSLANE

www.boilingbilly.com.au

A Boiling Billy Publication under license to Woodslane Press.
An imprint of Woodslane Pty Ltd
Unit 7/5 Vuko Place
Warriewood NSW 2102 Australia
Email: info@woodslane.com.au
Tel: 02 9970 5111 Fax: 02 9970 5002
www.woodslane.com.au

Concept
Boiling Billy Publications Pty Ltd
Printed for the publisher by
Bookbuilders, China
This fully revised 4th edition 2009

ISBN 9781921203671

Design/Layout: Erica McIntyre
Cartography: Tony Fakira

National Library of Australia Cataloguing-in-Publication entry
Author: Savage, Cathy.
Title: Camping guide to Victoria / Cathy Savage, Craig Lewis.
Edition: 4th ed.
ISBN: 9781921203671 (pbk.)
Notes: Includes index.
Subjects: Camping--Victoria--Directories.
                Camp sites, facilities, etc.--Victoria--Directories.
                National parks and reserves--Victoria--Directories.
                Other Authors/Contributors:
                Lewis, Craig (Craig William), 1966-
Dewey Number: 796.5409945

Your Help Please

Boiling Billy Publications welcomes feedback from readers. If you find things are different than what is stated in this guide, or you know of a suitable campsite that we can update in subsequent editions, then please write or e-mail us at

Boiling Billy Publications
Locked Bag 1 Wyndham NSW 2550
Tel: 02 6494 2727
E-mail: info@boilingbilly.com.au
Web: www.boilingbilly.com.au

ABOUT the authors

Craig Lewis and Cathy Savage established Boiling Billy Publications in 1995 to write and publish accurate and up-to-date guidebooks for people who love travelling and exploring Australia's great outdoors.

They have travelled extensively throughout Australia over the last 15 years on writing assignments, including an 18-month, 100,000km 4WD odyssey, visiting some of the very best outdoor destinations on offer across this vast country.

As part of their extensive field research schedule, the pair generally camp out around 100 nights each year.

When not on the road travelling they throw down their swag on their secluded farm in the New South Wales high country.

Craig and Cathy's website is at www.boilingbilly.com.au

Contents

Regional Map of Victoria

MAP REGIONS

- Close to Melbourne **18-54**
- Otways and South-West **55-87**
- Goldfields and Grampians **88-113**
- Mallee **114-137**
- Central Murray **138-182**
- East Gippsland **183-202**
- Gippsland **203-230**
- High Country **231-291**

REGIONAL MAPS LEGEND

Geelong ○   Town Major

Clunes ○   Town Medium

Talbot ●   Town Minor

Cobb Highway   Road Name

Freeway

Principal Road

Secondary Road

Railway

River

State Border

Waterbody

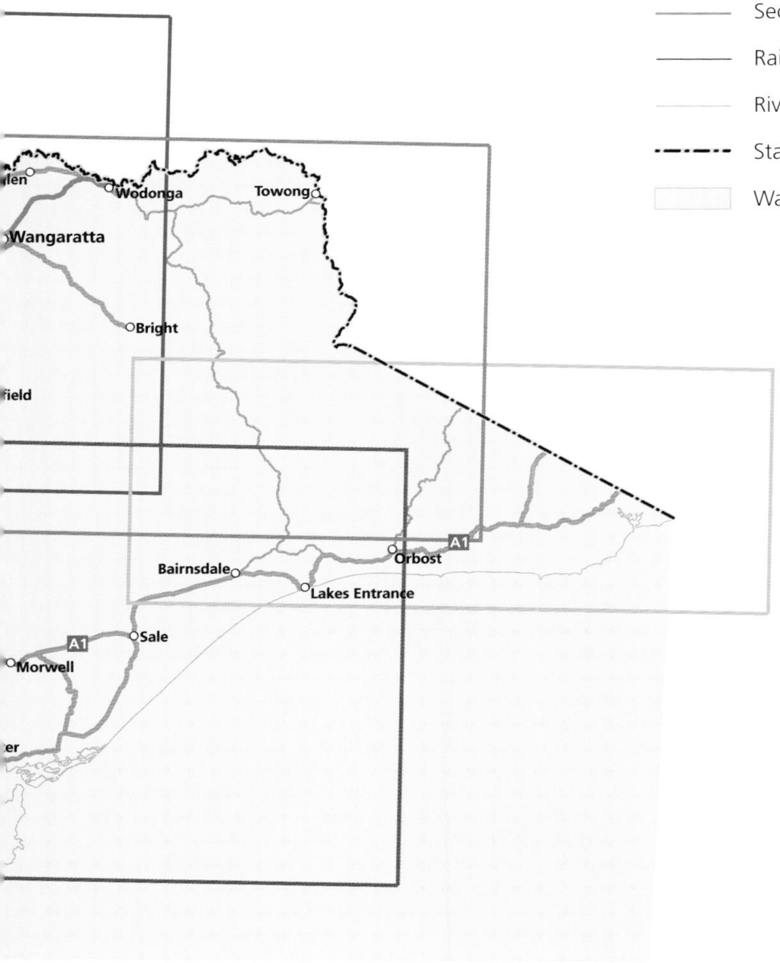

len

Wodonga   Towong

Wangaratta

Bright

field

Bairnsdale   Orbost **A1**

Lakes Entrance

Sale

A1 Morwell

er

How to use this Guide

Camping Guide to Victoria is designed in an easy-to-use format that makes finding that perfect campsite simple. The guide has been broken into different chapters covering the major tourism regions throughout Victoria.

In this book, each park, forest or reserve throughout the state that allows camping has its own entry. You can locate their approximate positions on the regional maps at the beginning of each chapter. These maps provide an overview of the region covered in the chapter and provide a starting reference point. There are also a number of more detailed maps for some of the national parks, forests and reserves throughout the guide. The grey boxes on the regional maps at the start of each region show the area covered by these maps in that region.

Each entry, whether it be a national park, forest reserve or riverside area, has detailed information relating to that site including access details, map references (MR) and some include GPS coordinates. These map references refer to the Touring Maps section and are useful for locating the campsite. For example, MR: Map 8 D6 refers to Touring Map 8 and the grid reference is D6 – this is the location of Blanket Bay camping area in Great Otway National Park.

We use symbols to detail the facilities and activities at each site.

We also include Further Information boxes for the authority to contact for making enquiries or bookings, along with prices and other details that apply to the camping site.

Although all care has been taken when compiling this guide and it is correct at the time of going to print, note that conditions at campsites are constantly changing, camping fees may rise or be introduced to previously free areas. Some areas may also be closed from time-to-time – fire and flood, for example, can have a marked affect on an area literally overnight.

Note for GPS Users

A substantial number of campsites in this guide have coordinates (latitude and longitude) which can be utilized by those with GPS receivers as an additional means of navigating to the campsite. The coordinates were acquired during field research using GDA 94 map datum and are in HDDD MM.MMM format.

Remember

After you have chosen your campsite we strongly recommend that you contact the park, forest or reserve office prior to your departure to obtain advice on current and upcoming conditions. Be aware that some sites may require advance bookings, especially during the popular holiday periods over Christmas/New Year and Easter. Booking requirements are detailed for these sites in the guide.

Camping in Victoria

Whether you like to rough it at a secluded bush camp by a mountain stream or prefer the convenience of amenities at a developed campground by the ocean, you will be sure to find a campsite to suit your tastes in the parks, forests and reserves scattered across Victoria that cater for campers. Marvel at platypus on Melbourne's doorstep, follow the footsteps of famous explorers in East Gippsland, try your luck fossicking for riches in the goldfields, pitch your tent on the banks of Australia's most famous river, or 'tickle' a trout in a crystal clear mountain stream. The activities available to you in Victoria's parks, forests and reserves are only bounded by your imagination. You will find symbols indicating possible activities at each campsite in this guide.

In this new fourth edition of Camping Guide to Victoria we've put together the most comprehensive and up-to-date directory of camping areas throughout Victoria. You'll find camping areas located beside the water's edge, whether at the seaside or on the banks of a meandering inland river, campsites tucked away in remote rainforest clearings and camping areas that offer visitors a range of amenities such as hot showers. No matter what type of camping you're into you are sure to find a site from among 690 plus sites listed in this guide.

Since the last edition of this guide we've had the opportunity to visit some new camping areas and revisit a large number of the sites listed, allowing us to bring you the latest information as far as facilities, amenities, activities and directional information. Some of the more popular parks have an excellent range of facilities, with some sites catering for people with disabilities. However, many of the more popular camping areas, especially those in the coastal regions, will require advance bookings for peak holiday periods. Some areas may require a ballot. On the other hand, there are numerous bush campsites that offer peace and tranquility far from the maddening crowds. All the sites listed throughout this guide are designated campsites where camping is allowed.

So what are you waiting for? For your next holiday or weekend away why not go camping. It's a great way to soak up the unforgettable sights and marvel at the stunning natural beauty that can be found throughout Victoria.

Happy Camping

Craig Lewis and Cathy Savage
Rocky Hall NSW

Planning

If you're an old hand at camping, travelling in a campervan or towing a caravan, you probably already have everything for a camping trip. However, if you're a camping novice or simply just rusty – that is, you're planning to go camping but it's not something you do regularly – then the following tips may be helpful.

Like many experienced campers, we've found over the years the key to hassle free camping is to follow the KIS principal – Keep It Simple. It's all about getting back to basics. Wander around any of the larger camping stores and you'll find a plethora of odds and ends which are claimed to make camp life easier and more comfortable. Stick to the basics. Travel light.

Your camping holiday will be much more enjoyable with the right gear. If you are setting up a camping outfit then buy the best gear you can afford. Quality gear will serve you well over a long period if looked after.

The warmer months of the year, from around October through to April are the best times for camping along Victoria's coastal fringe, the Murray River and in the mountain areas. Days

are generally warm and nights mild. The Mallee region in the far north-west corner of the state can experience extreme temperatures during summer and is best avoided at this time. Spring and autumn are the best times to visit here. Remember to always pack a warm jumper and long pants, even in summer.

Biting insects such as spiders, bees, wasps, ants, ticks or mosquitoes can turn a dream camping holiday into a nightmare. To help protect yourself from these unwelcome visitors wear long pants, long sleeve shirts and shoes and don't forget insect repellant.

Never pitch your tent directly under large trees, especially on river banks as they have a habit of dropping branches without warning.

When planning your camping trip, don't head off without:

- Good maps. See 'Maps, guidebooks and passes' in this section. If you plan on venturing off the beaten track, be it bushwalking, vehicle touring or fishing, be sure to carry a detailed map of the area you plan to visit.
- A gas/liquid fuel stove. If the campsite you want to visit doesn't allow you to light a fire or provide cooking facilities, then you will need to take your own. A small single burner gas stove is fine for 2-3 people; 2 burner stoves are needed for families.
- Insect repellent and a first aid kit. Mosquitoes, sand flies and bugs can be a nuisance while a good first aid kit is a necessity.
- Plenty of fresh drinking water.
- If you are camping in remote areas well away from shops be sure to take enough food with you – and always pack for an extra day or two in case inclement weather etc holds you up. When you're out in the fresh air, you often have a bigger appetite, especially if you combine some swimming, bike riding or bushwalking. Kids especially get very hungry on camping trips, so make sure you include healthy nibbles.

For a detailed equipment checklist see the Equipment Checklist section.

WE COULDN'T live without...

A comfortable folding chair is one luxury that we always pack. Sitting around the campfire with your drink of choice is just a whole lot more fun in a comfy chair.

A folding table, either the type with a hard top and folding legs or the newer aluminium slat type which pulls apart and rolls into a bag, makes camp life easier. We use both types, mostly the hard top but opt for the aluminium slat table when space is at a premium.

MAPS, PASSES AND PERMITS

All campsites in this guide are referenced to the Touring Map section in the back of the book (abbreviated to MR in campsite descriptions). This road atlas, which covers Victoria in detail, is used to locate campsites along with the regional maps and national park/forest maps in this guide.

Those who require detailed maps for regional areas and national park areas may be interested in maps by Meridian Maps, including: Hattah Kulkyne Map Guide, Lerderderg/Werribee Gorge, Mornington Peninsula, Otways, Victoria's Deserts and Wombat State Forests along with VicMaps National park maps: Cathedral Range, Grampians, Kinglake, Lake Eildon, Lake Tyers, Mallacoota, Marysville - Lake Mountain and Wilson Promontory.

Rooftop Maps publish a number of detailed maps to the High Country and surrounding regions. Spatial Vision publish a series of map guides to areas along the Murray River showing access tracks as well as other regions throughout Victoria. AFN (Australian Fishing Network) have a range of fishing maps for selected coastal and inland lakes areas of Victoria.

Guidebooks

There are numerous guidebooks available on Victoria covering a variety of subjects such as walking, fishing, cycling, fossicking, national parks and vehicle touring. Victoria's National Parks and Forests, published by Boiling Billy Publications, covers many of the states parks, forests and reserves and is a good reference for those venturing into these areas. Four-wheel drivers are provided with a wealth of information in the series of Boiling Billy Publications (www.boilingbilly.com.au) books titled 4WD Treks Close to Melbourne, 4WD Touring Victoria and The High Country 4WD and Camping Guide. These are indispensible for 4WD travel in the state.

National Park Passes

Annual, Multi-day and Day National Parks Passes are available for Wilsons Promontory, Mt Buffalo, Mornington Peninsula, Baw Baw, Yarra Ranges and Point Nepean national Parks. Passes can be purchased at the respective park offices or from the Parks Vic Information Centre (www.parkweb.vic.gov.au).

Permits

Generally, permits are not required for the majority of campsites in this guide. If a permit is required, this is detailed in the Further Information box.

For safety purposes, some remote walk-in sites or canoe access sites may require visitors to register their intentions with the land managers.

Camping Permits and Fees

Camping permits are required for many of the campsites in this guide.

For safety purposes, some remote walk-in sites or canoe access sites may require visitors to register their intentions with the land managers.

NOTE on camping fees

> The camping fees indicated in the Further Information box are correct at the time of research and generally reflect the low season fee. Peak season fees may be higher than those listed. Camping fees may rise or be introduced to areas which may have previously been free of charge. It is the responsibility of individuals to enquire with the land managers about the status of areas they wish to visit, including current fees, prior to departure.

FIRE WARNINGS AND RESTRICTIONS

On days of declared total fire bans you're not allowed to have any fire in the open, this includes solid fuel fires, gas cookers or barbeques. Fire bans are generally broadcast on local radio stations and it's your responsibility to be aware of these. On days of high fire danger it may be prudent to refrain from having open fires; use gas or fuel cooking appliances instead.

To protect the natural environment and local wildlife, you may find that a number of national parks and reserves listed in this guide do not permit campfires. For these parks and reserves, it's essential that you carry your own gas/fuel stove for cooking.

Firewood

Wood is becoming scarce in popular camping areas. Fallen and dead timer also provides habitats for the local wildlife. If you're camping where campfires are permitted, try to purchase or collect your wood prior to arrival to the campsite. Some parks prohibit the collection of firewood within the park and some parks may have signposted firewood collection points outside the park boundary. Also, to help protect the spread of exotic weeds and pests, some national parks and reserves request that collected firewood from outside the immediate area is not to be taken into the parks.

Vegetation

Please do not cut down any vegetation, either living or dead, and do not collect or use wood that may have habitat holes. If you use a campfire you must ensure that all combustible material is clear for 4 metres, never leave the campfire unattended and always put it out with water (never with sand or dirt). Never throw cans or glass into your campfire.

Remember the average-sized campfire...
- is capable of generating over 500 Degrees of heat after burning for only three hours.
- when extinguished with sand or dirt, retains up to 100 Degrees of heat for eight hours.
- when extinguished with a bucket of water retrains little or no heat after of period of ten minutes.

FURTHER Information

Country Fire Authority
(total ban updates, general enquiries and emergencies)
Bushfire Information Hotline Tel: 1800 240 667
Website: www.cfa.vic.gov.au

TREADING LIGHTLY IN VICTORIA

Victoria's parks and reserves are some of the state's most precious and at the same time sensitive recreational resources.

When enjoying these areas, whether it be camping, walking, canoeing, cycling, car touring, 4WDing or just going bush, it's important to tread lighting on the environment.

Minimal impact camping is the way to go. When setting up camp there are a few simple guidelines, which if followed ensure that Victoria's parks and reserves are preserved for everyone to enjoy in the future.

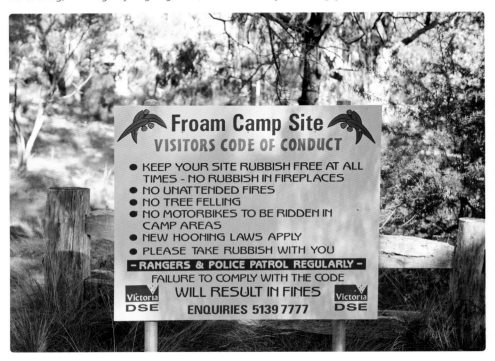

 Be prepared: Plan your trip carefully and make sure your gear is in good order (for good gear tips, see 'Planning' in this section).

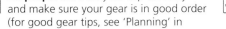 **Protect plants and animals:** If possible, make your camp to avoid trampling plants or disturbing animals. Do not feed wildlife as 'human food' can cause illness and disease to animals.

 Campfire safety: Use fireplaces where provided. Clear combustible material 4 metres away from the fire. Be sure the fire is out before leaving (for more, see the section 'Fire Warnings and Restrictions').

 Waterway care: Don't pollute waterways. Don't use soap or detergents in or close to waterways. Wash at least 100 metres from waterways.

 Toilet time: Use toilets if provided. If not, bury wastes at least 100 metres away from campsites and watercourses, in a hold at least 15cm deep.

 Clean camp: Leave campsites better than you found them.

 Neighbours: Be considerate of others when camping nearby.

WHAT TO PACK

Camping Equipment

- ❏ Bucket
- ❏ Chairs
- ❏ Dust pan & brush
- ❏ First Aid Kit
- ❏ Fluro light
- ❏ Ground sheet
- ❏ Head torch
- ❏ Mattress/s
- ❏ Mattress pump
- ❏ Pillows and cases
- ❏ Screen/mesh tent
- ❏ Sleeping bag
- ❏ Spare rope
- ❏ Swag
- ❏ Table
- ❏ Tent
- ❏ Tent pegs
- ❏ Tent poles
- ❏ Tent rope
- ❏ Torch
- ❏ Torch batteries
- ❏ Water container

Cooking Equipment

- ❏ Matches and/or lighter
- ❏ Firelighters
- ❏ Two burner gas stove and gas bottle
- ❏ BBQ plate
- ❏ Grill or grate
- ❏ 2 saucepans with lids
- ❏ Frying pan
- ❏ Camp oven

- ❏ Trivet - to fit camp oven
- ❏ Billy
- ❏ Tripod hanger and hooks
- ❏ Pie dish - to fit camp oven
- ❏ Pizza tray - to fit camp oven
- ❏ Camp oven lifters
- ❏ Shovel - long handled
- ❏ Leather gloves

Miscellaneous Cooking Items

- ❏ Roll of aluminium foil
- ❏ Roll of cling wrap
- ❏ Paper towel
- ❏ Plastic bottle for milk
- ❏ Plastic bottle for cordial
- ❏ Plastic bottle for extra water
- ❏ Storage containers with lids
- ❏ Zip lock bags

Personal Eating Equipment - 1 per person

- ❏ Bowl
- ❏ Fork
- ❏ Knife
- ❏ Mug
- ❏ Plate
- ❏ Spoon
- ❏ Steak Knife
- ❏ Tea spoon

Cooking Utensils

- ❏ Mixing bowls
- ❏ Measuring jug
- ❏ Tongs - short or long
- ❏ Bar-B-Q Mate
- ❏ Basting brush

- ❏ Serving spoon
- ❏ Slotted serving spoon
- ❏ Peelers
- ❏ Egg flip
- ❏ Flat grater
- ❏ Can opener with bottle opener
- ❏ Swiss Army Knife
- ❏ Flat Strainer
- ❏ Egg rings
- ❏ Large sharp knife
- ❏ Bread/Serrated edge knife
- ❏ Wooden spoons
- ❏ Cutting board
- ❏ Mesh toaster
- ❏ Measuring spoon and/or tablespoon
- ❏ Extra plate and bowl for serving
- ❏ General purpose scissors

Washing/Cleaning Equipment

- ❏ Cloth
- ❏ Clothesline and pegs
- ❏ Detergent
- ❏ Dish brush
- ❏ Garbage bags
- ❏ Scourer
- ❏ Scrubbing brush
- ❏ Sponge
- ❏ Tea towel/s
- ❏ Wash up bucket
- ❏ Washing powder for clothes

Personal Items

- ❏ Comb and/or brush
- ❏ Toothbrush
- ❏ Toothpaste
- ❏ Towel
- ❏ Face Washer
- ❏ Soap and container
- ❏ Shampoo & Conditioner
- ❏ Deodorant
- ❏ Sunblock
- ❏ Toilet paper
- ❏ Insect repellent

USEFUL RESOURCES AND CONTACTS

Parks Victoria
Tel: 131 963 (8am-6pm weekdays and 9am-6pm weekends)
Web: www.parkweb.vic.gov.au

Department of Sustainability & Environment - Customer Service Centre
Tel: 136 186
Web: www.dse.vic.gov.au

Fisheries: Department of Primary Industries – Fisheries & Aquaculture
Tel: 136 186
Web: www.dpi.vic.gov.au

Fossicking/Miners Rights: Department of Primary Industries - Minerals & Petroleum
Tel: 136 186
Web: www.dpi.vic.gov.au

Country Fire Authority
Headquarters – Burwood **Tel:** 03 9262 8444
Bushfire Information Hotline **Tel:** 1800 240 667
Web: www.cfa.vic.gov.au

RACV
Roadside Assistance **Tel:** 131 111
Memberships **Tel:** 137 228
Web: www.racv.com.au

VicRoads
Traffic Management Centre/Road Conditions
Tel: 03 9854 2666
Web: www.vicroads.vic.gov.au

Victorian Tourism Information Service
Tel: 132 842
Web: www.visitvictoria.com

Victoria's Tourism Regions and a number of Accredited Visitor Information Centres
– for other Information Centres visit the Victorian Tourism website

Melbourne – Melbourne Visitor Centre
Tel: 03 9658 9658

Yarra Valley & Dandenong Ranges – Dandenong Ranges Visitor Information Centre
Tel: 1800 645 505 and Yarra Valley Visitor Information Centre **Tel:** 03 5962 2600

Mornington Peninsula – Mornington Peninsula Visitor Information Centre
Tel: 1800 804 009

Daylesford & the Macedon Ranges – Daylesford Regional Visitor Information Centre
Tel: 03 5321 6123 and Seymour Visitor Information Centre **Tel:** 03 5799 0233

Phillip Island – Phillip Island Visitor Information Centre
Tel: 1300 366 422

Geelong and the Bellarine Peninsula – Geelong Visitor Information Centre
Tel: 1800 620 888

Great Ocean Road – 12 Apostles Visitor Information Centre, Part Campbell
Tel: 1300 137 255

Goldfields – Ballarat Visitor Information Centre
Tel: 1800 446 633 and Bendigo Visitor Information Centre **Tel:** 1800 813 153

Grampians – Halls Gap and Grampians Visitor Information Centre
Tel: 1800 065 599

High Country – Benalla Visitor Information Centre
Tel: 03 5762 1749 and Mansfield Visitor Information Centre **Tel:** 1800 039 049

Gippsland – Bairnsdale Visitor Information Centre
Tel: 1800 637 060 and Prom Country Visitor Information Centre **Tel:** 1800 630 704 and Wellington Visitor Information Centre, Sale **Tel:** 1800 677 520

The Murray – Albury Wodonga Gateway Visitor Information Centre
Tel: 1300 796 222 and Greater Shepparton Visitor Information Centre **Tel:** 1800 808 839 and Mildura Visitor Information Centre **Tel:** 1800 039 043

Bureau of Meterology
Web: www.bom.gov.au

Close to Melbourne

THE CLOSE TO MELBOURNE region arcs around the city and encompasses the bayside, along with the coastal areas of the Bellarine and Mornington Peninsulas. Inland, the delightful Yarra Valley and the Dandenongs await, as well as the gorges and ranges in the north-west. This region, stretching from the sea to the mountains, provides a swag of outdoor experiences for family campers, watersports enthusiasts or more adventurous four-wheel drivers, mountain bikers and bushwalkers.

BEST Campsites!

Frenchmans Creek camping area
Upper Big River State Forest

Suspension Bridge camping area
Murrindindi Scenic Reserve

Cooks Mill camping area
Cathedral Range State Park

Mount Franklin Reserve camping area
Mount Franklin Reserve

Jerusalem Creek camping area
Lake Eildon National Park

If the sound of ocean waves from your campsite appeals to you, then you can choose from camping reserves along the Bellarine and Mornington Peninsulas or camping areas dotted around Port Phillip Bay. Be warned — these reserves, being so close to Melbourne, are popular over the summer months, so be sure to book ahead.

If lakeside camping is more your thing, then inland and to the north-east of the city is the popular fishing and camping destination of Lake Eildon. Surrounded by national park, here you'll discover a variety of campsites including some that are accessible only by boat – perfect if you want to get away from crowds. Also located in this north-east corner is the delightful Murrindindi Scenic Reserve. You can camp here along the Murrindindi River among towering mountain forests.

If you have an urge for adventure you might like to explore the rugged Brisbane Ranges or the sheer-sided cliffs of Lerderderg Gorge. Both offer camping and are popular areas to explore on foot. Or if you're intent on finding your fortune, why not try panning for gold while camped around Blackwood or in Creswick Regional Park.

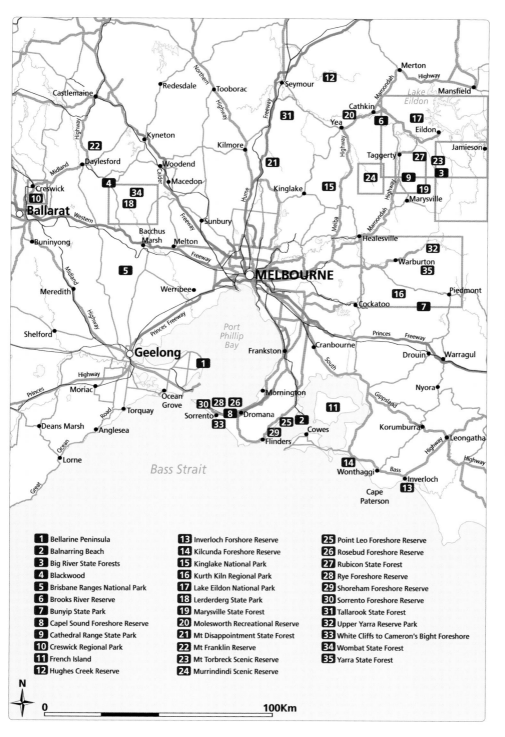

1 Bellarine Peninsula
2 Balnarring Beach
3 Big River State Forests
4 Blackwood
5 Brisbane Ranges National Park
6 Brooks River Reserve
7 Bunyip State Park
8 Capel Sound Foreshore Reserve
9 Cathedral Range State Park
10 Creswick Regional Park
11 French Island
12 Hughes Creek Reserve

13 Inverloch Forshore Reserve
14 Kilcunda Foreshore Reserve
15 Kinglake National Park
16 Kurth Kiln Regional Park
17 Lake Eildon National Park
18 Lerderderg State Park
19 Marysville State Forest
20 Molesworth Recreational Reserve
21 Mt Disappointment State Forest
22 Mt Franklin Reserve
23 Mt Torbreck Scenic Reserve
24 Murrindindi Scenic Reserve

25 Point Leo Foreshore Reserve
26 Rosebud Foreshore Reserve
27 Rubicon State Forest
28 Rye Foreshore Reserve
29 Shoreham Foreshore Reserve
30 Sorrento Foreshore Reserve
31 Tallarook State Forest
32 Upper Yarra Reserve Park
33 White Cliffs to Cameron's Bight Foreshore
34 Wombat State Forest
35 Yarra State Forest

The Bellarine Peninsula is a popular seaside and bayside holiday destination and water sports venue to the east of Geelong. The peninsula forms the northern entrance to Port Phillip Bay and is a good fishing spot. Many reserves along the foreshore offer camping.

Barwon Heads Caravan Park

Located on Ewing Blyth Drive, Barwon Heads. Foreshore location, close to surf beach. Camp kitchen. Laundry facilities. Gas/fuel stove only.
MR: Map 8 I3

Riverview Family Caravan Park

Located at Barwon Heads on Ocean Grove Road. Situated on the Barwon River close to Ocean Grove Beach. Natural sites. Laundry and kiosk. Gas/fuel stove only.
MR: Map 8 I3

Queenscliff Recreation Reserve caravan and camping area

Foreshore location at Hesse Street, Queenscliff. Good access to Port Phillip Bay. Laundry facilities. Gas/fuel stove only.
MR: Map 8 J3

FURTHER Information

Barwon Heads Caravan Park
Tel: 03 5254 1115. Bookings essential during peak periods: school and public holidays, Easter and Christmas.
Web: www.barwoncoast.com.au
Camping fees: Unpowered from $22 per site/night for 2 people. Powered from $28 per site/night for 2 people. Cabin and backpacker accommodation available.

FURTHER Information

Riverview Family Caravan Park
Tel: 03 5256 1600. Bookings essential during Christmas period.
Web: www.barwoncoast.com.au
Camping fees: Unpowered from $22 per site/night for 2 people. Powered from $28 per site/night for 2 people. Cabin accommodation available.

FURTHER Information

Queenscliff Recreation Reserve
Tel: 03 5258 1765. Bookings essential during peak periods: school and public holidays, Easter and Christmas.
Web: www.queensclifftouristparks.com.au
Camping fees: Unpowered from $21 per site/night for 2 people. Powered from $26 per site/night for 2 people.

CLOSE TO MELBOURNE

Royal Park caravan and camping area, Point Lonsdale

Located on Point Lonsdale Road, Point Lonsdale. Foreshore location close to The Heads. Gas/fuel stove only. Open 1 Dec–30 April.
MR: Map 8 J3

Victoria Park caravan and camping area, Queenscliff

Access via King Street, office located in Hesse Street. Gas/fuel stove only. Open 1 Dec–30 April.
MR: Map 8 J3

St Leonards Foreshore caravan and camping area

Signposted access via The Esplande, St Leonards. Foreshore frontage near The Bluff. Gas/fuel stove only. Two camping areas. Open Melbourne Cup Weekend–April.
MR: Map 8 J2

Indented Head Foreshore – Anderson Reserve, Batman Park and Taylors Reserve camping areas

Access via The Esplanade. Three reserves. Foreshore frontage to Port Phillip Bay. Gas/fuel stove only. Open Melbourne Cup Weekend–April.
MR: Map 8 J2

FURTHER Information

Royal Park caravan and camping area
Tel: 03 5258 1765. Bookings essential during peak periods: school and public holidays, Easter and Christmas.
Web: www.queensclifftouristparks.com.au
Camping fees: Unpowered from $21 per site/night for 2 people. Powered from $26 per site/night for 2 people.

FURTHER Information

St Leonards Foreshore
Tel: 03 5259 2764. Bookings essential during peak periods.
Web: www.portarlingtonresort.com.au
Camping fees: From $30 per site/night for 2 people.

FURTHER Information

Victoria Park caravan and camping area
Tel: 03 5258 1765. Bookings essential during peak periods: school and public holidays, Easter and Christmas.
Web: www.queensclifftouristparks.com.au
Camping fees: Unpowered from $21 per site/night for 2 people. Powered from $26 per site/night for 2 people.

FURTHER Information

Indented Head Foreshore
Tel: 03 5259 2764. Bookings essential during peak periods.
Web: www.portarlingtonresort.com.au
Camping fees: From $30 per site/night for 2 people.

CLOSE TO MELBOURNE

Portarlington Seaside Resort

Access via Sproat Street, Portarlington. Foreshore frontage to Port Phillip Bay. Camp kitchen. Gas/fuel stove only.
MR: Map 8 J2

FURTHER Information

Portarlington Seaside Resort
Tel: 03 5259 2764. Bookings essential during peak periods.
Web: www.portarlingtonresort.com.au
Camping fees: From $35 per site/night for 2 people.

2 Balnarring Beach Camping Reserves

Balnarring Beach is located 80km south of Melbourne on the eastern side of the Mornington Peninsula, and offers the closest ocean beaches to the city. The waters of Western Port provide for all types of aquatic recreation. Walking and nature trails.

A Reserve, B Reserve and C Reserve camping areas

Access is to A Reserve is along the signposted Mason Smith Road just south of the reserve office. Sites here are set among coastal vegetation, with some sandy sites. Access to B Reserve is signposted along Balnarring Beach Road at the reserve office, 1.6km south of the C777 road. Sites here are grassy and well protected beside the river. Access to C Reserve is along the signposted Fethers Road, which is opposite the reserve office. These sites are among coastal vegetation. All reserves are within walking distance to sheltered surf beach. Communal picnic tables, shelters and gas/electric barbeques.
GPS: A Reserve S:38 23.539 E:145 07.349. B Reserve S:38 23.374 E:145 07.460. C Reserve S:38 23.366 E:145 07.652
MR: Map 11 B3

FURTHER Information

Balnarring Beach Camping Reserves
Tel: 03 5983 5582 or 0419 596 549. Advance bookings recommended during peak periods.
Web: www.balnarring.net
Camping fees: Unpowered from $20 per family/night (2 adults and 3 children under 17). Powered from $25 per family/night (2 adults and 3 children under 17).

LOWER BIG RIVER STATE FOREST

Located 240km north-east of Melbourne and south-west of Jamieson. Access is via the unsealed Jamieson-Eildon Road. The Lower Big River State Forest offers good bushwalking, fishing, 4WD touring, trailbike riding, gold fossicking and camping opportunities.

Burnt Bridge camping ground

Signposted access along the Jamieson-Eildon Road, 24.4km from Jamieson, then in 300m to camping area with shady trees set high above the river. Steep, narrow access track. Popular trailbike area. Bring drinking water and firewood.
GPS: S:37 20.917 E:146 03.631
MR: Map 10 G4

Bulldog Flat camping area

Signposted access 600m south of Burnt Bridge camping area along Jamieson-Eildon Road. Two signposted access tracks lead to dispersed bushcamping areas among trees above the river; tracks to sites are tight and winding in sections. Bring drinking water and firewood.
GPS: S:37 21.188 E:146 03.768
MR: Map 10 G4

The Pines camping area

Signposted access 500m south of Bulldog Flat camping area along Jamieson-Eildon Road. Small area beneath stand of pines. Best suited for tent-based camping. Some limited sites for smaller camper trailers and caravans. Bring drinking water and firewood.
GPS: S:37 21.432 E:146 03.704
MR: Map 10 G4

Big River camping area

Located along Jamieson-Eildon Road 1.3km south of The Pines camping area on the northern end of the bridge over Big River. Well shaded, terraced camping area. Bring drinking water and firewood.
GPS S:37 22.004 E:146 03.330
MR: Map 10 G4

Jim Bullock camping area

Signposted access along Jamieson-Eildon Road 200m south of Big River camping area and at the southern end of the bridge over Big River. Well shaded sites. Bring drinking water and firewood.
GPS S:37 22.081 E:146 03.461
MR: Map 10 G4

Stockmans Reward camping area

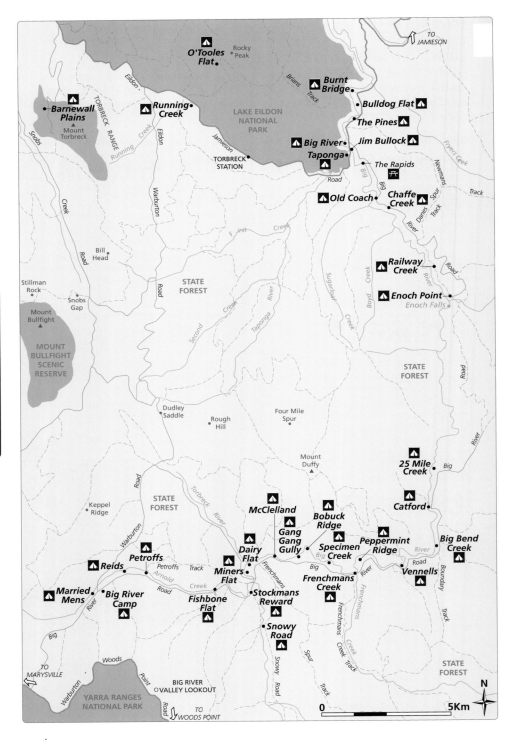

TO
JAMIESON

O'Tooles
Flat
Rocky
Peak

Burnt
Bridge

Briens
Track

Bulldog Flat

The Pines

Barnewall
Plains
Mount
Torbreck

TORBRECK RANGE

Running
Creek

LAKE EILDON
NATIONAL
PARK

Jim Bullock

Fryers Creek

Eildon

Jamieson

Running

Big River
Taponga

Old Coach

The Rapids

Chaffe
Creek

Newmans
Track

Danes Spur

Warburton

TORBRECK
STATION

Road

Big

Big River

Snobs

Creek

Railway
Creek

Road

Bill
Head

First
Creek

STATE
FOREST

Sugarloaf
Creek

Boy
Creek

Enoch Point
Enoch Falls

River

Stillman
Rock

Mount
Bullfight

Snobs
Gap

Road

STATE
FOREST

MOUNT
BULLFIGHT
SCENIC
RESERVE

Second
Creek

Taponga
River

Road

Dudley
Saddle

Rough
Hill

Four Mile
Spur

Mount
Duffy

25 Mile
Creek

Big

Keppel
Ridge

STATE
FOREST

Torbreck River

McClelland

Bobuck
Ridge

Catford

Warburton

Gang
Gang
Gully

Specimen
Creek

Peppermint
Ridge

Big Bend
Creek

Petroffs

Petroffs

Track

Dairy
Flat

Frenchmans

River

Vennells

Boundary Track

Reids

Arnold
Creek

Miners
Flat

Big
River

Frenchmans
Creek

Road

Married
Mens

Big River
Camp

Road

Fishbone
Flat

Stockmans
Reward

Big
River

Snowy
Road

Frenchmans Creek

Frenchmans Creek Track

STATE
FOREST

TO
MARYSVILLE

Woods
Point

Snowy
Road

Spur
Track

Warburton

BIG RIVER
VALLEY LOOKOUT

Road

TO
WOODS POINT

N

0   5Km

Taponga camping area

Signposted access along Jamieson-Eildon Road 100m south of Jim Bullock camping area. Smaller area in clearing among trees. Bring drinking water and firewood.
GPS S:37 22.194 E:146 03.486
MR: Map 10 G4

Running Creek camping area

Signposted access along Jamieson-Eildon Road 8.9km south of Taponga camping area. Then proceed in 400m to small cleared area beside the track. Bring drinking water and firewood.
GPS S:37 21.154 E:145 59.132
MR: Map 10 G4

Old Coach camping area

Signposted access 3.5km along Big River Road, which is signposted off Jamieson-Eildon Road 1.2km south of The Pines camping area and 100m north of Big River camping area. Camping area located above the river, best suited to tent-based camping with some sites a short distance carry-in. Bring drinking water and firewood.
GPS S:37 23.163 E:146 04.218
MR: Map 10 G4

Chaffe Creek camping area

Signposted access along Big River Road 1km south of Old Coach camping area. Large, well-shaded area with some grassed sites. Bring drinking water and firewood.
GPS S:37 23.439 E:146 04.375
MR: Map 10 G4

Taponga camping area

Railway Creek camping area

Signposted access along Big River Road south of Chaffe Creek camping area. Bring drinking water and firewood.
MR: Map 10 G4

FURTHER Information

> **DSE Customer Service Centre**
> **Tel:** 13 61 86

UPPER BIG RIVER STATE FOREST

Located 130km north-east of Melbourne and east of Marysville. Access to the forest is via Big River State Forest road, which is signposted east of Cumberland Junction. Cumberland Junction is situated 19km east of Marysville via the Marysville-Woods Point Road and 42km north of Warburton via the Warburton-Woods Point Road. The forest is popular for gold fossicking, bushwalking, fishing, trailbike riding, camping and 4WD touring.

Big River Camp camping area

Located on Big River Road at its junction with the Eildon-Warburton road, 5.8km north-east of the Marysville-Woods Point Road. Bring drinking water and firewood.
GPS S:37 31.725 E:145 56.691
MR: Map 10 G5

Stockmans Reward camping area

Signposted access along Big River Road 7.7km east of Big River Camp. Bring drinking water and firewood.
GPS S:37 31.545 E:146 00.704
MR: Map 10 G5

Frenchmans Creek camping area

Signposted access along Big River Road 6km east of Stockmans Reward CA and 1.7km east of Specimen Creek CA access track. Bring drinking water and firewood.
GPS S:37 31.332 E:146 03.516
MR: Map 10 G5

Snowy Road bush camping area

Located 1.7km along Snowy Road south of Big River Road. Snowy Road is signposted 7.3km east of Big River Camp CA. Bring drinking water and firewood.
GPS S:37 32.519 E:146 00.977
MR: Map 10 G5

2WD Access bush camping areas

Each camping area is signposted along Big River Road. Access is possible by 2WD vehicles in dry weather only. Bring drinking water and firewood.

Married Mens: Access track is located to the west of the Big River Road and the Eildon-Warburton road junction, 5.8km north-east of the Marysville-Woods Point Road.
GPS S:37 31.754 E:145 56.580
MR: MR: Map 10 G5

Reids: Access via signposted Reeds Quarry Road off Big River Road, 900m east of Big River Camp CA.
Access track **GPS** S:37 31.402 E:145 57.153
MR: MR: Map 10 G5

McClelland: Access signposted off Big River Road, 1km east of Dairy Flat CA access track.
Access track **GPS** S:37 31.034 E:146 01.295
MR: Map 10 G5

Gang Gang Gully: Access signposted off Big River Road, 1km east of McClelland CA access track, then in 400m to camping area.
Access track **GPS** S:37 31.173 E:146 01.888
MR: Map 10 G5

Bobuck Ridge: Access signposted off Big River Road, 700m east of Gang Gang Gully CA, then in 800m to camping area.
Access track **GPS** S:37 31.133 E:146 02.226
MR: Map 10 G5

Peppermint Ridge: Access signposted off Big River Road, 700m north of Frenchmans Creek CA.
MR: Map 10 G5

Vennells: Access signposted off Big River Road, 2km east of Peppermint Ridge CA.
MR: Map 10 G5

Big Bend Creek: Access signposted off Big River Road, 3.2km east of Vennells CA.
MR: Map 10 G5

Catford: Access signposted off Big River Road, 2.2km north of Big Bend Creek CA.
MR: Map 10 VR G5

25 Mile Creek: Access signposted off Big River Road, 1.8km north of Catford CA.
MR: Map 10 G5

4WD Access bush camping areas

Each camping area is signposted along Big River Road. Bring drinking water and firewood.

Petroffs: Access off Big River Road via signposted Petroffs Road 1.2km east of Reeds Quarry Road.
Access track **GPS** S:37 31.372 E:145 57.937.
MR: Map 10 G5

Fishbone Flat: Access signposted off Big River Road 3.1km east of Petroffs Road.
Access track **GPS**: S:37 31.646 E:145 59.788
MR: Map 10 G5

Miners Flat: Access signposted off Big River Road, 600m north of Stockmans Reward CA.
Access track **GPS** S:37 31.276 E:146 00.721
MR: Map 10 G5

Dairy Flat: Access signposted off Big River Road, 100m north of Miners Flat access track.
Access track **GPS** S:37 31.232 E:146 00.737
MR: Map 10 G5

Specimen Creek: Access signposted off Big River Road, 800m east of Bobuck Ridge CA access track, then in 500m to camping area.
Access track **GPS** S:37 31.247 E:146 02.651
MR: Map 10 G5

Enoch Point: Access signposted off Big River Road north of 25 Mile Creek CA and south of Railway Creek CA in Lower Big River State Forest.
MR: Map 10 G4

FURTHER Information

> **DSE Customer Service Centre**
> **Tel:** 13 61 86
> **DSE Marysville**
> **Tel:** 03 5957 7111

CLOSE TO MELBOURNE

4 Blackwood

Once a gold rush site, Blackwood is situated north of Bacchus Marsh and the Western Freeway, and west of Lerderderg State Park. Located nearby are numerous gold panning areas and mineral springs.

Blackwood Mineral Springs Caravan Park

Signposted access along Golden Point Road, 400m east of village.
GPS S:37 28.332 E:144 18.700
MR: Map 7 H5

FURTHER Information

Blackwood Mineral Springs Caravan Park
Tel: 03 5368 6539. Bookings recommended during peak periods.
Camping fees: Unpowered from $18 per site/night for 2 people. Powered from $22 per site/night for 2 people.

5 Brisbane Ranges National Park

The national park is located 80km west of Melbourne between Bacchus Marsh and Anakie. The park's rugged ranges were formed millions of years ago by a fault line. The area offers scenic walks, lookouts, picnic areas, diverse plant species, wonderful wildflower displays and abundant wildlife. Note: Mountain bike riders are not permitted to access trails behind management gates.

Boar Gully camping area

Access via Reids Road off Brisbane Ranges Road off the Geelong-Ballan Road. Seven sites. Boil water first. Bring drinking water and firewood. Gas/fuel stove preferred.
MR: Map 7 H7

Bush Camping
Walk-in bush camping is possible for self-sufficient walkers in the Brisbane Ranges NP. Contact Parks Vic Bacchus Marsh for details and map. **Tel** 03 5367 2922.

FURTHER Information

Parks Vic Info Line
Tel: 13 19 63. Advance bookings essential for holiday periods.
Bookings: Parks Vic Info Line or online at www.parkstay.vic.gov.au
Camping fees: From $12.50 per site/night up to 6 people.

6 Brooks River Reserve

Situated beside the Goulburn River west of Alexandra. From the Maroondah Highway take the signposted Swann Road 2km north of Alexandra.

Brooks River Reserve camping area

From Maroondah Highway take signposted Swann Road and follow for 1.8km, then turn right into Brooks Cutting Road and follow for 600m to signposted reserve access. Located high above the river with little shade, walk to river.

Limited tent-based camping due to rocky ground, best suited for camper trailers and caravans. Bring drinking and firewood.
GPS S:37 11.402 E:145 40.327
MR: Map 10 E3

FURTHER Information

> **Parks Vic Info Line**
> **Tel:** 13 19 63.

7 Bunyip State Park

Bunyip State Park is located 65km east of Melbourne and just east of Gembrook. The park has magnificent Mountain Ash forests in the north, whereas the lower sections are dominated with swamp heathland. The forests come alive at night with nocturnal animals such as possums, gilders, owls and bats. You can check out the numerous walking tracks, go mountain bike riding, explore Four Brothers Rocks, or look for the legendary Bunyip. Popular park for trailbike riding. The unsealed Tonimbuk Road is the park's main access road.

Nash Creek camping area

Signposted access along Black Snake Creek Road, 1.5km east of Dyers Picnic Ground. Then drive 100m to open area encircled by forest. Sites are generally bare ground. Bring drinking water and firewood.
GPS S:37 56.796 E:145 41.264
MR: Map 10 E8

Blue Range camping area

Cleared bush camping area along Bunyip Ridge Track accessed from Bunyip River Road. Bring drinking water and firewood.
GPS S:37 57.726 E:145 43.142 (access track along Bunyip River Road)
MR: Map 10 E8

> **Parks Vic Info Line**
> **Tel:** 13 19 63.

8 Capel Sound Foreshore Reserves

Capel Sound Foreshore Reserves is situated on the Mornington Peninsula on Port Phillip Bay near Rosebud. This foreshore location has many sites stretching from Rosebud West to Tootgarook. Access is signposted along Point Nepean Road.

Capel Sound Foreshore Reserves – Rosebud West & Tootgarook

Camping permit required from Rangers Office in Rosebud West. Signposted access on Point Nepean Road in Rosebud West. Large area. Laundry. Gas/fuel stove only.
GPS S:38 21.796 E:144 52.627
MR: Map 8 K3

FURTHER Information

> **Capel Sound Foreshore Reserves**
> **Tel:** 03 5986 4382. Rosebud West camping available all year. Tootgarook camping available between November and April. Bookings essential during peak Christmas/New Year period.
> **Web:** www.foreshore.net.au
> **Camping fees:** Unpowered from $21 per site/night. Powered from $26 per site/night. Rate includes up to 4 adults or 2 adults and children under 16.

CLOSE TO MELBOURNE

Cathedral Range State Park is located 100km north-east of Melbourne. Access to the park is signposted off the Maroondah Highway, 2km south of Taggerty. From highway take signposted Cathedral Lane and follow for 2.5km to signposted access road to park. Follow access road for 2.6km to carpark for Neds Gully camping area. There are numerous walking trails of varying lengths and difficulty. The park has great vistas, clear mountain streams and is a great destination for camping, rock climbing and fishing.

Neds Gully camping area

Located along Little River Road 2.6km south of Cathedral Lane. From carpark walk over bridge to large grassed clearing surrounded by trees. Bring drinking water and firewood.
Carpark **GPS** S:37 21.355 E:145 45.170
MR: Map 10 E4

Cooks Mill camping area

Located along Little River Road 3km south of Neds Gully carpark. Some sites carry gear over bollards. Well sheltered, grassed sites. Site of old sawmill beside Little River. Communal tables and shelter. Bring drinking water and firewood.
GPS S:37 22.780 E:145 45.637
MR: Map 10 E4

The Farmyard camping area

Walk-in site. No facilities, self-sufficient camping. Access from Jawbone carpark on Cerberus Road west of Cooks Mill CA, or 2 hour walk from Neds Gully CA. Carry drinking water. Gas/fuel stove only.
MR: Map 10 E4

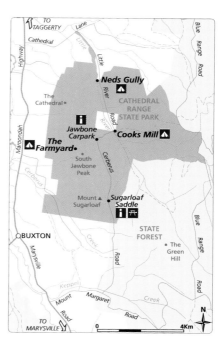

FURTHER Information

> **Parks Vic Info Line**
> **Tel:** 13 19 63. Advance bookings required.
> **Bookings:** Parks Vic Info Line or online at www.parkstay.vic.gov.au
> **Camping fees:** From $13.00 per site/night.
> **Note:** Wood collection is prohibited in Cathedral Range State Park.

CLOSE TO MELBOURNE

Located 18km north of Ballarat near Creswick. Access to the park is via the Bungaree-Creswick Road (C291) off Midland Highway south of Creswick. Follow the C291 for 1.9km then take the signposted gravel road to Slatey Creek Picnic Ground. Follow this road for 1.3km to a Y-junction, keep left here this is Slatey Creek Road and follow this for 1.7km to the first camping and picnic ground. Activities include fossicking, bushwalking, mountain biking, picnicking, canoeing and nature study.

Slatey Creek Campground No 1

Signposted access on Slatey Creek Road 3km south of the Creswick-Bungaree Road (C291). Well-shaded area beside the road. Short-term camping only. Bring drinking water and firewood.
GPS S:37 27.769 E:143 54.247
MR: Map 7 F5

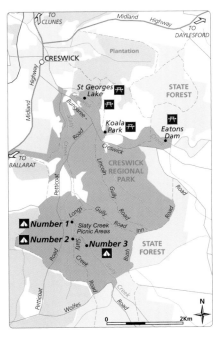

Slatey Creek Campground No 2

Signposted access on Slatey Creek Road 300m south of campground No 1, then in 100m via narrow track to camping area stretched along creek. Short-term camping only. Bring drinking water and firewood.
GPS S:37 27.927 E:143 54.287
MR: Map 7 F5

Slatey Creek Campground No 3

Signposted access on Slatey Creek Road, 200m past campground No 2 then in 400m to camping area. Short-term camping only. Bring drinking water and firewood.
GPS S:37 28.079 E:143 54.510
MR: Map 7 F5

FURTHER Information

Parks Vic Info Line
Tel: 13 19 63.

Slatey Creek Campground No.1 Creswick Regional Park

11 French Island

French Island is situated in Western Port. Two thirds of the island is national park. The island is generally flat with gentle undulations making it ideal for walking and cycling. Bird watchers will delight in the range of birds on the island, with over 230 species recorded. Populations of koalas and long-nosed potaroos are also on the island. Access via passenger ferry from Stony Point and Phillip Island (contact Inter Island Ferries, Tel: 03 9585 5730 or visit www.interislandferries.com.au).

Fairhaven Camping Area

Camping permit required. Located on the island's western foreshore, 5km north of Tankerton along Coast Road. Walk or cycle from ferry terminal at Tankerton. Bring drinking water. Gas/fuel stove only.
MR: Map 11 C3

Airs Farm camping ground

Private campground situated on 3ha of bushland, 10km east of Tankerton on Bayview Road. Cycle or walk from ferry or book pickup through Airs Farm. Firewood supplied.
MR: Map 11 C3

FURTHER Information

> **Parks Vic Info Line**
> **Tel:** 13 19 63. Advance bookings required as maximum camper numbers apply. No camping fees.
> **Bookings:** Parks Vic Rosebud
> **Tel:** 03 5986 9108.

FURTHER Information

> **Airs Farm**
> **Tel:** 03 5980 1241. Bookings recommended.
> **Web:** www.frenchislandtours.com.au
> **Camping fees:** From $6 per adult/night.

12 Hughes Creek Reserve

This large reserve is located north-east of Seymour and situated beside Hughes Creek. From the Goulburn Valley Highway, take the signposted Tarcombe Rd, which is 20km north of Seymour, and proceed in south-easterly direction for 12.1km. Then turn right onto road signposted Dry Weather Access Only (this is Wickett Hill Road). Follow this road for 4.8km to entrance to Hughes Creek Reserve. Wickett Hill Road is a narrow, winding road.

Hughes Creek Reserve camping area

Signposted access along unsealed Wicket Hill Road 17km south-east of the Goulburn Valley Highway. Very large grassed area beside the road and along Hughes Creek. Some shaded sites (note: do not camp under large trees). Walk to creek from camping area. The reserve is surrounded by private property with grazing stock.
GPS S:36 58.833 E:145 20.956
MR: Map 10 C1

FURTHER Information

> **Parks Vic Info Line**
> **Tel:** 13 19 63.

13 Inverloch Foreshore Reserve

Inverloch is accessed via the Bass Highway, 13km east of Wonthaggi and 26km south-west of Leongatha. The foreshore reserve is situated along The Esplande and offers fishing and swimming.

Inverloch Foreshore Reserve caravan and camping area

Foreshore location. Accessed via The Esplande in Inverloch. Gas/fuel stove only. Open all year round.
MR: Map 11 E5

FURTHER Information

Inverloch Foreshore Reserve
Tel: 03 5674 1236. Bookings required for Dec–Feb peak season.
Camping fees: Unpowered from $21 per site/night for 2 people. Powered from $24 per site/night for 2 people.

14 Kilcunda Foreshore

Kilcunda is located on the Bass Highway west of Wonthaggi and south-east of the Phillip Island Tourist Road. This beachside location is popular for walking, swimming and fishing.

Kilcunda Caravan Park

Located in Kilcunda and accessed from the Bass Highway. Gas/fuel stove only.
MR: Map 11 D4

FURTHER Information

Kilcunda Caravan Park
Tel: 03 5678 7260. Bookings required for peak seasons: Easter and Christmas.
Camping fees: Unpowered from $20 per site/night for 2 people. Powered from $27 per site/night for 2 people. Dog bond applies, refer to park pet policy.

15 Kinglake National Park

Kinglake National Park is the largest national park close to Melbourne. Situated on the Great Dividing Range, the park has scenic lookouts, beautiful forests and fern-filled gullies, along with many walking trails, making it a great site for bird watching and nature study. Located near Kinglake, access is off the Melba Highway.

The Gums camping area

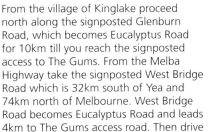

From the village of Kinglake proceed north along the signposted Glenburn Road, which becomes Eucalyptus Road for 10km till you reach the signposted access to The Gums. From the Melba Highway take the signposted West Bridge Road which is 32km south of Yea and 74km north of Melbourne. West Bridge Road becomes Eucalyptus Road and leads 4km to The Gums access road. Then drive in 100m to camping area with 10 sites (4 suitable for small caravan access). Bring drinking water. Some firewood supplied.

GPS S:37 28.204 E:145 23.596
MR: Map 10 C5

FURTHER Information

Parks Vic Info Line
Tel: 13 19 63. Advance bookings required.
Bookings: By phone or online at www.parkstay.vic.gov.au
Camping fees: From $13 per site/night.

16 Kurth Kiln Regional Park

Kurth Kiln Regional Park is home to historic kilns that once produced charcoal for gas producer units fitted to cars during the World War II. The park is located 9km north of Gembrook. Access to the park is via Beenaak Road off Gembrook-Launching Place Road. Activities include bushwalking, mountain bike riding and horse riding.

Kurth Kiln picnic and camping area

From the Gembrook-Launching Place Road following Beenak Road for 4.5km to signposted access. Tiered camping area, carry gear over bollards to sites. Located close to the kiln area and Tomahawk Creek Walking Circuit. Horses to be camped at the nearby corral area on Scout Camp Track. Bring drinking water and firewood.
GPS S:37 53.977 E:145 34.531
MR: Map 10 E7

FURTHER Information

Parks Vic Info Line
Tel: 13 19 63.

KURTH KILN History

During WWII when petrol rationing was introduced an alternative fuel was required, the most practical of which was charcoal. The charcoal burning kiln and plant at Kurth Kiln Regional Park was developed by Professor Ernest Kurth and produced 20 tonnes of charcoal a week when run continuously. However, charcoal was not a successful replacement for fuel as it produced 40 per cent less power, was dirty to use and at the time a conversion unit for a car was nearly 20 times the weekly wage. The plant closed in 1944 when the war ended. The eight metre high kiln is the only one of its type in Australia. Repair works, rebuilding and maintenance of the kiln plant and other structures are done by the Friends of Kurth Kiln, who have erected informative display boards at the site.

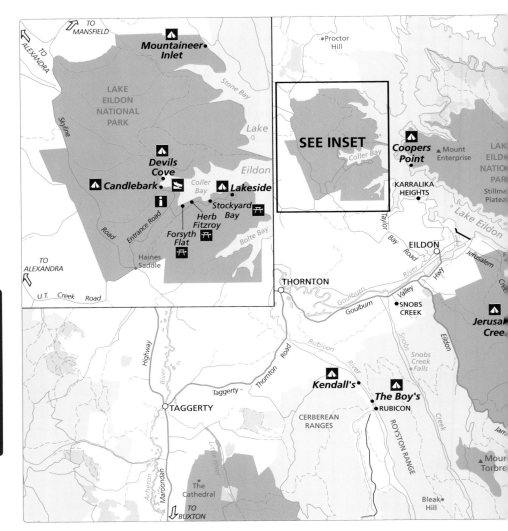

17 Lake Eildon National Park

Lake Eildon National Park, a large park surrounding Lake Eildon, is located 145km north-east of Melbourne. The lake's waters are popular for fishing, sailing and canoeing. There are numerous camping areas around the lake's foreshore. Access is signposted from Alexandra via UT Creek Road, which is signposted off the Goulburn Valley Highway just east of Alexandra. Follow UT Creek Road for 16km to a roundabout at the park entrance, office and Fraser store. The forests surrounding the lake are home to large kangaroo populations along with many different bird species. Bushwalking, mountain biking, four-wheel driving.

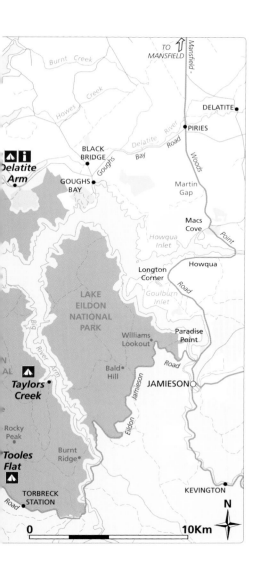

good flat areas. Communal fire pits and electric BBQs in day use area. Water is untreated; boil or treat first or bring own drinking water. Fire bins are available for hire from Fraser Store.
GPS S:37 10.739 E:145 51.691
MR: Map 10 F3

Candlebark camping area

From the roundabout on UT Creek Road follow the signposted access to Candlebark CA and follow for 700m to the camping area. Large open camping area with flat sites. Communal fire pits in day use area. Water is untreated, so boil or treat first or bring own drinking water.
GPS S:37 10.572 E:145 50.515
MR: Map 10 F2

Devils Cove camping area

Seasonally opened. Access road signposted 500m past Candlebark CA. Water is untreated; boil or treat first or bring own drinking water.
GPS S:37 10.389 E:145 50.350
MR: Map 10 F2

FURTHER Information

Parks Vic Info Line
Tel: 13 19 63. Advance bookings required.
Bookings: Parks Vic Info Line **Tel:** 13 19 63 or online at www.parkstay.vic.gov.au
Camping fees: From $16.50 per site/night.

Lakeside camping area

From the roundabout on UT Creek Road take the signposted access road to the Lakeside CA and follow for 2.8km to the very large, terraced camping area with

Jerusalem Creek camping area

From the southern side of the river in Eildon, follow signposts to Jerusalem Creek and at 7.1km at the Y-junction follow signposts to Lake Eildon National Park. At 1.8km you arrive at the first signposted camping area, providing seven camping areas, each with 20 campsites. All areas are signposted along this access road. Dispersed camping among vegetation with flat sites. Camping areas set well back from the lake. Bring drinking water and firewood.
GPS S:37 15.705 E:145 57.922
MR: Map 10 G3

FURTHER Information

Parks Vic Info Line
Tel: 13 19 63. Advance bookings required for areas 1, 5 and 6.
Bookings: Parks Vic Info Line **Tel:** 13 19 63 or online at www.parkstay.vic.gov.au
Camping fees: From $12.50 per site/night. Non booked areas, payable to ranger.

O'Tooles Flat camping area

Access via Gap Track, which is signposted along Jamieson-Eildon Road 9.5km from Taponga CA in Lower Big River State Forest. Then proceed in 600m to cleared area among trees beside the track. Bring drinking water and firewood.
GPS S:37 20.614 E:145 59.265
MR: Map 10 G4

Taylors Creek camping area

Boat-based or walk-in campsite located at Big River Arm. Bring own drinking water and firewood. Contact ranger for details.
MR: Map 10 G3

Mountaineer Inlet camping area

Boat-based or walk-in campsite located at Stone Bay. Bring own drinking water and firewood. Contact ranger for details.
MR: Map 10 F2

Coopers Point camping area

Boat-based campsite located on eastern foreshore of Lake Eildon opposite Coller Bay. Bring own drinking water. Contact ranger for details.
MR: Map 10 F2

FURTHER Information

Parks Vic Info Line
Tel: 13 19 63.

Delatite Arm Reserve camping areas

Delatite Arm Reserve has 24 camping zones located on the southern shore of the Delatite Arm of Lake Eildon. Access is via signposted Walshes Road from Goughs Bay, which is access off the Mansfield-Jamieson Road 14km south of Mansfield and 21km north of Jamieson.

Follow Walshes Road for 5.8km to the information bay, which has all details of the camping areas. Open fires prohibited November to April. Gas/fuel stove preferred.
Information bay **GPS** S:37 10.873 E:146 00.555
MR: Map 10 G2

FURTHER Information

> **DSE Mansfield**
> **Tel:** 03 5733 1200

18 Lerderderg State Park

Lerderderg State Park is located north of Bacchus Marsh and east of Blackwood. The park's dominant feature is the 300-metre deep Lerderderg Gorge. There are numerous walks through the park of varying lengths and difficulty. In the south of the park is the delightful picnic area of Mackenzies Flat, which is accessed via Lerderderg Gorge Road off the Bacchus Marsh-Gisborne Road. Access to the park from the east via Firth Road off the Bacchus Marsh-Gisborne Road; and access from the west is via Golden Point Road from Blackwood.

CLOSE TO MELBOURNE

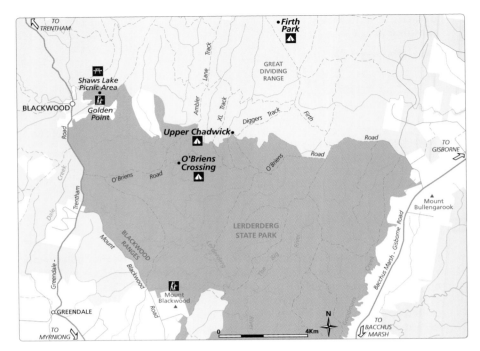

O'Briens Crossing camping area

Located 8km east of Blackwood on the Lerderderg River. From Blackwood take Golden Point Road then onto O'Briens Road. Access road is steep in places. Bring drinking water and firewood.
GPS S:37 29.798 E:144 21.678
MR: Map 7 I5

Upper Chadwick Campground

Located along Upper Chadwick Track, which is signposted off O'Briens Road east of O'Briens Crossing. Bring drinking water and firewood.
MR: Map 7 I5

Walk-in bush camping areas

Walk-in bush campsites located through the park for self-sufficient, experienced walkers. Contact ranger for details.

FURTHER Information

Parks Vic Info Line
Tel: 13 19 63
Parks Vic Bacchus Marsh
Tel: 03 5367 2922

19 Marysville State Forest

Located north-east of Marysville. Access via Lady Talbot Drive. Spectacular waterfalls and rainforests en route in the Yarra Ranges National Park.

Keppel Hut camping area

4WD (seasonal) only access via Keppel Hut Track off Lady Talbot Drive. Bring drinking water and firewood. Small walk-in camping area near hut. Part of the Bi-centennial National Trail.
MR: Map 10 F5

FURTHER Information

> **DSE Marysville**
> **Tel:** 03 5957 7111

20 Molesworth Recreational Reserve

Molesworth Recreational Reserve is situated beside the Goulburn River in the village of Molesworth on the Goulburn Valley Highway, 14km north-east of Yea. Fish, canoe and go boating on the Goulburn River.

Molesworth camping ground

Signposted access on the Goulburn Valley Highway in Molesworth, then in 300m to reserve. Laundry facilities. Bring drinking water and firewood.
GPS S:37 09.822 E:145 32.400
MR: Map 10 D2

FURTHER Information

> **Molesworth Recreational Reserve**
> **Tel:** 03 5797 6278
> **Camping fees:** Unpowered tent site from $10 per site/night for 2 people. Powered sites from $12 per site/night. Limited powered sites, call in advance for availability.

21 Mount Disappointment State Forest

Mt Disappointment was named by Hamilton Hume and William Hovell in 1824 while seeking an overland route to Port Phillip Bay from the Southern Highlands of NSW. Mt Disappointment State Forest is located 60km north of Melbourne, south-east of Broadford. Access to the forest from the west is via North Mountain Road from Heathcote Junction; or from the north via Reedy Creek Road and Murchison Spur Road off the Broadford-Strath Creek Road. Enjoy the scenic views to Port Phillip Bay from Mt Disappointment, tour the forests by car or bike, on foot or horse back.

No 1 Camp camping area

Located at the junction of Main Mountain and Flowerdale roads. Main Mountain

Road is accessed off North Mountain Road from Heathcote Junction. Large area suited to groups. Bring drinking water and firewood.
MR: Map 10 B4

Regular Camp camping area

Located along Main Mountain Road, which is accessed off North Mountain Road or off Spur Road from the Broadford-Wallan Road north of Wandong. Camping area bollarded, carry in gear. Bring drinking water and firewood.
MR: Map 10 B4

> **DSE Broadford**
> **Tel:** 03 5784 0600

22 Mount Franklin Reserve

Mount Franklin Reserve has signposted access off the Midland Highway 10.5km north of Daylesford and 4.2km north of the access road to Hepburn Springs. Excellent views can be had on the drive from the highway to the summit of Mount Franklin.

Mount Franklin Reserve camping area

Signposted access off Midland Highway 10.5km north of Daylesford and then in 1.7km to large attractive and scenic camping area. Short-term camping. Bring drinking water and firewood.
GPS S:37 15.946 E:144 09.043
MR: Map 7 H4

FURTHER Information

> **Parks Vic Info Line**
> **Tel:** 13 19 63

23 Mount Torbreck Scenic Reserve

Located 14km south of Eildon. The main access is signposted via Barnewall Plains Road. Access roads and tracks are subject to seasonal closures during winter. Walk to the summit of Mt Torbreck, 2 hours return.

Barnewall Plains camping area

Located 6km along Barnewall Plains Road from its junction with the Eildon-Jamieson Road. Shaded site among snow gums. Bring drinking water and firewood.
MR: Map 10 F4

FURTHER Information

> **DSE Customer Service Centre**
> **Tel:** 13 61 86

CLOSE TO MELBOURNE

24 Murrindindi Scenic Reserve

Murrindindi Scenic Reserve is situated in the northern end of Toolangi State Forest and can be accessed from the west via Murrindindi Road off the Melba Highway south of Yea. Or, from the south take the signposted Sylvia Creek Road 2km south-east of Toolangi and follow for 11km to Siberia Junction and the start of Murrindindi Road, which proceeds north pass all the camping areas en route to the Melba Highway. The reserve has picturesque Mountain Ash forests, fern-filled gullies, cascading waterfalls and the delightful Murrindindi River, which provides excellent riverside camping and refreshing waters to paddle in on a hot day. Activities include picnicking, walking trails, motorbike riding, 4WD touring, mountain bike riding and fishing.

Bull Creek camping area

Signposted access on Murrindindi Road 10.2km north of Siberia Junction. Then proceed 200m in to reach the camping area, which has approximately 23 sites individually fenced off along the river. Access track to the sites winds around trees in some sections and is narrow and tight, which limits access for some camper trailers and caravans. Bring drinking water and firewood.
GPS S:37 25.879 E:145 34.494
MR: Map 10 E4

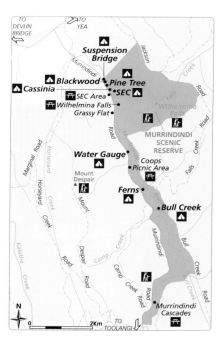

Walking bridge to SEC camping area

Ferns camping area

Ferns camping area

Signposted access on Murrindindi Road 600m north of Bull Creek CA. Small area with individually fenced sites, best suited for tents and smaller camper trailers. Bring drinking water and firewood.
GPS S:37 25.572 E:145 34.121
MR: Map 10 E4

Water Gauge camping area

Signposted access on Murrindindi Road 1.3km north of Ferns CA. Small area suitable for 5 or 6 sites. Bring drinking water and firewood.
GPS S:37 24.932 E:145 33.893
MR: Map 10 E4

SEC camping area

Walk-in site. Carpark is located along Murrindindi Road 2.6km north of Water Gauge CA, then walk and carry gear across bridge to camping area. Bring drinking water. Car park.
GPS S:37 23.706 E:145 33.483
MR: Map 10 E4

Cassinia camping area

Signposted access on Murrindindi Road 200m north of SEC CA carpark. Eight sites with carry in over bollards. Bring drinking water and firewood.
GPS S:37 23.598 E:145 33.355
MR: Map 10 E4

Pine Tree camping area

Signposted access on Murrindindi Road 100m north of Cassinia CA. A number of sites are suitable for larger camper trailers and caravans. Bring drinking water and firewood.
GPS S:37 23.543 E:145 33.318
MR: Map 10 E4

Blackwood camping area

Signposted access on Murrindindi Road 200m north of Pine Tree CA. Bring drinking water and firewood.
GPS S:37 23.409 E:145 33.182
MR: Map 10 E4

Suspension Bridge camping area

Signposted access on Murrindindi Road 100m north of Blackwood CA. Well grassed area suitable for six sites, some suitable for groups. Suitable for small caravans. Bring drinking water and firewood.
GPS S:37 23.341 E:145 33.171
MR: Map 10 E4

FURTHER Information

DSE Customer Service Centre
Tel: 13 61 86
Camping fees: From $5 per vehicle/night. Fees payable at self-registration station at Suspension Bridge camping area.

TOTAL Fire Bans

 On days that are declared a total fire ban it is illegal to light any fire in the open, in tents and in canvas camping trailers. This includes any naked flame (portable stoves, gas and solid fuel BBQ). It's your responsibility to be aware of which fire district your campsite falls under. Fire bans are usually broadcast on the local radio station.

25 Point Leo Foreshore Reserve

Attractive reserve adjacent to Western Port on the Mornington Peninsula at Point Leo. Good surfing beaches nearby.

Point Leo Foreshore caravan and camping area

Located at the foreshore in Point Leo. Attractive, grassed area with some shelter and light coastal vegetation set above the shoreline. Communal barbecue area in day use area. Laundry facilities. Store nearby. Generally open all year.
GPS S:38 25.007 E:145 04.606
MR: Map 11 B3

FURTHER Information

Point Leo Foreshore Reserve
Tel: 03 5989 8333. Bookings recommended during peak periods.
Camping fees: Contact office for current fee structure.

Located on Mornington Peninsula 5km west of Dromana. Situated on the foreshore of Port Phillip Bay and stretches for nearly 7km from McCrae to Rosebud West. Popular watersports area. Boat hire facilities nearby.

Rosebud Foreshore caravan and camping area

Signposted access along Point Nepean Road, numerous access points. Very large area with 665 sites and good beach access. Gas/fuel stove only.
GPS S:38 21.670 E:144 53.117
MR: Map 8 K3

FURTHER Information

Rosebud Foreshore Reserve, Mornington Peninsula Shire
Tel: 03 5986 8286. Bookings recommended. Camping available between November and April.
Web: www.mornpen.vic.gov.au
Camping fees: Unpowered from $20 per site/night. Powered from $26 per site/night.

Beach boxes along Rosebud Foreshore

CLOSE TO MELBOURNE

Rubicon River

27 Rubicon State Forest

Located 150km north-east of Melbourne. Access via Rubicon Road, which is signposted 3km south of Thornton and 10km north-east of Taggerty on the Thornton-Taggerty-Thornton Road. The forest and surrounds are popular for 4WD touring, bushwalking, fishing and horse riding.

Kendall's camping area

Signposted access 5.7km south of the Thornton-Taggerty Road along Rubicon Road, sealed to this camping area. Travel another 100m to large grassed camping area with plenty of shade. Walk short distance to river. Bring drinking water and firewood.
GPS S:37 18.603 E:145 51.150
MR: Map 10 F3

The Boy's camping area

Signposted access 1.5km south of Kendall's CA along Rubicon Road. Rubicon Road is unsealed from Kendall's CA. Grassed, well-shaded area close to the river. Bring drinking water and firewood.
GPS S:37 19.253 E:145 51.643
MR: Map 10 F3

FURTHER Information

> **DSE Customer Service Centre**
> **Tel:** 13 61 86

28 Rye Foreshore Reserve

Located adjacent to Port Phillip Bay on the Mornington Peninsula at Rye. Signposted access along Point Nepean Road.

Rye Beach Camping Ground

Signposted access along Point Nepean Road in Rye. Large area with sites situated between Point Nepean Road and the foreshore. Gas/fuel stove only.
GPS S:38 22.237 E:144 49.505
MR: Map 8 K3

FURTHER Information

Rye Foreshore Reserve,
Mornington Peninsula Shire
Tel: 03 5986 8286. Bookings essential. Camping available between November and April.
Web: www.mornpen.vic.gov.au
Camping fees: Unpowered from $20 per site/night. Powered from $26 per site/night.

29 Shoreham Foreshore Reserve

Located at Shoreham on the south-east side of Mornington Peninsula. From the Frankston-Flinders Highway take the signposted Byrnes Road to Shoreham and follow the signage to the Shoreham Camping Ground via Prout-Webb Road. Foreshore frontage to the entrance of Western Port.

Shoreham Camping Ground

Accessed via Prout-Webb Road in Shoreham. Scattered camping among coastal vegetation; well-protected sites. Gas/fuel stove only.
GPS S:38 25.721 E:145 03.041
MR: Map 11 B3

FURTHER Information

Shoreham Foreshore Reserve
Tel: 03 5989 8325. Bookings recommended during peak periods.
Camping fees: From $25 per site/night for 2 people.

30 Sorrento Foreshore Reserve

Foreshore frontage to Port Phillip Bay on the Mornington Peninsula. Signposted access along Point Nepean Road, 1km east of Sorrento shopping village.

Sorrento Foreshore caravan and camping area

Located 1km east of Sorrento, signposted on Point Nepean Road. Small area, well sheltered, located beside the sailing club. Gas/fuel stove only
GPS S: 38 20.665 E:144 45.154
MR: Map 8 K3

FURTHER Information

Sorrento Foreshore Reserve, Mornington Peninsula Shire
Tel: 03 5986 8286. Bookings essential during peak period mid-December to end of January. Camping available between November and April.
Camping fees: Unpowered from $20 per site/night. Powered from $26 per site/night.

31 Tallarook State Forest

Located 80km north of Melbourne between Broadford and Seymour. Access via Ennis Road off the Hume Freeway. Conventional vehicle access to Freemans camping area. Activities include 4WD touring, motorbike riding, bushwalking and horse riding. Note: The forest is a gazetted military training area.

Freemans picnic and camping area

Located 11km east of the Hume Freeway on Freemans Road, which is signposted off Ennis Road. Ennis Road leaves the freeway north of the Broadford exit and 2km south of the C383 Tallarook exit. Ideal area for groups and families. Bring drinking water.
MR: Map 10 B3

Falls Creek Reservoir camping area

4WD (seasonal closures apply) access via East Falls Road off Freemans Road or Ennis (Main) Road. Site located beside old water supply dam. Water from dam, boil or treat first.
MR: Map 10 B3

FURTHER Information

DSE Broadford
Tel: 03 5784 0600

32 Upper Yarra Reservoir Park

Upper Yarra Reservoir Park is located 24km east of Warburton. Access is via the Woods Point-Warburton Road. The park is the upper most point of the Yarra River that's accessible to the public. The reservoir is the third largest of Melbourne's water supplies. View the restored McVeigh's Water Wheel, go bushwalking or take in the views from the lookout points.

Upper Yarra Reservoir Park camping area

Signposted access via the Woods Point Road 24km east of Warburton. Park open 8.30am–5pm and 6pm summer time. Ideal area for groups and families. Bring own firewood.
MR: Map 10 F6

FURTHER Information

Parks Vic Info Line
Tel: 13 19 63. Advance bookings required.
Bookings: By phone or online at www. parkstay.vic.gov.au
Camping fees: From $5.70 per adult/night and $3.40 per child/night.site/night.

33 White Cliffs to Cameron's Bight Foreshore

Foreshore area stretched along Port Phillip Bay at Blairgowrie, with two separate camping areas. Signposted access off Point Nepean Road.

Stringer Road Caravan Park

Signposted access on Point Nepean Road at Blairgowrie, 2km south-east of Sorrento. Sites along the foreshore, grassed with some good shelter. Cold outdoor shower. Gas/fuel stove only.
GPS S:38 21.318 E:144 45.874
MR: Map 8 K3

Tyrone Road Caravan Park

Signposted access on Point Nepean Road at White Cliffs, east of Blairgowrie. Open

area on foreshore with flat grassed sites. Gas/fuel stove only.
GPS S:38 22.010 E:144 48.407
MR: Map 8 K3

FURTHER Information

White Cliffs to Cameron's Bight Foreshore, Mornington Peninsula Shire
Tel: 03 5985 3288. Bookings essential during peak period Christmas and Easter. Camping available between November and April.
Web: www.foreshore.net.au
Camping fees: From $30 per site/night.

34 Wombat State Forest

Located to the north-east of Melbourne between Macedon in the east and Daylesford in the west. Access to Wombat State Forest is via Firth Road off Carrolls Lane, which leaves the Bacchus Marsh–Gisborne Road, south of Gisborne. The forest is popular for vehicle touring, bushwalking, mountain bike riding and horse riding. View the old logging relics at Firth Park.

Firth Park picnic and camping area

Signposted access along Firth Road off Carrolls Lane from the Bacchus Marsh–Gisborne Road. Old sawmill site. Bring drinking water and firewood.
GPS S:37 26.125 E:144 24.583
MR: Map 7 I5

Nolan's Creek picnic and camping area

Located 11km west of Blackwood on Lerderderg Road (Wombat Forest Drive). Bring drinking water and firewood.
MR: Map 7 I5

Bush camping
Camping in the bush is permitted within the forest. Contact the ranger for details.

Firth Park

FURTHER Information

> **DSE Customer Service Centre**
> **Tel:** 13 61 86
> **DSE Daylesford**
> **Tel:** 03 5348 2211

35 Yarra State Forest

Located 75km east of Melbourne near Powelltown. Access via Warburton, Powelltown, Yarra Junction and Nojee. Yarra State Forest contains the upper reaches of the Yarra, Latrobe and Bunyip River systems. Popular area for forest drives. More than 100km of walking trails criss-cross these forests, including the Walk Into History, a two-day hike from Powelltown to East Warburton. Visit the Ada Tree, a giant mountain ash that's one of the largest trees in Victoria. Other activities include 4WD touring, horse riding and mountain biking.

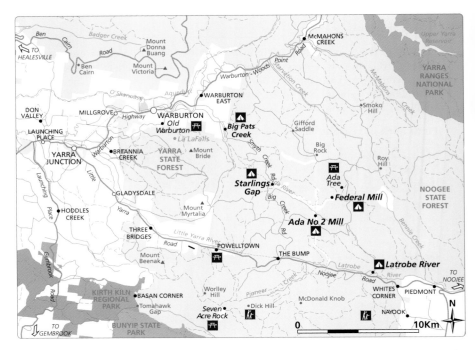

Starlings Gap camping area

Located on Big Creek Road. Best access is via signposted Black Sands Road off the Yarra Junction–Noojee Road. The turn off is just south-east of small village of Gladysdale.
MR: Map 10 F7

Latrobe River camping area

Located on Ada River Road off the Noojee-Powelltown Road. Situated beside the Latrobe River.
MR: Map 10 F7

Big Pats Creek, Ada No 2 Mill and Federal Mill camping areas

Walk-in sites located along the Walk Into History Trail. No facilities; toilet located at Big Pats Creek. Trail brochure available from DSE.

Bush camping

Bush camping is permitted within the forest. Contact the ranger for details.

FURTHER Information

DSE Customer Service Centre
Tel: 13 61 86
DSE Powelltown
Tel: 03 5966 7203

Otways and South-West

VICTORIA'S most popular and most visited regions, the Otways and South-West is blessed with kilometre after kilometre of stunning coastline featuring pristine white sandy beaches interspersed with rugged headlands and rocky outcrops.

This region offers some excellent bushwalking, camping and sightseeing destinations. Popular locations include stunningly diverse Great Otway National Park, Discovery Bay Coastal Park and the many scenic coastal towns along one of Australia's greatest drives, the spectacular Great Ocean Road. The towering verdant forests of the Otway Ranges

tucked in behind Lorne offer a selection of wonderful walking and camping areas. Hidden away in the forests is the picturesque Lake Elizabeth, formed by a landslip in the 1950s. A walking track leads to the lake from the camping area.

Campers in Great Otway National Park can take in the spectacular coastal vistas from numerous lookouts scattered throughout the park or visit any number of waterfalls for which the area is renowned. For the energetic there are marked bushwalking tracks to explore while mountain bikers and four-wheel drivers will also find tracks to enjoy. Be sure to pack a raincoat, though, because this region receives Victoria's highest yearly rainfall.

Bushwalkers looking for multi-day adventures will find top campsites along the long distance Great South West Walk. Starting in Portland, the trek winds its way through forests and coastline before finishing back at Portland. Lower Glenelg National Park in the far west of the region has some wonderful camping along the banks of the river where canoeing, fishing and swimming are popular water based activities. Many of the towns along the coast have camping reserves which are generally in prime foreshore locations.

The preferred time to visit this region is during spring, summer and early autumn. Many campsites close to the coast will require prior booking over the busy summer period.

BEST Campsites!

 Cumberland River Holiday Park
Cumberland River Reserve

 Blanket Bay camping area
Otway National Park

 Lake Elizabeth camping area
Great Otway National Park

 Pritchards camping area
Lower Glenelg National Park

 Sawpit Gully picnic and camping area
Mount Clay State Forest

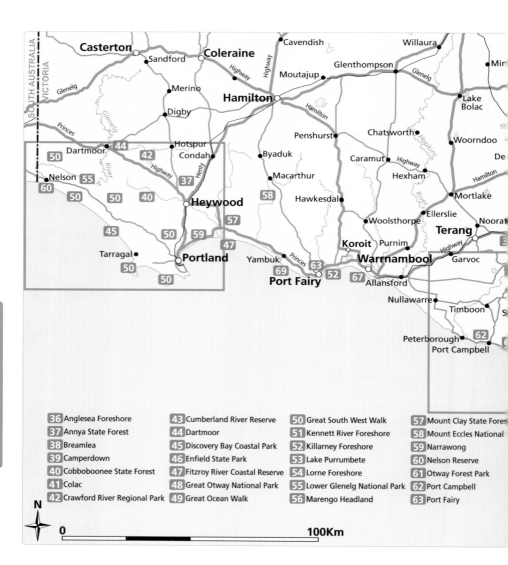

Legend:
- 36 Anglesea Foreshore
- 37 Annya State Forest
- 38 Breamlea
- 39 Camperdown
- 40 Cobboboonee State Forest
- 41 Colac
- 42 Crawford River Regional Park
- 43 Cumberland River Reserve
- 44 Dartmoor
- 45 Discovery Bay Coastal Park
- 46 Enfield State Park
- 47 Fitzroy River Coastal Reserve
- 48 Great Otway National Park
- 49 Great Ocean Walk
- 50 Great South West Walk
- 51 Kennett River Foreshore
- 52 Killarney Foreshore
- 53 Lake Purrumbete
- 54 Lorne Foreshore
- 55 Lower Glenelg National Park
- 56 Marengo Headland
- 57 Mount Clay State Forest
- 58 Mount Eccles National
- 59 Narrawong
- 60 Nelson Reserve
- 61 Otway Forest Park
- 62 Port Campbell
- 63 Port Fairy

N

0 ————————————— 100Km

36 Anglesea Foreshore

Located at Anglesea close to shopping centre. Signposted access on Cameron Road from The Great Ocean Road. Beach and river frontage.

Anglesea Family Caravan Park

Access via Cameron Road in Anglesea. Camp kitchen. Gas/fuel stove only.
MR: Map 8 H4

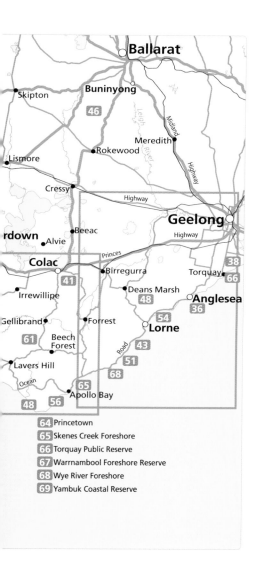

64 Princetown
65 Skenes Creek Foreshore
66 Torquay Public Reserve
67 Warrnambool Foreshore Reserve
68 Wye River Foreshore
69 Yambuk Coastal Reserve

FURTHER Information

Anglesea Family Caravan Park
Tel: 03 5263 1583. Bookings recommended at peak times.
Web: www.angleseafcp.com.au
Camping fees: Powered from $32 per site/night for 2 people. Cabin accommodation available.

TUCKER Time

If one thing is for sure, it's that your appetite certainly increases when camping. Choose your meals on personal preference. It's quite easy to cook when out camping what you'd cook at home – with a little thought. But then again, why not try something new. BBQ's are fine for a few days but may get a little monotonous every night for two weeks!

As for cooking equipment, a folding grate for the fire, a BBQ plate, frying pan, a few pots with lids and a couple of billies are generally all that's required for camp cooking. A gas stove – a single burner for a couple of people or a two burner LPG or fuel stove for families and groups are essential for when campfires are not allowed or impractical. For example, many outback national parks do not allow fires, campfires are not permitted in many coastal reserves while some regions have fire bans in place over the summer months each year.

37 Annya State Forest

Annya State Forest is located to the north of Heywood near Drumborg. Access is via the Portland-Casterton Road off the Princes Highway.

Annya Camp camping area

Access via Portland-Casterton Road off the Princes Highway. Bring drinking water.
MR: Map 4 R5

> **DSE Heywood**
> **Tel:** 03 5527 0444

38 Breamlea

Breamlea is located 18km south of Geelong between Barwon Heads and Torquay. Good fishing destination with a patrolled ocean beach and tidal estuary.

Breamlea Caravan Park

Access via Horwood Drive in Breamlea. Gas/fuel stove only. Open all year round
MR: Map 8 I3

FURTHER Information

> **Breamlea Caravan Park**
> **Tel:** 03 5264 1352. Bookings recommended at peak times.
> **Camping fees:** Off-peak: Unpowered from $20 per site/night for 2 adults. Powered from $23 per site/night for 2 adults.

39 Camperdown

Lake Bullen Merri is part of an extinct volcanic crater. The lake is located 3km south-west of Camperdown and is a popular watersports venue.

Camperdown Lakes & Craters Holiday Park

Located south-west of Camperdown on Park Road. Signposted access from Camperdown. Fires are permitted, bring own fire drum and firewood.
MR: Map 8 B2

FURTHER Information

> **Camperdown Lakes & Craters Holiday Park**
> **Tel:** 03 5593 1253. Bookings recommended at peak times (Easter and Christmas) for powered sites and cabin accommodation.
> **Camping fees:** Contact office for current fee structure. Cabin accommodation available.

Cobboboonee State Forest is situated north-west of Portland and west of Heywood. The forest has a range of walks where visitors can view the diverse vegetation of the forest and do some wildlife spotting. The main access road T+W Road is signposted off the Portland-Nelson Road 22km west of Portland and off the Princes Highway north-west of Heywood.

Jackass Fern Gully camping area

Located 9km along T+W Road. T+W Road is signposted 22km west of Portland along the Portland-Nelson Road. Proceed north along T+W Road for 20km to signposted turn off to Jackass Fern Gully, then campsite is located 300m west. Bring drinking water and firewood.
GPS: S:38 04.487 E:141 25.550
MR: Map 4 E6

Jackass Fern Gully camping area

Surrey Ridge picnic and camping area

Located 300m south of Cut Out Dam Road. Take T+W Road signposted 22km west of Portland along the Portland-Nelson Road. Follow T+W Road for 6.1km to signposted Cut Out Dam Road. Camping area is signposted 3.6km along Cut Out Dam Road. Bring drinking water.
GPS: S:38 11.042 E:141 30.275
MR: Map 4 E6

FURTHER Information

> **DSE Heywood**
> **Tel:** 03 5527 0444

OTWAYS AND SOUTH-WEST

41 Colac

Colac is situated 75km west of Geelong along the Princes Highway. The town is located on the southern shores of Lake Colac, a popular watersports venue.

Lake Colac Caravan Park

Access via Fyans Street in Colac.
MR: Map 8 D3

Central Caravan Park

Located on Bruce Street in Colac. Camp kitchen, laundry facilities.
MR: Map 8 D3

Meredith Park camping area

Situated on edge of Lake Colac, on Meredith Park Road. Access signposted off the Colac-Ballarat Road, 10km north-west of Colac.
MR: Map 8 D3

FURTHER Information

> **Lake Colac Caravan Park**
> **Tel:** 03 5231 5971. Bookings recommended at peak times.
> **Camping fees:** Unpowered from $20 per site/night for 2 people. Powered from $25 per site/night for 2 people.

FURTHER Information

> **Central Caravan Park**
> **Tel:** 03 5231 3586. Bookings preferred.
> **Camping fees:** Unpowered from $12 per site/night for 2 people. Powered from $18 per site/night for 2 people.

FURTHER Information

> **Colac Tourist Information Centre**
> **Tel:** 03 5231 3730
> **Colac Fire Restrictions:** Fire Danger Period November to May — check with locals prior to lighting a fire. Fires only in regulation built fire places.

42 Crawford River Regional Park

Access via The Boulevard off the Lyons-Hotspur Road either off the Princes Highway 22km north-west from Heywood (17km south-east of Dartmoor) or from Hotspur along the Portland-Casterton Road.

Hiscocks Crossing camping area

Dispersed camping along the Crawford River between Hotspur and Dartmoor. Access via The Boulevard. Access suitable for camper trailers with four-wheel drive tow vehicles. Bring drinking water and firewood.
MR: Map 4 D4

FURTHER Information

> **Parks Vic Nelson**
> **Tel:** 08 8738 4051

OTWAYS AND SOUTH-WEST

43 Cumberland River Reserve

Located 7km south-west of Lorne. Signposted access via Great Ocean Road. River frontage surrounded by cliffs. Close to beach. Many walking trails nearby.

Cumberland River Holiday Park

Signposted access along the Great Ocean Road, 7km south-west of Lorne. Laundry facilities.

GPS: S:38 34.486 E:143 56.948
MR: Map 8 F5

FURTHER Information

> **Cumberland River Holiday Park**
> **Tel:** 03 5289 1790. Bookings recommended at peak times, Easter and Christmas.
> **Camping fees:** Unpowered from $10 per person/night. Cabin accommodation available.

44 Dartmoor

The village of Dartmoor is accessed along the Princes Highway 38km north-west of Heywood. The Glenelg River passes to the east of the town and has a canoe put set-down area. The river here is a section of the Major Mitchell Trail.

Fort O'Hare camping area

Located 800m east of Dartmoor at the end of Gambier Road, follow the Major Mitchell Trail signs. Situated on the banks of Glenelg River. Canoe set-down area. Bring drinking water and firewood.
GPS: S:37 55.578 E:141 17.103
MR: Map 4 D4

FURTHER Information

> **Nelson Visitor Information Centre**
> **Tel:** 08 8738 4051

OTWAYS AND SOUTH-WEST

Discovery Bay Coastal Park is located south-east of Nelson between Portland and Nelson. Access roads to the camping areas are signposted off the Nelson-Portland Road. Attractions include lakes, seal colonies, blowholes, petrified forests and sweeping beaches.

Lake Monibeong camping area

Located 7km south of the Nelson-Portland Road on Lake Monibeong Road. Lake Monibeong Road is signposted off the Nelson-Portland Road 16.3km south-east of Nelson and 20.9km north-east of the Swan Lake Road. A 1.2km walk leads from the camping area to the beach. Bring drinking water and firewood.
GPS: S:38 08.085 E:141 11.078
MR: Map 4 C5

Swan Lake camping area

Located 5.8km south of the Nelson-Portland Road on Swan Lake Road. Swan Lake Road is signposted off the Nelson-Portland 30km west of Portland and 21km south-east of the Lake Monibeong Road. Unsealed, loose gravel access road has steep descents and sharp bends, suitable for caravans with 4WD tow vehicle. Bring drinking water and firewood.
GPS: S:38 12.847 E:141 18.744
MR: Map 4 D6

FURTHER Information

Parks Vic Info Line
Tel: 13 19 63. Advance bookings and payment required.
Bookings: Nelson Visitor Information Centre
Tel: 08 8738 4051
Camping fees: Off-peak: From $11.50 per site/night.

46 Enfield State Park

Enfield State Park is home to numerous gold mining sites and relics from the mid to late 1800s. Try your luck fossicking for gold. Wildflower displays in spring.

Surface Point camping area

Located 30km south of Ballarat. Access is via Misery Creek Road signposted off the Ballarat-Colac Road, 25km south of Ballarat. Bring drinking water and firewood.
MR: Map 7 E7

FURTHER Information

Parks Vic Info Line
Tel: 13 19 63

Located at the mouth of the Fitzroy River half way between Portland and Yambuk. Access is via the signposted turn off along the Princes Highway. The reserve provides access to beautiful sandy beaches along the Discovery Coast.

Fitzroy River Reserve camping area

Situated on the eastern side of the Fitzroy River mouth. Located 4.1km along Thompsons Road which is signposted off the Princes Highway 21.5km west of Yambuk and 32km east of Portland. Two camping areas, one caters for overnight stays and one area for longer stays, area located 400m east of the boat ramp. Bring drinking water and firewood.
GPS: S:38 15.588 E:141 50.878
MR: Map 4 G6

FURTHER Information

> **Portland Visitor Information Centre**
> **Tel:** 03 5523 2671
> **Web:** www.glenelg.vic.gov.au
> **Camping fees:** From $6 per site/night. Fees collected daily.

OTWAYS AND SOUTH-WEST

Great Otway National Park encompasses 102,500 hectares and incorporates Otway National Park, Angahook-Lorne State Park, Carlisle State Park, Melba Gully State Park and areas of state forest. The park stretches from Torquay in the north-east to Princetown in the south-west and is home to some of the Otway's most beautiful natural and scenic features — verdant rainforests, spectacular coastline and towering mountain forests. A diverse range of activities are on offer. Visit spectacular waterfalls, take a short walk or a multiday hike along one of the many walking trails, picnic in wonderful forests, fish along the magnificent coastline, go daytripping in your car or mountain-bike riding, or just relax and enjoy the scenery. Access to various sections of the park is possible from the Great Ocean Road, or from the north via the Princes Highway from Colac via the Colac-Lavers Hill Road.

Hammonds Road camping area

Located in the northern section of the park, on Hammonds Road 10km from Aireys Inlet. Access via Bambra Road from Aireys Inlet. Gas/fuel stove only. Bring drinking water.
MR: Map 8 G3

Big Hill Track camping area

Located on Bill Hill Track. Signposted access off Deans Marsh Road 11km from Lorne heading towards Deans Marsh. Gas/fuel stove only.
MR: Map 8 G4

OTWAYS AND SOUTH-WEST

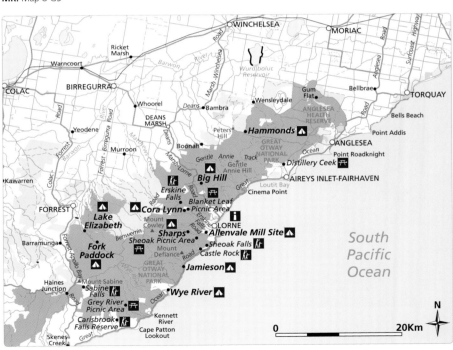

Allenvale Mill Site camping area

Accessed along Allenvale Road 2km south-west of Lorne. Walk-in access to camping area, 2 to 5 minute walk. Large partly grassed and partly shaded area. Gas/fuel stove only.
GPS: S:38 33.007 E:143 57.575
MR: Map 8 F4

Sharps Track camping area

Located on Sharps Track. Signposted access off Garvey Track off Allenvale Road. Conventional vehicle access in dry weather only, 4WD recommended. Gas/fuel stove only.
GPS: S:38 33.088 E:143 55.922
MR: Map 8 F4

Cora Lynn camping area

Located on Cora Lynn Walking Track. Walk-in only access from Blanket Leaf picnic area on the Erskenville Falls Road. Gas/fuel stove only. Contact ranger for details.
MR: Map 8 F5

Jamieson Track camping area

Located on Jamieson Track (seasonally closed). Access via Jamieson Track 10km south of Lorne on The Great Ocean Road. 4WD only access. Small area with five campsites, each site suitable for one vehicle only. Gas/fuel stove only.
MR: Map 8 F5

Wye River Road camping area

Located on Wye River Road. Sites begin 1.7km north of the Great Ocean Road. Wye River Road is signposted 14km south of Lorne along the Great Ocean Road. Twelve sites with five sites suitable for camper trailer with four-wheel drive tow vehicle. Gas/fuel stove only.
GPS: S:38 37.467 E:143 54.170
MR: Map 8 F5

Lake Elizabeth camping area

Signposted access along Kaanglang Road from Forrest. Walk in/carry gear from car park to camping site — 50 metres. Walk to picturesque Lake Elizabeth, which was formed by a natural landslip in 1952.
GPS: S:38 32.988 E:143 44.684
MR: Map 8 E4

Fork Paddock camping area

Located on West Barwon Track (seasonally closed), 6.4km north of Benwerrin Road and 100m south of the Barwon River crossing. Bush camping, no facilities. Dry weather access only, access tracks are extremely slippery and difficult after and during rain.
GPS: S:38 34.733 E:143 43.369
MR: Map 8 E4

Rainforest walk Great Otway National Park

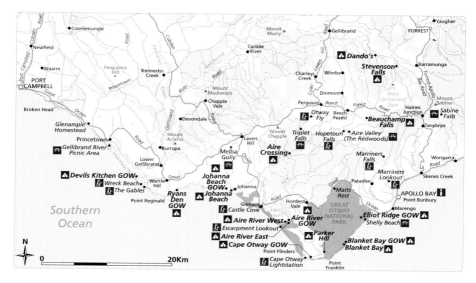

Blanket Bay camping area

Located 6.2km along Blanket Bay Road, signposted 9.3km along Cape Otway Lighthouse Road. Cape Otway Lighthouse Road is signposted off Great Ocean Road 20.4km west of Apollo Bay. Bring drinking water and firewood.
GPS: S:38 49.708 E:143 34.960
MR: Map 8 D6

Aire River East camping area

Signposted access along Horden Vale Road 5.5km south of the Great Ocean Road. Horden Vale Road is signposted off Great Ocean Road 3.3km west of Cape Otway Lighthouse Road. Located on eastern bank of Air River near its mouth. Bring drinking water and firewood.
GPS: S:38 48.032 E:143 28.914
MR: Map 8 D6

Aire River West camping area

Located on Sand Road (seasonally closed) 5.3km south of the Great Ocean Road. Sand Road is signposted off the Great Ocean Road at Glenaire. Alternative access is to continue pass Aire River East for 700m to camping area, note crossing of bridge with 5 tonne limit this way. Situated on bank of Aire River near its mouth. Gas/fuel stove only. Bring drinking water.
GPS: S:38 48.046 E:143 28.652
MR: Map 8 D6

Johanna Beach camping area

Located 4.7km south of the Great Ocean Road along Red Johanna Road. Red Johanna Road is signposted off the Great Ocean Road 12km south of Laves Hill. Alternative access via Blue Johanna Road, which is signposted off Great Ocean Road 3.5km south of Lavers Hill. Blue Johanna Road is not suitable for camper trailers or carvans, due to steep, winding narrow road. Travel along Blue Johanna Road for 8.3km. Campsites behind sand dunes. Popular surfing beach. Dogs must be kept on a leash at all times in this camping area. Gas/fuel stove only.
GPS: S:38 45.721 E:143 22.732
MR: Map 8 C6

Parker Hill camping area

Access signposted off Blanket Bay Road, 900m east of Cape Otway Lighthouse Road. Then 1.5km to camping area with 3 sites. Bring drinking water. Gas/fuel stove only.
GPS: S:38 50.811 E:143 33.500
MR: Map 8 D6

Aire Crossing camping area

Access via Wait-A-While Road from Colac-Lavers Hill Road or Aire Crossing Track from the Great Ocean Road. Sites beside Aire River.
MR: Map 8 D6

FURTHER Information

> **Parks Vic Info Line**
> **Tel:** 13 19 63. Ballot booking system for Blanket Bay for Easter and Christmas through Parks Vic Info Line.
> **Portland Visitor Information Centre**
> **Tel:** 03 5523 2671
> **Web:** www.glenelg.vic.gov.au
> **Camping fees:** Only apply during peak periods of Easter and Christmas for Blanket Bay CA from $13.50 per site/night.

WATERFALL Wonderland

Narrow valleys combined with high rainfall make the Otway Ranges the ideal destination for campers who love viewing waterfalls. Ranging from the impressive sheer drop of the easily accessible Erskine Falls near Lorne to the remote and little visited Sabine Falls high up on the escarpment, there are fourteen waterfalls available for visitors to explore in these verdant ranges.

Behind Aireys Inlet is Currawong Falls. At their best after good rain, it's a 4-hour return walk to reach this secluded drop.

Tucked away in the ranges behind Lorne, and easily the most visited falls in the Otways is Erskine Falls, located around eight kilometres from Lorne. A viewing platform offers glimpses across to the sheer 30 metre drop while the more adventurous can take the stepped path to the fern-lined pool at the base of the falls. Other falls to visit here include the delightful Cora Lynn Cascades and Phantom Falls on the St Georges River.

Near Beech Forest is Hopetoun Falls, probably one of the area's more photogenic waterfalls. A 30-minute return walk from the carpark will take you to the base of the falls which are rimmed with fern trees. Other popular falls to explore and photograph are Triplet Falls, Beauchamp Falls and Stevenson Falls.

Hopetoun Falls, Otway Ranges

49 Great Ocean Walk

This scenic walk with spectacular coastal views follows the coastline off the Great Ocean Road for 91km, from Apollo Bay to the information bay on the Great Ocean Road at the 12 Apostles south-east of Port Campbell. The walk has been designed so that walkers can either complete it in one go (an 8-day, 7-night walk) or access different sections for shorter walks. Note: When doing the complete walk, you must walk from east to west.

Great Ocean Walk camping areas

Access via the Great Ocean Walk walking trail. Limited tank water at sites with untreated rainwater, water to be boiled and/or treated first. Gas/fuel stoves only. Obtain a copy of the walk brochure and maps.

12 Apostles

Trackhead: Apollo Bay
MR: Map 8 E6
Elliot Ridge campsite: 9.9km from Apollo Bay
Blanket Bay campsite: 11.6km from Elliot Ridge
Cape Otway campsite: 10.5km from Blanket Bay
Aire River campsite: 9.7km from Cape Otway
Johanna campsite: 13.6km from Aire River
Ryans Den campsite: 12.4km from Johanna
Devils Kitchen campsite: 15.3km from
Ryans Den
Glenample Homestead Trackhead: 12.9km
from Devils Kitchen,
MR: Map 8 B5

FURTHER Information

> ### Parks Vic Info Line
> **Tel**: 13 19 63. Advance bookings necessary.
> **Web:** www.greatoceanwalk.com.au (Online
> booking system operational from October/
> November 2008.)
> **Camping fees:** From $20 per individual
> camp pad/night, plus a one-off $5
> administration fee.

Great South West Walk

Stretching for 250km, the Great South West Walk begins and ends in Portland. Leaving Portland the walk heads north through native forests before reaching the Glenelg River, then on to the coast near the South Australian border. The walk then heads east along the coast back to Portland.

The Great South West Walk camping areas

Access via The Great South West Walk walking trail. Facilities vary at sites. Water from creeks or rivers may not always be reliable — always carry extra. Gas/fuel stove preferred. Obtain a copy of the walk brochure and maps.

Trackhead: Portland
MR: Map 4 E7
Cubby's Camp: 20km from Portland
Cut-out Camp: 15km from Cubby's Camp
Cobbooboonee Camp: 9.4km from Cut-Out Camp
Fitzroy River Camp: 12.5km from Cobbooboonee Camp
Moleside Camp: 22km from Fitzroy Camp
Post and Rail Camp: 12km from Moleside Camp
Murrells Camp: 9.5km from Post and Rail Camp
Pattersons Camp: 8.5km from Murrells Camp

Simsons Camp: 17km from Pattersons Camp
White Sands Camp: 13km from Simsons Camp
Lake Monibeong: 13km from White Sands Camp (see Discovery Bay CP)
Swan Lake: 16.5km from Lake Monibeong (see Discovery Bay CP)
The Springs Camp: 21km from Swan Lake Camp
Trewalla Camp: 15km from The Springs Camp
Mallee Camp: 17km from Trewalla Camp and 16.5km from Portland Visitor Information Centre,
MR: Map 4 E7

FURTHER Information

> ### Parks Vic Info Line
> **Tel:** 13 19 63.
> ### Portland Visitor Information Centre
> **Tel:** 03 5523 2671
> **Web:** www.glenelg.vic.gov.au
> **Note:** Walkers are advised to register their intentions with the Portland Police or Portland Visitor Information Centre. Don't forget to de-register on completion of walk.

Kennett River Foreshore

Located at Kennett River between Lorne and Apollo Bay. Signposted access via The Great Ocean Road. River frontage. Popular surfing area.

Kennett River Caravan Park

Signposted access off the Great Ocean Road at Kennett River.
MR: Map 8 F5

FURTHER Information

> ### Kennett River Caravan Park
> **Tel:** 13 19 63.
> **Tel:** 03 5289 0272. Bookings required at peak times.
> **Camping fees:** Off-peak: Unpowered from $22 per site/night for 2 people. Powered from $25 per site/night for 2 people.

Killarney Foreshore

Set among coastal vegetation Killarney Foreshore is a well-sheltered grassy site. Killarney Beach offers safe swimming, fishing and walking. Access via the signposted route to Killarney Beach.

Killarney Beach camping ground

Signposted access on Mahoneys Road 11km east of Port Fairy.
MR: Map 4 I7

FURTHER Information

Killarney Beach Caretaker
Tel: 0407 504 049. Bookings recommended during Christmas holiday period.
Killarney Beach booking line
Tel: 0428 314 823
Camping fees: Unpowered from $14 per site/night. Powered from $18 per site/night. Fees collected by caretaker.

Lake Purrumbete

Lake Purrumbete is a popular fishing venue. The lake is located 10km east of Camperdown along Purrumbete Estate Road, off the Princes Highway.

Lake Purrumbete Caravan Park

Located on Purrumbete Estate Road, close to the lake.
MR: Map 8 C3

FURTHER Information

Lake Purrumbete Caravan Park
Tel: 03 5594 5377. Bookings recommended at peak times.
Camping fees: Unpowered from $8 per person/night. Powered from $20 per site/night for 1 to 2 people.

Lorne Foreshore

Lorne is a popular tourist destination, located on the coast along the Great Ocean Road. The region is blessed with natural beauty: great beaches, beautiful coast, magnificent rainforests, waterfalls and scenic views.

Erskine River camping area

Located on the northern bank of Erskine River. Signposted access on the Great Ocean Road in Lorne.
MR: Map 8 F4

Kia-Ora camping area

Located on the southern bank of Erskine River. Signposted access on Great Ocean Road in Lorne. Gas/fuel stove only.
MR: Map 8 F4

FURTHER Information

Lorne Foreshore Reserve
Tel: 03 5289 1382 or 1300 736 533.
Bookings required at peak times: Victorian school and public holidays, Easter and Christmas.
Web: www.gorcc.com.au
Camping fees: From $25 per site/night for 2 people. Cabin accommodation available.

55 Lower Glenelg National Park

Lower Glenelg National Park is located east of Nelson. The tranquil waters of the Glenelg River is its major attraction and is ideal for canoeing and fishing. Explore Princess Margaret Rose Cave, go bushwalking or just relax by the river. The park's camping areas are located on the southern and northern shores of the river. Access to the southern shore of the river is via Glenelg Drive, which is signposted 2km north of Nelson along North Nelson Track and accessible via signposted access tracks along the Nelson-Winnap Road. Access to the northern shore of the river is via River Fireline, which is signposted 14.8km south of Dartmoor off Wanwin Road. Camping areas are also signposted along Wanwin Road, which runs parallel and north of River Fireline.

Glenelg River at Red Gum camping area

CAMPING AREAS ON THE SOUTHERN SHORE OF RIVER

Forest Camp South camping area

Signposted access along Glenelg Drive 13.1km east of North Nelson Track. Then 200m north to camping area with 8 sites. Bring drinking water and firewood.
GPS: S:38 01.863 E:141 08.323
MR: Map 4 C5

Battersbys camping area

Signposted access along Glenelg Drive 3km east of Forest Camp South access track and 16km east of North Nelson Track. Then 300m north to camping area with 4 sites. Bring drinking water and firewood.
GPS: S:38 02.773 E:141 09.652
MR: Map 4 C5

Pritchards camping area

Signposted access off the Nelson-Winnap Road, 1.5km east of Glenelg Drive and 8.8km north of the Nelson-Portland Road. Then 1.1km into the 20-site camping area. Sites 11 to 20 suitable for camper trailers and caravans. Bring drinking water and firewood.
GPS: S:38 03.377 E:141 13.138
MR: Map 4 C5

Wild Dog Bend camping area

Access is off the Nelson-Winnap Road, 5.1km north-east of the Pritchards access track. Access track is not signposted. Then 3.1km into camping area. Bring drinking water and firewood.
GPS: S:38 02.290 E:141 14.746
MR: Map 4 C5

CAMPING AREAS ON THE NORTHERN SHORE OF RIVER

Red Gum camping area

From Dartmoor follow Wanwin Road for 14.8km, then take road signposted Red Gum, and after 2.9km turn west into signposted River Fireline. Access track to Red Gum camping area is signposted 1.9km along River Fireline. Then 200m south into large camping area. Bring drinking water and firewood.
GPS: S:38 02.064 E:141 09.320
MR: Map 4 C5

Forest Camp North camping area

Signposted access along River Fireline, 2km west of Red Gum access road. Then 200m south to large open camping area. Access track is steep; 4WD vehicle recommended. Bring drinking water and firewood.
GPS: S:38 01.792 E:141 08.411
MR: Map 4 C5

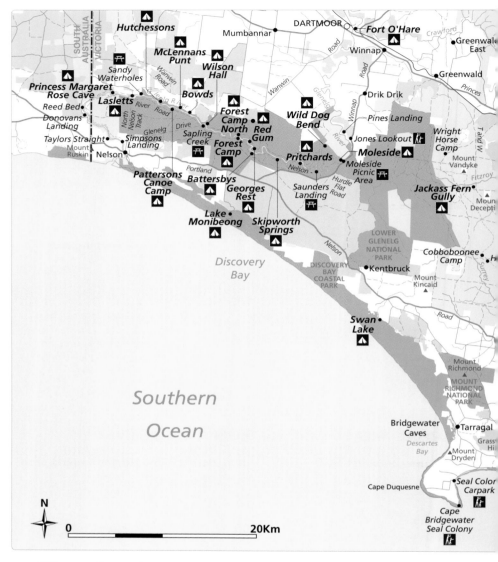

Wilson Hall camping area

Signposted access along River Fireline 3.4km west of Forest Camp North access road. Then 350m to camping area with 12 sites. Bring drinking water and firewood.
GPS: S:38 01.320 E:141 06.376
MR: Map 4 C5

McLennans Punt camping area

Signposted access along River Fireline 3.6km west of Wilson Hall access road. Then in 250m to camping area with 3 sites. Bring drinking water and firewood.
GPS: S:38 00.306 E:141 04.473
MR: Map 4 C5

of River Fireline. Bring drinking water and firewood.

GPS: S:37 59.907 E:141 02.808
MR: Map 4 C5

CANOE ACCESS CAMPING AREAS

Lasletts, Pattersons, Bowds, Georges Rest, Skipworth Springs, Moleside, Pines Landing, Fort O'Hare

Canoe/boat access sites along the Glenelg River. Permit required. Obtain a copy of the Glenelg River Canoeing Guide from Parks Vic.
MR: Map 4 C5

FURTHER *Information*

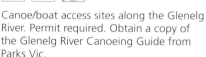

Parks Vic Info Line

Tel: 13 19 63. Advance bookings and permits are required for all sites in Lower Glenelg National Park.
Bookings: Nelson Visitor Information Centre, 08 8738 4051.
Camping fees: Southern and Northern Shore sites: Off-peak From $11.50 per site/night. Peak From $15.50 per site/night. Canoe access sites From $3.20 per person/night.

Hutchessons camping area

Signposted access along River Fireline 900m west of McLennans Punt access track. Then in 250m to camping area with 2 sites. Access is also signposted off Wanwin Road, which is 1.9km north

Princess Margaret Rose Caves camping area

Located 19km along Princess Margaret Rose Caves Road, which is signposted off the Princes Highway 10km east of Mt Gambier. Or access off Nelson Road 3km south of Mt Gambier, then 26km to camping area. Camp kitchen.
MR: Map 4 B4

FURTHER Information

Princess Margaret Rose Caves
Tel: 08 8738 4171. Advance bookings recommended.
Camping fees: Unpowered from $15 per site/night. No powered sites.

Canoeing Glenelg River

OTWAYS AND SOUTH-WEST

Situated just south of Apollo Bay, Marengo Headland offers superb beach frontage. As well as the excellent views, the area offers great fishing and surfing.

Marengo Holiday Park

Located on Marengo Crescent in Marengo. Signposted off the Great Ocean Road.
MR: Map 8 E6

FURTHER Information

> **Marengo Holiday Park**
> **Tel:** 03 5237 6162. Bookings required during peak periods or Christmas and Easter.
> **Web:** www.vicnet.net.au/~marengo
> **Camping fees:** Off-peak: Unpowered from $24 per site/night for 2 people. Powered from $25 per site/night for 2 people. Cabin accommodation available.

Mount Clay State Forest is located 15km to the east of Portland near Narrawong. Access to the forest is via Boyers Road off the Princes Highway. Take the short walk to Whalers Lookout for excellent whale watching.

Sawpit picnic and camping area

Signposted access along Goodes Road north of the Princes Highway. From Narrawong take the signposted Boyers Road 600m west of the store. Follow for 1.2km north to a T-intersection, then turn left into Goodes Road. Follow Goodes Road for 1.6km to the signposted access track, then in 200m to camping and picnic area. Old sawmill site. Bring drinking water and firewood.
GPS: S:38 14.142 E:141 41.268
MR: Map 4 F6

FURTHER Information

> **DSE Heywood**
> **Tel:** 03 5527 0444

OTWAYS AND SOUTH-WEST

Sawpit picnic and camping area, Mount Clay State Forest

58 Mount Eccles National Park

Located 10km west of Macarthur, via Mount Eccles Road. Mt Eccles was formed by volcanic activity 20,000 years ago. Lava caves and tunnels. Swim in the springwater-filled crater of Lake Surprise or explore one of the park's walking trails.

Lake Surprise camping area

Access via Mount Eccles Road from Macarthur. Bring drinking water and firewood. Firewood is available for purchase at stall 3km prior to park entrance.
MR: Map 4 G5

FURTHER Information

Parks Vic Info Line
Tel: 13 19 63. Advance bookings and payment required.
Bookings: Parks Vic Mt Eccles
Tel: 03 5576 1338
Camping fees: From $14 per site/night.

59 Narrawong

Narrawong is located on the Princes Highway, 13km east of Portland. Coastal and river frontage make it a popular area for swimming and fishing.

Narrawong Holiday Park

Located south of the Princes Highway in Narrawong. Access signposted off the Princes Highway. Camp kitchen. Laundry facilities.
MR: Map 4 F6

FURTHER Information

Narrawong Holiday Park
Tel: 03 5529 5282 or 1800 055 066.
Bookings recommended during peak periods.
Web: www.narrawong.contact.com.au
Camping fees: Unpowered from $22 per site/night for 2 people. Powered from $25 per site/night for 2 people.

60 Nelson Reserve

Nelson Reserve is located on North Nelson Road at Nelson. The reserve is close to the Lower Glenelg River National Park, the Vic/SA Border, the Great South West Walk walking trail and the Historic Shipwreck Trail.

Kywong Caravan Park

Located on North Nelson Road 1km north of the Portland-Nelson Road and 500m from the Nelson River. North Nelson Road is signposted off the Portland-Nelson Road. Laundry facilities.
MR: Map 4 B5

FURTHER Information

Kywong Caravan Park
Tel: 08 8738 4174. Advance bookings recommended during peak periods of Christmas and Easter.
Web: www.kywongcp.com
Camping fees: Unpowered from $15 per site/night for 2 people. Powered from $20 per site/night for 2 people.

COLLECTING Firewood

 Most camping areas, especially the more popular ones, are usually devoid of any firewood. If firewood is not supplied by the land managers, it's best to collect enough wood for your needs well before getting to your campsite, or to bring some from home. Please do not cut down any trees, either living or dead, from around the camping area.

OTWAYS AND SOUTH-WEST

Otway Forest Park is a newly proclaimed park which will cover nearly 40,000 hectares of forests located along the north-western edge of the Otway Ranges. The forests in the park are home to a number of beautiful waterfalls, providing excellent photographic opportunities. Access to the park is along the Beech Forest-Mt Sabine Road or along the Forrest-Apollo Bay Road.

Beauchamp Falls camping area

Located 33km north-west of Skens Creek along Beauchamp Falls Road. From Skenes Creek proceed in a northerly direction along Skenes Creek Road, then take Beech Forest Road and travel for 17km to Aire Valley Road. From Aire Valley Road turn into Flannagan Road and then turn into Beauchamp Falls Road. Bring drinking water and firewood.
MR: Map 8 D5

Stevenson Falls camping area

Located 4km west of Barramunga. Signposted access via Upper Gellibrand Road. Bring firewood. Walk 1.8km to falls. Good swimming in the falls rock pools.
MR: Map 8 E5

Dandos camping area

Access via Lardner Track near Gellibrand Track from Great Ocean Road.
Water from river, boil or treat first.
Bring firewood.
MR: Map 8 D5

Beauchamp Falls

FURTHER Information

Parks Vic Info Line
Tel: 13 19 63

OTWAYS AND SOUTH-WEST

62 Port Campbell

Port Campbell is located along the Great Ocean Road adjacent to Port Campbell National Park. The area is popular for swimming, fishing and canoeing.

Port Campbell Holiday Park

Located along Morris Street, Port Campbell. At head of Campbells Creek. Gas/fuel stove only. Camp kitchen. Laundry facilities.
MR: Map 8 A5

FURTHER Information

Port Campbell Holiday Park
Tel: 03 5598 6492. Bookings required at peak times: school and public holidays, Easter and Christmas.
Web: www.pchp.com.au
Camping fees: Unpowered from $22 per site/night for 2 people. Powered from $28 per site/night for 2 people. Cabin accommodation available.

63 Port Fairy

Port Fairy is located along the Princes Highway 28km west of Warrnambool. At the mouth of the Moyne River. Swimming, fishing and canoeing.

Port Fairy Gardens Caravan Park

On Griffiths Street, Port Fairy. Moyne River frontage. Camp kitchen. Laundry facilities. Gas/fuel stove only.
MR: Map 4 I7

FURTHER Information

Port Fairy Gardens Caravan Park
Tel: 03 5568 1060. Bookings required at peak times.
Camping fees: Unpowered from $26 per site/night for 2 people. Powered from $29 per site/night for 2 people. Cabin accommodation available.

OTWAYS AND SOUTH-WEST

Port Fairy

64 Princetown

Princetown is a small village on the Great Ocean Road 19km east of Port Campbell. Activities include swimming, canoeing and fishing.

Princetown Recreation Reserve

[icons]

Located 1km south of Princetown on Old Coach Road beside Gellibrand River.
MR: Map 8 B5

FURTHER Information

Reserve Caretaker
Tel: 0429 985 176
Camping fees: Unpowered from $15 per site/night for 2 people. Powered from $20 per site/night for 2 people. Fees collected daily.

RECREATIONAL fishing licence

A Recreational Fishing Licence (RFL) covers all forms of recreational fishing in all of Victoria's marine, estuarine and freshwaters. Unless you are exempt, a RFL is required when taking, or attempting to take, any species of fish by any method including line fishing, bait collection, gathering shellfish, yabby fishing, prawning and spear fishing.

A RFL is available from many DPI offices and more than 980 retail businesses throughout Victoria, including most retail fishing tackle stores. For details visit www.dpi.vic.gov.au

Skenes Creek Foreshore

Located at Skenes Creek 6km north of Apollo Bay. Signposted access via The Great Ocean Road. Ocean frontage.

Skenes Creek Beachfront Caravan Park

Located at Skenes Creek 4km north of Apollo Bay.
MR: Map 8 E6

FURTHER Information

Skenes Creek Beachfront Caravan Park
Tel: 03 5237 6132. Bookings required at peak times.
Camping fees: Contact office for current fee schedule.
Dog fee: A daily fee applies for dogs.

Torquay Public Reserve

Located in Bell Street, Torquay. Signposted access via Surf Coast Highway. Close to beach and Spring Creek. Torquay is a popular holiday and surfing destination.

Torquay Foreshore Caravan Park

Located in Bell Street, Torquay. Gas/fuel stove only.
MR: Map 8 H3

FURTHER Information

Torquay Foreshore Caravan Park
Tel: 03 5261 2496. Bookings required at peak times.
Web: www.gorcc.com.au
Camping fees: From $27 per site/night for 2 people. All sites are powered.

67 Warrnambool Foreshore Reserve

Located on Pertobe Road in Warrnambool. Foreshore frontage to Lady Bay and close to Merri River.

Surfside Holiday Park

Located on Pertobe Road in Warrnambool. Gas/fuel stove only. Dogs on lead okay during off-season; confirm with park prior to arrival.
MR: Map 4 J7

FURTHER Information

Surfside Holiday Park
Tel: 03 5561 2611. Bookings required at peak periods: public holidays, Easter and Christmas.
Web: www.surfsidepark.com.au
Camping fees: Off-peak From $28 per site/night for 2 people. Cabin accommodation available.

OTWAYS AND SOUTH-WEST

68 Wye River Foreshore

Located at Wye River 15km south of Lorne. Signposted access via Great Ocean Road in Wye River. Beach frontage to Bass Strait and beside Wye River.

Wye River Foreshore Reserve

Open first week of December to end of April. Gas/fuel stove only. Bring drinking water.
MR: Map 8 F5

FURTHER Information

> **Wye River Foreshore Reserve**
> **Tel:** 03 5289 0412. Bookings required.
> **Camping fees:** Contact office for current fee schedule.

Coastline along Great Ocean Road

69 Yambuk Coastal Reserve

Located at mouth of the Eumeralla River in Yambuk, 15km west of Port Fairy. Great fishing and beach combing opportunties.

Yambuk Lakes Camping Ground

Small area set above Yambuk Lake with limited level sites. Access from the east is via Carrolls Road which is signposted off the Princes Highway 15km west of Port Fairy. Access from the west is via Yambuk Lake Road which is signposted off the Princes Highway in Yambuk, then travel 3km to camping area. Laundry facilities.

Gas/fuel stove only.
GPS: S:38 20.387 E:142 03.216
MR: Map 4 H7

FURTHER Information

Yambuk Lakes Camping Ground Caretaker
Tel: 0419 006 201. Bookings essential during Easter and Christmas holidays - contact caretaker for bookings.
Moyne Shire Council
Tel: 03 5568 2600
Camping fees: Unpowered from $14 per site/night for 2 people. Powered from $18 per site/night for 2 people.

Goldfields and Grampians

THE JEWEL IN THE CROWN OF THIS REGION is the spectacular Grampians National Park. On offer to visitors are a host of different experiences; you can walk from your campsite to scenic lookouts, waterfalls and Aboriginal rock art, or jump on a push bike and explore the park's roads and tracks. Campers are spoilt for choice with numerous sites scattered throughout the park.

A little to the east of Ararat are idyllic campsites set among the Yellowbox woodlands of Langi Ghiran State Park. Campers can easily

access this park from the Western Highway. In the far east of the region keen fisherfolk may wish to dangle a line in the Loddon River whilst camped at Newbridge Recreation Reserve near the village of Newbridge on the Wimmera Highway.

Other scenic destinations which provide camping include the remote Little Desert National Park, a popular spot to explore by four-wheel drive and the forested mountain area of Mount Cole near Beaufort. Kooyoora State Park, near Inglewood, has caves to explore and offers panoramic vistas from a number of marked walking tracks.

Near Horsham watch in awe as rock climbers cling to the sheer rock walls in Mt Arapiles-Tooan State Park or set up camp beside the large water storage of Rocklands Reservoir. Here a number of sites can be found within the state forest and around the lake's edge. Campers with dogs on a lead are welcome here.

Other delightful destinations to pitch camp are at the picturesque Waterfalls Picnic and Camping Area within the Pyrenees Forest, just the spot after a day of touring the local wineries, or in Mount Buangor State Park while exploring the Major Mitchell Trail.

Best seasons to visit this region are spring, early summer and autumn.

BEST Campsites!

Buandik camping area
Grampians National Park

Smith Mill camping area
Grampians National Park

Langi Ghiran camping area
Langi Ghiran State Park

Waterfalls picnic and camping area
Pyrenees Forest

Ditchfields camping area
Mt Cole State Forest

70 Balmoral

Located 10km north of Balmoral near Kanagulk on the banks of the Glenelg River. Access via Natimuk-Hamilton Road. 4WD vehicle access - seasonal track closures may apply. Canoeing on the Glenelg River.

Fulham Streamside Reserve camping area

Signposted access off Natimuk-Hamilton Road. Sandy track will require 4WD. Bush camping, no facilities.
MR: Map 3 G7

FURTHER Information

> **Parks Vic Info Line**
> **Tel:** 13 19 63

71 Dergholm State Park

Located 40km north-west of Casterton near Dergholm. Access via Casterton-Naracoorte Road. The park features large granite tors and unique vegetation. Take a stroll along the Baileys Rocks Loop Walk. Activities include bushwalking, orienteering and four-wheel driving.

Baileys Rocks picnic and camping area

Access via Baileys Rocks Road off the Casterton-Naracoorte Road.

Water from tank, boil first. Bring drinking water and firewood.
MR: Map 3 C7

FURTHER Information

> **Parks Vic Info Line**
> **Tel:** 13 19 63

72 Dunolly State Forest

Situated 10km north-east of Dunolly township, there are a range of activities available for visitors including walking trails, the Golden Triangle Bicycle Track and the 4.2km Waanyarra Forest Drive.

Waanyarra Recreation Area

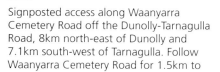

Signposted access along Waanyarra Cemetery Road off the Dunolly-Tarnagulla Road, 8km north-east of Dunolly and 7.1km south-west of Tarnagulla. Follow Waanyarra Cemetery Road for 1.5km to

open camping area with some shaded sites. Limited tank water. Bring drinking water and firewood.
GPS S:36 48.971 E:143 48.008
MR: Map 6 F8

FURTHER Information

> **DSE Customer Service Centre**
> **Tel:** 13 61 86
> **DSE Maryborough**
> **Tel:** 03 5461 0800

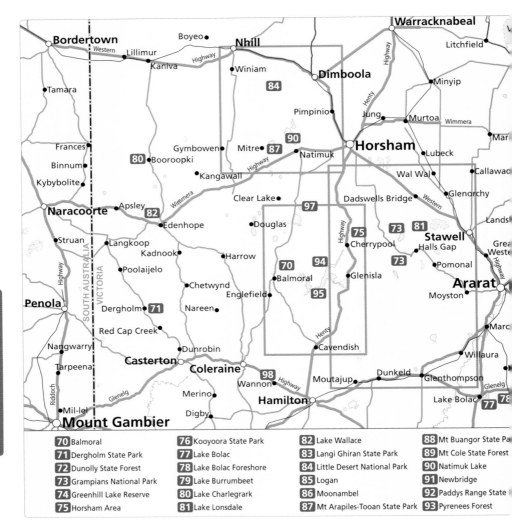

70 Balmoral	**76** Kooyoora State Park	**82** Lake Wallace	**88** Mt Buangor State Pa
71 Dergholm State Park	**77** Lake Bolac	**83** Langi Ghiran State Park	**89** Mt Cole State Forest
72 Dunolly State Forest	**78** Lake Bolac Foreshore	**84** Little Desert National Park	**90** Natimuk Lake
73 Grampians National Park	**79** Lake Burrumbeet	**85** Logan	**91** Newbridge
74 Greenhill Lake Reserve	**80** Lake Charlegrark	**86** Moonambel	**92** Paddys Range State
75 Horsham Area	**81** Lake Lonsdale	**87** Mt Arapiles-Tooan State Park	**93** Pyrenees Forest

73 Grampians National Park

73 Grampians National Park

Located 45km west of Ararat. Main access is via Grampians Road in the east, Northern Grampians Road in the north and Henty Highway in the west. The area is renowned for its spectacular scenery, brilliant wildflower displays in spring and many species of wildlife. Abundant Aboriginal art sites. Activities include bushwalking, picnicking, cycling, rock climbing and vehicle based touring (both 2WD and 4WD).

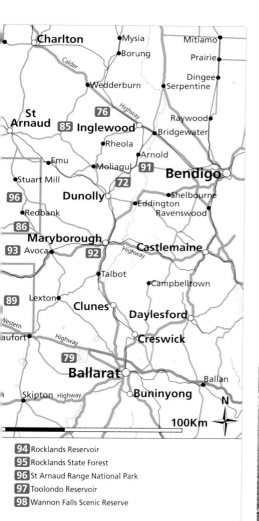

SLEEP *easy*

Self-inflating camp mattresses are by far the best choice for tent-based campers and offer a comfortable nights sleep. Mattresses range from ultra light ¾ length models for bushwalkers through to heavier and more bulky double models which are perfect for vehicle-based campers. We use a double one as our swag mattress. Self-inflating mattresses roll up to form a compact cylinder which can easily be stowed in your vehicle. Although they rarely leak, don't forget a puncture repair kit just in case.

Comfortable bedding is also a must. Winter nights in the outback can fall below freezing while summer on the coast is far more temperate. A good, zero degrees rated sleeping bag will cover most camping scenarios, although we prefer sheets and a doona. And don't forget your pillow.

94 Rocklands Reservoir
95 Rocklands State Forest
96 St Arnaud Range National Park
97 Toolondo Reservoir
98 Wannon Falls Scenic Reserve

NORTHERN GRAMPIANS

Troopers Creek camping area

Signposted access via Roses Gap Road, 10.6km west of Mt Victory Road. Limited space for small vans and camper trailers. Bring drinking water and firewood.
MR: Map 3 J6

Smith Mill camping area

Accessed from the McKenzie Falls Road, which is signposted off the Halls Gap-Horsham Road, 16.8km west of Halls Gap. From the Halls Gap-Horsham Road take the road signposted to McKenzie Falls, then at 400m turn right at T-intersection. At 600m are crossroads, turn right here and after 400m is the attractive camping area with a number of individual sites with good shade beneath pines. Limited space for small vans and camper trailers. Bring firewood.
GPS S:37 06.499 E:142 25.443
MR: Map 3 J6

Plantation camping area

Access via Pines Road off Halls Gap-Mt Zero Road. Situated at the base of the Mount Difficult Range. Bring firewood.
MR: Map 3 J6

Stapylton camping area

Access via Plantation Road off Northern Grampians Road or Horsham-Halls Gap Road. Large area. Aboriginal art site nearby. Bring firewood.
MR: Map 3 J5

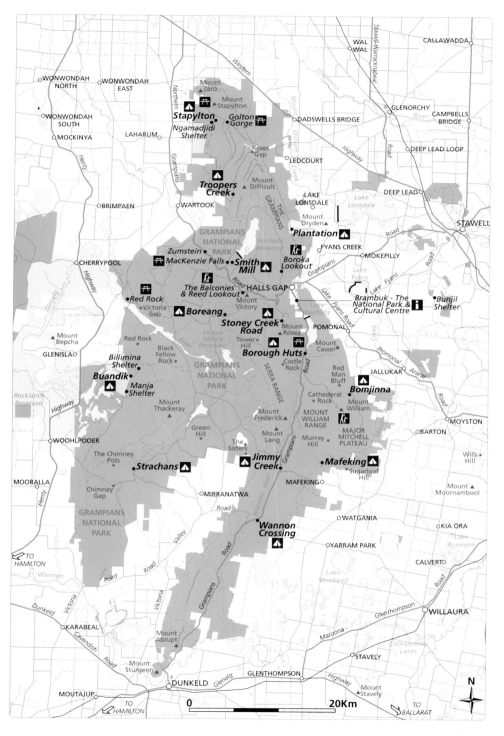

WONWONDAH NORTH

WONWONDAH EAST

WONWONDAH SOUTH

MOCKINYA

LAHARUM

WAL WAL

CALLAWADDA

GLENORCHY

CAMPBELLS BRIDGE

Mount Zero

Mount Stapylton

Stapylton

Golton Gorge

Ngamadjidi Shelter

DADSWELLS BRIDGE

DEEP LEAD LOOP

BRIMPAEN

Northern

Grampians

Western

Wimmera River

Roses Gap

LEDCOURT

Mount Difficult

Troopers Creek

WARTOOK

THE GRAMPIANS

Mount William Creek

LAKE LONSDALE

Lake Lonsdale

DEEP LEAD

Highway

Mount Dryden

STAWELL

Plantation

FYANS CREEK

CHERRYPOOL

GRAMPIANS NATIONAL PARK

Zumstein

MacKenzie Falls

Wartook Reservoir

Boroka Lookout

Smith Mill

MOKEPILLY

The Balconies & Reed Lookout

Red Rock

Victoria Gap

HALLS GAP

Mount Victoria

Boreang

Grampians

Lake Fyans

Lake Fyans

Brambuk - The National Park & Cultural Centre

Bunjil Shelter

Mount Bepcha

GLENISLA

Red Rock

Moora Moora Reservoir

Black Fellow Rock

Stoney Creek Road

Mount Rosea

Lake Bellfield

POMONAL

Promonal - Ararat

Borough Huts

Tower Hill

Mount Cassel

Billimina Shelter

Buandik

Manja Shelter

GRAMPIANS NATIONAL PARK

Castle Rock

Red Man Bluff

JALLUKAR

SERRA RANGE

Mount Thackeray

Cathedral Rock

Bomjinna

MOYSTON

Rocklands Reservoir

Green Hill

Mount Frederick

Mount Lang

Murray Hill

MOUNT WILLIAM RANGE

Mount William

MAJOR MITCHELL PLATEAU

BARTON

Wills Hill

WOOHLPOOER

Highway

Henty

The Chimney Pots

Strachans

Chimney Gap

MOORALLA

The Sisters

Jimmy Creek

MIRRANATWA

Grampians

MAFEKING

Sugarloaf Hill

Mafeking

Mount Moornambool

KIA ORA

Lake Buninjon

GRAMPIANS NATIONAL PARK

Wannon River

WATGANIA

YARRAM PARK

CALVERTO

TO HAMILTON

Wannon

Point

Road

Valley

Road

Grampians

Road

Wannon Crossing

Lake Muirhead

Lockaterning Lakes

WILLAURA

KARABEAL

Dunkeld

Victoria

Cavendish

River

Mount Abrupt

Glenelg

Mount Sturgeon

DUNKELD

MOUTAJUP

TO HAMILTON

GLENTHOMPSON

Glenthompson

Maroona -

Highway

Mount Stavely

STAVELY

TO BALLARAT

0   20Km

N

CENTRAL GRAMPIANS

Borough Huts camping area

Signposted access along Grampians Road, 10km south of the Brambuk Cultural Centre. Very large, grassed and shady camping area near Fyans Creek. Bring firewood.

GPS S:37 13.439 E:142 32.395
MR: Map 3 J7

Borough Huts camping area

Stoney Creek Road camping areas

Bush campsites located along Stoney Creek Road, which is signposted off Silverband Road, 5.4km west of Grampians Road. Camp only in signposted areas. Bring drinking water and firewood.

MR: Map 3 J7

Boreang camping area

Signposted access along Glenelg River Road, 200m north of Moora Track. Glenelg River Road is signposted off the Halls Gap-Horsham Road 8km west of Halls Gap. Bring drinking water and firewood.

GPS S:37 10.489 E:142 25.072
MR: Map 3 I7

GOLDFIELDS AND GRAMPIANS

MacKenzie Falls, Grampians National Park

SOUTH-WEST GRAMPIANS

Buandik camping area

Signposted access along Harrop Track which can be accessed via Billywing Road off Henty Highway. Walk to Billimina Shelter (Aboriginal rock art). Large, well shaded campground with separate areas for tent based camping and trailer/caravan camping. Bring drinking water. Limited firewood supplied. No generators.
GPS S:37 15.144 E:142 16.715
MR: Map 3 I7

Strachans camping area

Located along Sawmill Track, 3.5km south of its junction with Victoria Range Rd. Well shaded camping area situated at old sawmill site beside creek. Suitable for tent based camping, carry gear over bollards. Bring drinking water and firewood.
GPS S:37 22.563 E:142 16.921
MR: Map 3 I8

SOUTH-EAST GRAMPIANS

Mafeking camping area

Access via Jimmy Creek Road from Grampians Road or Mafeking Road from Moyston-Dunkeld Road. Situated near old goldmining site. Bring drinking water and firewood.
MR: Map 3 J8

Bomjinna camping area

Access via Mitchell Road. Small secluded site. Bring drinking water and firewood.
MR: Map 3 K8

Wannon Crossing camping area

Access via Grampians Road. Situated beside Wannon River. Bring drinking water and firewood.
MR: Map 3 J8

Jimmy Creek camping area

Access via Grampians Road. Situated beside Wannon River. Bring drinking water and firewood.
MR: Map 3 J8

Bush camping

Bush camping is allowed within the park except in the Wonderland Range and the watershed of Lake Wartook. Contact rangers for details.

FURTHER Information

Parks Vic Info Line
Tel: 13 19 63
Brambuk – The National Park and Cultural Centre
Tel: 03 5361 4000
Camping fees: From $12.50 per site/night up to 6 people. Fees are payable at Brambuk in Halls Creek.

GOLDFIELDS AND GRAMPIANS

74 Greenhill Lake Reserve

Located 4km east of Ararat city centre. Signposted access off Western Highway. Popular summer watersports and fishing venue.

Greenhill Lake Reserve camping area

Signposted access off Western Highway. Then drive in 200 metres north from highway, crossing railway to very large area with some shade beside the lake. Camp only in areas signposted. Bring drinking water and firewood. Gas/fuel stove preferred.
MR: Map 7 A4

FURTHER Information

Ararat Visitor Information Centre
Tel: 1800 657 158
Camping fees: Free camping during off-peak periods. Peak periods fee of $6.00 per night/site applies. Fees payable to patrolling council ranger.

75 Horsham Area

Horsham is a major centre in the western region of the state and is at the junction of the Western, Henty and Wimmera highways. Located 50km south of Horsham is a highway park suitable for an overnight stop.

Cherrypool Highway Park

Located beside Glenelg River. Signposted access along the Henty Highway, 50km south of Horsham. Suitable for overnight stop. Bring drinking water and firewood.
MR: Map 3 H6

FURTHER Information

Parks Vic Info Line
Tel: 13 19 63

Kooyoora State Park

Located 15km west of Inglewood and north of Rheloa. Access from the west is from the locality of Logan on the Wimmera Highway. From Inglewood proceed west via the Inglewood-Rheloa Road. From Logan follow the road to Inglewood for 17km to the signposted access to Kooyoora State Park. Panoramic views from the park's granite tors. Activities include bushwalking - trek the 2km Kooyoora Summit Walk or the longer Eastern Walking Circuit, try your hand at fossicking, rock climbing and horse riding.

Melville Caves Campground

Located 3km along the signposted Kooyoora State Park access road, which is signposted 17km east of Logan via the Inglewood road. Dispersed camping in large open area, some sites have good shade. Bring drinking water and firewood. Gas/fuel stove preferred.
GPS S:36 36.065 E:143 41.922
MR: Map 6 E7

Glenalbyn Campground

Located along the Brenanah-Glenalbyn Road, 3.2km south of the Calder Highway. This road is signposted off the highway 13km north-west of Inglewood. Dispersed bush camping at site of dam at road junction. Bring drinking water and firewood. Gas/fuel stove preferred.
GPS S:36 32.093 E:143 44.583
MR: Map 6 E6

FURTHER Information

Parks Vic Info Line
Tel: 13 19 63

Melville Caves Campground

77 Lake Bolac

Located adjacent to Lake Bolac township, 100km west of Ballarat. Popular summer watersports venue.

Lake Bolac Caravan Park

Signposted access via Frontage Road from the Glenelg Highway.
MR: Map 4 L3

FURTHER Information

Lake Bolac Caravan Park
Tel: 03 5350 2329. Bookings required at peak times.
Camping fees: Unpowered from $18.00 per site/night for 2 people. Powered from $20.00 per site/night for 2 people. Cabin accommodation also available.

78 Lake Bolac Foreshore

The lake is located 2km east of Lake Bolac township on the Glenelg Highway. Activities include watersports and walking trails.

Lake Bolac Foreshore camping area

Access to the camping area is via the signposted Montgomery Street (Mortlake Road) off the Glenelg Highway in Lake Bolac. Follow this road south to the signposted access to the lake's foreshore. Many campsites around lake's edge. Showers in main area and toilets at scattered locations. Bring firewood.
MR: Map 4 L3

FURTHER Information

Lake Bolac Information Centre
Tel: 03 5350 2204
Camping fees: From $10.00 per site/night for 2 people. Ranger collects fees daily.

79 Lake Burrumbeet

Lake Burrumbeet is a popular trout and redfin fishing destination as well as a summer watersports venue. The lake is situated west of Ballarat near Burrumbeet on the Western Highway.

Lake Burrumbeet Caravan Park

Access via Avenue of Honour from Burrumbeet.
MR: Map 7 E5

FURTHER Information

Lake Burrumbeet Caravan Park
Tel: 03 5344 0583. Bookings required for Christmas and Easter.
Camping fees: Unpowered from $8.00 per person/night. Powered from $19.00 per site/night up to 2 people. Cabin accommodation available.

80 Lake Charlegrark

Located 35km north of Edenhope near Booroopki. Access along the Kaniva-Edenhope Road. Popular watersports venue.

Lake Charlegrark Camping and Cottages

Signposted access along Kaniva-Edenhope Road. Lakeside location.
MR: Map 3 C4

FURTHER Information

Lake Charlegrark Camping and Cottages
Tel: 03 5386 6281. Bookings recommended.
Camping fees: Unpowered from $5.00 per person/night. Powered from $15.00 per site/night for 2 people. Cabin accommodation available.

81 Lake Lonsdale

Situated 12km west of Stawell. Access via the Sandbar Road off the Western Highway, north of Stawell. Popular watersports venue when lake is at full capacity.

Lake Lonsdale camping area

Access via signposted Sandbar Road off the Western Highway. Campsites are on the northern shore of the lake, camp only in designated zones.
MR: Map 3 K6

FURTHER Information

GWM Waters
Tel: 1300 659 961

82 Lake Wallace

Situated in the township of Edenhope. Located on Lake Street off the Wimmera Highway. Popular summer watersports venue.

Edenhope Lakeside Tourist Park

Signposted access along Lake Street. Lakeside location.
MR: Map 3 D6

FURTHER Information

Lake Wallace Caravan Park
Tel: 03 5585 1659. Bookings required at peak times.
Camping fees: Unpowered from $16.00 per site/night for 2 people. Powered from $22.00 per site/night for 2 people.

GOLDFIELDS AND GRAMPIANS

Langi Ghiran State Park

Located 12km east of Ararat. Signposted access via Kartuk Road off Western Highway. Panoramic views from the park's granite peaks amongst attractive red gum and yellowbox woodlands. Explore the two decommissioned water reservoirs that once served Ararat. Activities include bushwalking and vehicle touring.

Langi Ghiran camping area

Signposted access via Kartuk Road off the Western Highway. Located 5km north of the highway.
GPS S:37 17.386 E:143 05.512
MR: Map 7 B4

Bush camping

Bush camping is allowed within the mountainous sections of the park. Take own water. Contact ranger for details.

FURTHER Information

> **Parks Vic Info Line**
> **Tel:** 13 19 63

Little Desert National Park

Comprising of three 'blocks', the park is located south of the Western Highway and to the east of Dimboola (Wimmera River), stretching across to the VIC/SA Border. Sealed access roads are off the Western Highway or Natimuk Road. Conventional vehicle access to camping areas. Most other roads and tracks are sandy and require 4WD. The park is home to the Mallee Fowl plus a large number of bird and animal species. Activities include bushwalking (short half day walks through to the four day 84km Desert Discovery Walk), bird watching, fishing and 4WD vehicle touring.

Kiata camping area

Situated in the park's eastern block. Signposted access via Kiata South Road from Kiata on Western Highway. Bring drinking water and firewood.
MR: Map 3 F2

Horseshoe Bend camping area

In the park's eastern block on the Wimmera River. Signposted access via Horseshoe Bend Road from Dimboola on Western Highway. Bring drinking water and firewood.
MR: Map 3 H2

GOLDFIELDS AND GRAMPIANS

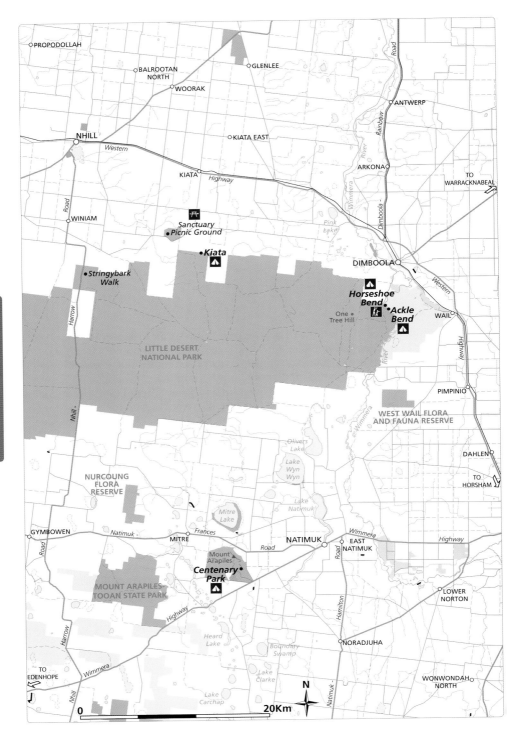

PROPODOLLAH

BALROOTAN NORTH

GLENLEE

WOORAK

ANTWERP

NHILL

Western

KIATA EAST

KIATA

Highway

ARKONA

TO WARRACKNABEAL

WINIAM

Road

Harrow

Rainbow River

Wimmera

Dimboola -

Pink Lake

Sanctuary
Picnic Ground

Kiata

DIMBOOLA

Western

Stringybark Walk

Horseshoe Bend

Ackle Bend

WAIL

One Tree Hill

LITTLE DESERT NATIONAL PARK

Nhill -

River

Highway

PIMPINIO

WEST WAIL FLORA AND FAUNA RESERVE

Olivers Lake

DAHLEN

Lake Wyn Wyn

TO HORSHAM

NURCOUNG FLORA RESERVE

Mitre Lake

Lake Natimuk

GYMBOWEN

Natimuk -

Frances

MITRE

Road

NATIMUK

EAST NATIMUK

Wimmera

Highway

Road

Road

Mount Arapiles

Centenary Park

MOUNT ARAPILES TOOAN STATE PARK

Highway

Hamilton

LOWER NORTON

Heard Lake

RD

Boundary Swamp

NORADJUHA

TO EDENHOPE

Nhill

Wimmera

Lake Clarke

Lake Carchap

N

20Km

WONWONDAH NORTH

Ackle Bend camping area

Located in the park's eastern block on the Wimmera River. Signposted access via Horseshoe Bend Road from Dimboola on Western Highway. Bring drinking water and firewood.

MR: Map 3 H2

Central and Western block bush camping

Vehicle based bush camping is allowed within the Central and Western Blocks of the park away from campgrounds and picnic areas. Take own water. Contact ranger for details.

FURTHER Information

> **Parks Vic Info Line**
> **Tel:** 13 19 63
> **Camping fees:** Fees apply at all camping areas within the park and are subject to change. Fees are payable at self-registration stations at each camping area. Contact Parks Vic Info Line for current fees.

 ## Logan

The small hamlet of Logan is situated 21km east of St Arnaud at the junction of the Bendigo-St Arnaud Road and the Logan-Wedderburn Road.

Logan Pub camping area

Free camping area at rear of hotel, check with publicans prior to setting up. Small fee for power if required.

GPS S:36 37.293 E:143 29.475
MR: Map 6 D7

FURTHER Information

> **Logan Pub**
> **Tel:** 03 5496 2220
> Budget accommodation available.

Moonambel

The small hamlet of Moonambel is on the C220 road, 6.5km west of the Sunraysia Highway. The C220 is signposted 12km north-west of Avoca.

Mountain Creek picnic and camping area

Located 300m north of Moonambel along the signposted Greens Lane. Best suited for tents with carry gear in over bollards. Smaller camper trailers and caravans park in parking area. Area set above small creek.
GPS S:36 59.112 E:143 19.151
MR: Map 7 C2

FURTHER Information

> **DSE Maryborough**
> **Tel:** 03 5461 0800

87 Mount Arapiles—Tooan State Park

Mt Arapiles is Australia's best known rock climbing destination. The first European to climb it was explorer Major Sir Thomas Mitchell in 1836. The park is located 9km west of Natimuk with signposted access via Centenary Park Road off Wimmera Highway. Activities include rock climbing, walking and cycling.

Centenary Park camping area

Access via the signposted Centenary Park Road, 8.3km west of Natimuk off the Wimmera Highway. Then travel 2.1km to camping area. Limited vehicle based camping, generally carry in over bollards. Bring firewood. Gas/fuel stove preferred.
GPS S:36 45.566 E:141 50.866
MR: Map 3 F4

FURTHER Information

> **Parks Vic Info Line**
> **Tel:** 13 19 63
> **Camping fees:** Fees apply and are subject to change. Current fee structure is detailed at the self-registration station in the camping area. Collection of firewood is not permitted in the park.

GOLDFIELDS AND GRAMPIANS

Located 21km west of Beaufort. Access via Ferntree Gully Road from Western Highway. Mt Buangor is the area's highest peak. Activities include camping, bushwalking and mountain biking.

Middle Creek picnic and camping area

Signposted access via Jimmy Smith Road from Ferntree Gully Road. Large area suitable for groups. Bring drinking water and firewood.
MR: Map 7 C4

Ferntree picnic & camping area

Signposted access via Ferntree Waterfall Road. 5 sites only. Bring firewood.
MR: Map 7 C4

FURTHER Information

> **Parks Vic Info Line**
> **Tel:** 13 19 63

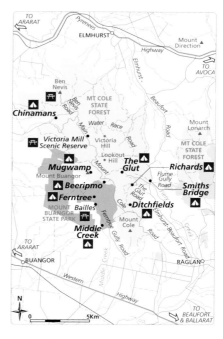

WATER Wise

> Fresh water for drinking and cooking is one aspect of camping which needs to be taken into consideration. You can't always rely on creeks and rivers – they may be polluted by animals, muddy or even dry. Allow around 7 litres of water per person per day – plus a couple of extra litres if you are heading into remote areas. We find storing water in a couple of 20 litre containers more convenient than in one larger container. Besides being easier to lift in and out of the vehicle and easier to handle around camp, if one container springs a leak you don't risk losing all your drinking water

This large forested area is located 25km north-west of Beaufort. Access via Mt Cole Road from Raglan. Access roads may be rough at times. Activities include bushwalking, mountain biking and four-wheel drive touring.

Beeripmo camping area

Located on the Beeripmo overnight walking track. Access via Richards camping area (trackhead).
MR: Map 7 C4

Chinamans camping area

Access via Mt Cole Road from Warrak. Located 5km from Warrak, beside Chinaman Creek.
MR: Map 7 C4

Ditchfields camping area

Signposted access via Camp Road from Mt Cole Road. Located near a small creek and old forest hut.
MR: Map 7 C4

Smiths Bridge camping area

Located 19km north-west of Beaufort and 13km south of Elmhurst on the Beaufort-Elmhurst Road.
MR: Map 7 C4

Mugwamp camping area

Access via Dawson Rock Road from Mt Cole Road, located near Mugwamp Creek. Old hut.
MR: Map 7 C4

Richards camping area

Access via The Glut Road. Located beside Fiery Creek. Short walk to campsites from car park, carry gear in.
MR: Map 7 C4

Bush camping
Bush camping is allowed within the forest. Contact ranger for details.

FURTHER Information

> **DSE Customer Service Centre**
> **Tel:** 13 61 86

GOLDFIELDS AND GRAMPIANS

90 Natimuk Lake

Located 4km north of Natimuk township. Access via Lake Road. Popular summer watersports venue.

Natimuk Lake Caravan Park

Located north of Natimuk via Lake Road. Lakeside location (beach).
MR: Map 3 G3

FURTHER Information

> **Natimuk Lake Caravan Park**
> **Tel:** 0407 800 753. Bookings required at peak times.
> **Camping fees:** Unpowered from $14.00 per site/night for 2 people. Powered from $20.00 per site/night for 2 people.

91 Newbridge

The Newbridge Recreation Reserve is situated on the eastern bank of the Loddon River in the picturesque town of Newbridge, 40km west of Bendigo. The reserve is a good place for bird watching, fishing and canoeing.

Newbridge Recreation Reserve camping area

Signposted access along the Maldon-St Arnaud Highway in Newbridge, on the eastern side of bridge over Loddon River. Shady, grassed sites on the river bank. Bring drinking water and firewood.
GPS S:36 44.350 E:143 54.174
MR: Map 6 F8

FURTHER Information

> **Caretaker**
> **Tel:** 03 5438 7469
> **Newbridge General Store**
> **Tel:** 03 5438 7201
> **Camping fees:** From $5.50 per site/night. Fees collected daily or payable at general store.

GOLDFIELDS AND GRAMPIANS

92 Paddys Range State Park

Located south-west of Maryborough via Old Avoca Road, which is signposted off the B180 highway, 3.7km from Maryborough. Follow Old Avoca Road for 1.3km to the signposted Karri Track. Many old gold mining sites and relics. Stunning wildflowers in spring. Activities include bushwalking, exploring old mine workings, bird watching, horse riding and fossicking.

Karri Track camping area

Signposted access 1.8km along Karri Track from Old Avoca Road. Shaded sites surrounded by box forest. Bring drinking water and firewood.
GPS S:37 04.980 E:143 41.442
MR: Map 7 E2

FURTHER Information

> **Parks Vic Info Line**
> **Tel:** 13 19 63
> Notify ranger before camping.
> No bush camping.

93 Pyrenees Forest

Located in the Pyrenee Range west of Avoca. Access via Vinoca Road from the Sunraysia Highway at the northern end of Avoca.

Waterfalls picnic and camping area

Located 11km west of Avoca. From highway in Avoca, take signposted Duke Street and follow for 200m to T-intersection with signposted Vinoca Road/Waterfalls Lookout. Turn right here and follow for 7.8km to Y-junction and signposted access to the camping area. Bring drinking water and firewood.
MR: Map 7 C2

Camerons Track Shelter camping area

Located on Camerons Track which is accessed off Main Break Track, 20km west of Avoca. Limited tank water. Bring firewood.
MR: Map 7 C2

FURTHER Information

> **DSE Maryborough**
> **Tel:** 03 5461 0800

This large reservoir is 68km south of Horsham and to the east of the Grampians near Black Range. Access via Henty Highway in the east and Natimuk-Hamilton Road in the west. Main function as water storage and also popular watersports and fishing venue.

ROCKLANDS RESERVOIR – EAST

Hynes Reserve Camping Ground

Located 50km north of Cavendish near Glenisla. Access via signposted Hynes Road off Henty Highway. Lakeside location. Bring firewood.
MR: Map 3 H7

ROCKLANDS RESERVOIR – WEST

Rocklands Caravan Park

Located 15km east of Balmoral. Access via Rocklands Road from Balmoral. Water untreated, bring own drinking water. Lakeside location.
MR: Map 3 G7

FURTHER Information

Hynes Reserve Camping Ground
Tel: 0418 546 028
GWM Waters
Tel: 1300 659 961
Camping fees: Currently not applicable, however may be introduced at a later date.

FURTHER Information

Rocklands Caravan Park
Tel: 03 5570 1438. Bookings required for Christmas, Easter and long weekends.
Camping fees: From $9.00 per adult/per night.

GOLDFIELDS AND GRAMPIANS

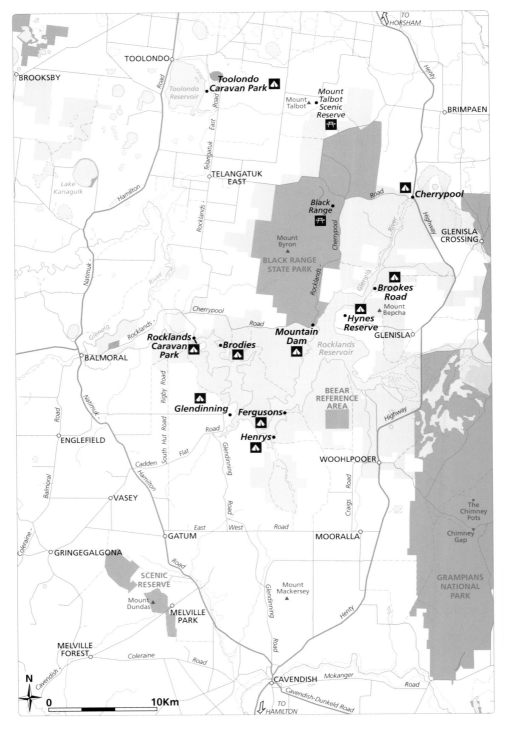

TO HORSHAM

TOOLONDO

BROOKSBY

Toolondo Reservoir

Telangatuk East

Road

Hamilton

Road

Mount Talbot

Toolondo Caravan Park

Mount Talbot Scenic Reserve

BRIMPAEN

Lake Kanagulk

Rocklands

TELANGATUK EAST

Glenelg River

Natimuk

Road

Hamilton

River

Black Range

Mount Byron

BLACK RANGE STATE PARK

Cherrypool

Road

Rocklands

Road

Cherrypool

River

Glenisla

Highway

GLENISLA CROSSING

Cherrypool

Road

Road

Rocklands Caravan Park

Brodies

Mountain Dam

Brookes Road

Mount Bepcha

Hynes Reserve

GLENISLA

BALMORAL

Rocklands Reservoir

BEEAR REFERENCE AREA

Rigby Road

South Hut Road

Glendinning

Fergusons

Glendinning

Road

Flat

Road

Henrys

Natimuk

Road

Cadden

Hamilton

ENGLEFIELD

Balmoral

Road

VASEY

GATUM

East

West

Road

Highway

WOOHLPOOER

Craigs

Road

MOORALLA

The Chimney Pots

Chimney Gap

Coleraine

Road

GRINGEGALGONA

SCENIC RESERVE

Mount Dundas

MELVILLE PARK

Glendinning

Road

Mount Mackersey

GRAMPIANS NATIONAL PARK

MELVILLE FOREST

Coleraine

Road

Cavendish

Henty

CAVENDISH

Mokanger

Road

Cavendish-Dunkeld Road

TO HAMILTON

N

0   10Km

This collection of forests are located to the west of the Grampians National Park and surround Rocklands Reservoir. Main access is via Rocklands-Cherrypool Road and Henty Highway. The area is popular for a wide range of activities which include camping, fishing, bushwalking and nature study.

Brodies camping area

Located on the northern shore of Rocklands Reservoir. Access via Rockland-Cherrypool Road. Bring drinking water.
MR: Map 3 G7

Mountain Dam camping area

Situated on the northern point and western foreshore of Rocklands Reservoir. Access via Rockland-Cherrypool Road. Bring drinking water and firewood.
MR: Map 3 H7

Brookes Road camping area

Located on northern point on the eastern foreshore of Rocklands Reservoir. Access via Brookes Road off the Henty Highway (access through private property). Bring drinking water.
MR: Map 3 H7

Henrys camping area

On the southern shore of Rocklands Reservoir. Access via Halls Road off East-West Road off the Henty Highway (access through private property). Bring drinking water.
MR: Map 3 H8

Glendinning camping area

Located on the southern point on the western foreshore of Rocklands Reservoir. Access via Glendinning Road or Yarramyljup Road. Bring drinking water and firewood.
MR: Map 3 G7

Fergusons camping area

On southern point and eastern foreshore of Rocklands Reservoir. Access via Fergusons Road off Gartons Road off the Henty Highway. Bring drinking water.
MR: Map 3 H8

Bush camping
Bush camping is allowed within these forests. Contact the ranger for details.

FURTHER Information

> **DSE Cavendish**
> **Tel:** 03 5574 2308

Located near the locality of Stuart Mill, 28km north-west of Avoca and 21km south of St Arnaud. Access via Teddington Road, which is signposted off the Sunraysia Highway at Stuart Mill. St Arnaud Range National Park is home to box-ironbark forests and in the 1860s was mined for alluvial and reef gold. Visitors can enjoy the timbered forests, go bushwalking, fossicking, and wildlife and bird spotting.

Teddington camp and picnic area

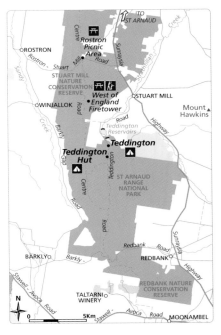

Signposted access along Teddington Road, 6.2km west of Sunraysia Highway at Stuart Mill. Attractive area with dispersed camping above the Upper Teddington Reservoir. Bring firewood. Gas/fuel stove preferred.
GPS S:36 50.593 E:143 15.732
MR: Map 6 C8

Teddington Hut camping area

Accessed along Teddington Road, 1.5km south of the camping area. Group camping in hut vicinity. Shower room, bring own canvas shower bag. Some firewood supplied.
GPS S:36 51.358 E:143 15.697
MR: Map 6 C8

FURTHER Information

Parks Vic Info Line
Tel: 13 19 63. Bookings required for Teddington Hut.
Bookings: Parks Vic Inglewood
Tel: 03 5431 7120
Collection of firewood is prohibited in the park.

GOLDFIELDS AND GRAMPIANS

Teddington Hut

97 Toolondo Reservoir

Located adjacent to Toolondo, 40km south of Horsham. Access via Natimuk-Hamilton Road. Popular fishing (trout and redfin) and watersports venue.

Toolondo Caravan Park

Signposted access along John McPhees Road off Telangatuk Road. Lakeside location.
MR: Map 3 G6

FURTHER Information

> **Toolondo Caravan Park**
> **Tel:** 03 5388 2231. Bookings required at peak times for caravan sites.
> **Camping fees:** From $7.70 per person/night. Power additional $3.50 per site/night.

97 Wannon Falls

Located near Wannon, 18km north-west of Hamilton and south-east of Coleraine. Signposted access off Glenelg Highway. Scenic waterfall on Wannon River.

Wannon River picnic and camping area

Signposted access via Glenelg Highway at Wannon. Take own drinking water, or boil/treat water first.
MR: Map 4 G2

FURTHER Information

> **Hamilton Visitor Information Centre**
> **Tel:** 03 5572 3746 or 1800 807 056
> **Web:** www.sthgrampians.vic.gov.au
> **Maximum stay:** 2 nights

Mallee

LOCATED IN THE FAR NORTH-WEST CORNER of the state, The Mallee is named after the region's unique vegetation, the Mallee scrub, which once covered the area. Much of this 'scrub' was cleared during the 18 and 1900's for farmland, however pockets remain and are preserved within some of the region's national parks. This vast region stretches from the South Australian border east along the Murray River to Swan Hill, and south towards Wycheproof and Nhill. Located in the region are three spectacular, and remote national parks; Murray-Sunset, Wyperfeld and Big Desert.

Lying just to the north of Underbool is the scenic Murray-Sunset National Park. Campers can set up beside Lake Crosbie in the Pink Lakes section of the park. These salt lakes take on an attractive pink hue at certain times and are a highlight for photographers. Also within the park are a number of four-wheel drive only accessible campsites.

In the far south of the region is the large Wyperfeld National Park. This park protects some of the Mallee's original habitat for native wildlife and birds. One of the highlights of this park are beautiful wildflower displays in spring. The park has three camping areas from where campers can enjoy the Eastern Lookout Nature Drive or undertake numerous marked walking tracks.

Along the Murray River campers will find numerous state forests and reserves between Mildura and Swan Hill. Swimming, fishing and canoeing are the popular recreational activities.

Although this region can be visited year round, spring and autumn are the best seasons to visit when daytime temperatures are more moderate than summer.

BEST Campsites!

Lake Hattah camping area
Hattah-Kulkyne National Park

Mopoke Hut camping area
Murray-Sunset National Park

Lake Crosbie camping area
Murray-Sunset National Park

Kings Billabong bush camping
Kings Billabong Wildlife Reserve

Wonga camping area
Wyperfeld National Park

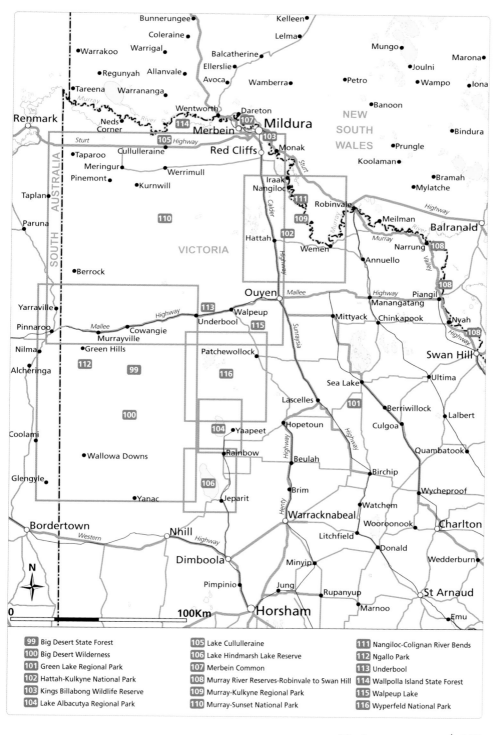

99 Big Desert State Forest	**105** Lake Cullulleraine	**111** Nangiloc-Colignan River Bends
100 Big Desert Wilderness	**106** Lake Hindmarsh Lake Reserve	**112** Ngallo Park
101 Green Lake Regional Park	**107** Merbein Common	**113** Underbool
102 Hattah-Kulkyne National Park	**108** Murray River Reserves-Robinvale to Swan Hill	**114** Wallpolla Island State Forest
103 Kings Billabong Wildlife Reserve	**109** Murray-Kulkyne Regional Park	**115** Walpeup Lake
104 Lake Albacutya Regional Park	**110** Murray-Sunset National Park	**116** Wyperfeld National Park

Big Desert State Forest is located to the south of the Mallee Highway and north of the Big Desert Wilderness. The forest is home to pine plantation, red gums, mallee and landscapes of sand dunes and flood plains. Access to the forest is via Firebreak Track which is signposted off Murrayville Track, 10km south of Murrayville. Four-wheel drive vehicle access is recommended and all roads are dry weather access only. The forest's black soil plains are extremely slippery during and after wet weather. Although dogs are permitted in state forests, due to wild dog activity in these forests it is recommended that the family pet is not taken.

Coburns Pines camping area

Located in the western section of the forest, north of Big Desert Wilderness. Signposted access at junction of Firebreak Track and Coburns Track, 12.4km west of Murrayville Track. Then 2.2km south of junction to large open camping area with dispersed bush camping. Self sufficient campers. Bring drinking water and firewood. Camping area named after Samuel S Coburn, a Mallee pioneer who planted pines in 1928 for harvesting.
GPS S:35 23.851 E:141 04.272
MR: Map 2 B2

Red Gums camping area

Located in the western section of the forest. Signposted access along Coburns Track, 5.3km south of Firebreak Track. Coburns Track is 12.4km west of Murrayville Track. Dispersed bush camping. Sandy access track. Dry weather access only. Self sufficient campers. Bring drinking water and firewood. A stand of flood plain red gums are located here, these are the only ones in the area with the nearest stand being 75km away.
GPS S:35 24.955 E:141 06.128
MR: Map 2 C2

Blue Gums camping area

Located 350m south of Firebreak Track along Blue Gums Track. Blue Gums Track is signposted along Firebreak Track 6.7km east of Coburns Track and 5.2km west of Murrayville Track. Very large area with dispersed bush camping. Dry weather access only. Self sufficient campers. Bring drinking water and firewood.
GPS S:35 21.788 E:141 08.233
MR: Map 2 C2

FURTHER Information

DSE Customer Service Centre
Tel: 13 61 86

MALLEE

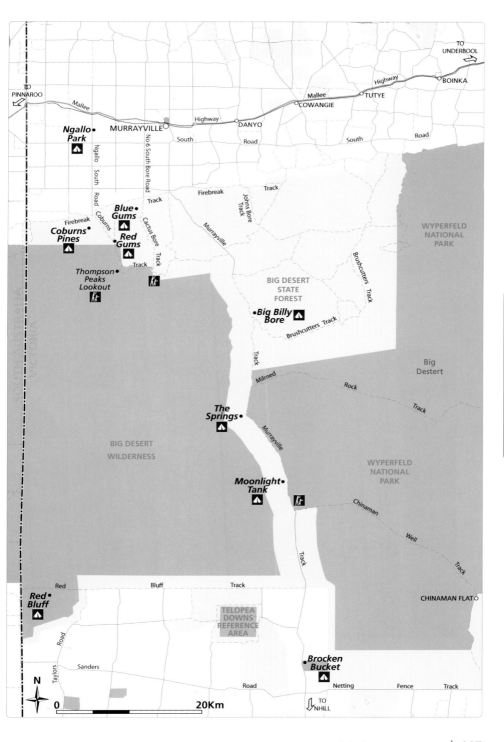

TO
UNDERBOOL

TO
PINNAROO

BOINKA

Highway

Mallee   TUTYE
COWANGIE

Mallee   DANYO
MURRAYVILLE   Highway

*Ngallo
Park*

South   Road   South   Road

Firebreak   Track

WYPERFELD
NATIONAL
PARK

*Blue
Gums*

Firebreak
*Coburns
Pines*

*Red
Gums*

*Thompson
Peaks
Lookout*

BIG DESERT
STATE
FOREST

*Big Billy
Bore*

Big
Destert

Big
Rock   Track

*The
Springs*

BIG DESERT
WILDERNESS

WYPERFELD
NATIONAL
PARK

*Moonlight
Tank*

Chinaman

Well   Track

CHINAMAN FLAT

*Red
Bluff*

Red   Bluff   Track

TELOPEA
DOWNS
REFERENCE
AREA

Taylors

Sanders

*Brocken
Bucket*

Road   Netting   Fence   Track

N

0   20Km

TO
NHILL

Located south of Murrayville and adjoins the SA border. Access via Murrayville-Nhill Track between Murrayville and Yanac. Conventional vehicle access in dry weather (4WD required after rain). Road may be rough at times. Big Desert was Victoria's first wilderness park. Exploration of the park is best undertaken on foot by experienced walkers with map and compass knowledge. Take own water. NB: Camping areas are outside park boundary. Use of fuel/gas stove preferred.

Big Billy Bore camping area

Signposted access along Murrayville Track, 33.3km south of Murrayville, then in 650m to camping area. Dry weather access only. Murrayville Track is unsealed and extremely slippery during and after wet weather. Bring drinking water and firewood. Gas/fuel preferred.
GPS S:35 30.713 E:141 19.373
MR: Map 2 D3

The Springs camping area

Signposted access along Murrayville Track, 14.8km south of Big Billy Bore CA. Small site. Dry weather access only. Murrayville Track is unsealed and extremely slippery during and after wet weather. Bring drinking water and firewood. Gas/fuel preferred.
GPS S:35 38.531 E:141 18.549
MR: Map 2 D4

Big Billy Bore camping area

Moonlight Tank camping area

Signposted access along Murrayville Track, 10km south of The Springs CA. Dry weather access only. Murrayville Track is unsealed and extremely slippery during and after wet weather. Bring drinking water and firewood. Gas/fuel preferred.
MR: Map 2 D4

Broken Bucket camping area

Signposted access along Murrayville Track, 39.7km south of The Springs CA. Dry weather access from the north. Located 53.5km north of Nhill via Murrayville Track, which is sealed from Nhill camping area turnoff. Bring drinking water and firewood. Gas/fuel preferred.
GPS S:35 58.049 E:141 23.969
MR: Map 2 D6

Red Bluff camping area

4WD access only, via Border Track or Red Bluff Track off Murrayville Track. Bring drinking water and firewood. Gas/fuel stove preferred.
MR: Map 2 B6

FURTHER Information

> **Parks Vic Info Line**
> **Tel:** 13 19 63

101 Green Lake Regional Park

Green Lake Regional Park is located 10km south of Sea Lake. Signposted access via Birchip-Sea Lake Road. Natural lake filled by irrigation channel surrounded by mallee woodland. Popular camping area. Watersports on lake.

Green Lake camping area

Signposted access along the Birchip-Sea Lake Road, south of Sea Lake. Laundry facilities. Coin operated BBQs and hot showers (10 cent pieces required for showers).
MR: Map 2 L4

FURTHER Information

> **Shire of Buloke**
> **Tel:** 03 5070 1218
> **Camping fees:** Unpowered from $6.00 per site/night up to 4 people. Powered from $12.00 per site/night up to 4 people. Fees payable at self-registration station.

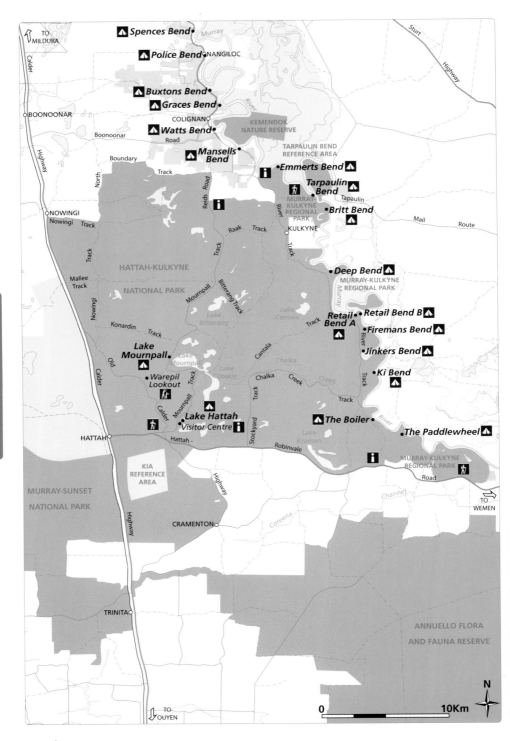

Spences Bend
Murray
TO
MILDURA
Calder
Police Bend NANGILOC
Buxtons Bend
Graces Bend
River
BOONOONAR
COLIGNAN
KEMENDOK
NATURE RESERVE
Watts Bend
Boonoonar
Road
TARPAULIN BEND
REFERENCE AREA
Boundary
Mansells Bend
North
Track
Emmerts Bend
Reids
MURRAY-
KULKYNE
REGIONAL
PARK
Tarpaulin Bend
River
Tapaulin
Road
NOWINGI
Track
Nowingi
Track
Britt Bend
Mail
Route
Raak
Track
Track
KULKYNE
Track
HATTAH-KULKYNE
Mournpall
Bitterang Track
Deep Bend
MURRAY-KULKYNE
REGIONAL PARK
Mallee
Track
NATIONAL PARK
Lake
Bitterang
Lake
Cantala
Track
Retail Bend B
Murray
Retail Bend A
Firemans Bend
Nowingi
Konardin
Track
Lake
Mournpall
Cantala
River
Jinkers Bend
Lake
Mournpall
Lake
Mournpall
Chalka
Creek
Track
Ki Bend
Lake
Mournpall
Warepil
Lookout
Chalka
Creek
Track
Old
Calder
Mournpall
Track
Stockyard
The Boiler
River
The Paddlewheel
HATTAH
Lake Hattah
Visitor Centre
Hattah -
Robinvale
Lake
Kramen
MURRAY-KULKYNE
REGIONAL PARK
KIA
REFERENCE
AREA
Road
TO
WEMEN
Highway
Channel
MURRAY-SUNSET
NATIONAL PARK
CRAMENTON
Coreena
Highway
TRINITA
ANNUELLO FLORA
AND FAUNA RESERVE
TO
OUYEN

N

0   10Km

MALLEE

Sturt
Highway

Located east of Hattah between the Calder Highway and the Murray River and centered around the tranquil Hattah and Mournpall Lakes systems. Access to the park's lake systems and main visitor facilities is signposted off the Robinvale Road 3.7km east of Hattah on the Calder Highway. Then drive in 1.7km to the park's visitor information centre. Access to the Murray River section of the park is signposted along River Track, which is signposted off the Robinvale Road 18.8km further east of the main access. Conventional vehicle access, roads can be rough at times. Caravan access with care. All park roads are dry weather only. Visitors are requested to check conditions prior to visiting. Some tracks may be seasonally flooded. Activities include walking, canoeing, swimming, fishing, cycling and vehicle touring.

Lake Hattah camping area

Signposted access on the main park entrance road, 300m east of the visitor information centre. Then in 200m to very large camping area with individual sites, some well shaded and protected others open. Bring drinking water. Some firewood supplied. Gas/fuel stove preferred.
GPS S:34 45.154 E:142 20.524
MR: Map 1 J6

Lake Mournpall camping area

Signposted access along Mournpall Track 8.9km north of the visitor information centre. Mournpall Track is signposted at visitor information centre. Bring drinking water. Some firewood supplied. Gas/fuel stove preferred.
GPS S:34 42.284 E:142 20.119
MR: Map 1 I5

Murray River bush camping areas

Bush camping areas beside the Murray River. Signposted access along the River Track, which is signposted off Robinvale Road, 22.5km east of Hattah on the Calder Highway. No facilities. Bring drinking water. Gas/fuel stove preferred.
Ki Bend: Three access tracks signposted along River Track, 6.3km, 8.5km and 9.5km north of the park information board (this information board is on River Track 100m north of the Robinvale Road.)
Southern access track: **GPS** S:34 43.966 E:142 30.071
MR: Map 1 J5

Jinkers Bend: Signposted access along River Track 500m north of the northern access track to Ki Bend, then in 200m to the river.
GPS S:34 41.928 E:142 29.990
MR: Map 1 J5

Firemans Bend: Signposted access along River Track 1.3km north of Jinkers Bend access track. Then in 700m river and boat ramp.
GPS S:34 40.953 E:142 30.070
MR: Map 1 J5

FURTHER Information

Parks Vic Info Line
Tel: 13 19 63
Camping fees: Fees change annually. Contact Parks Vic for current fees. Fees payable at self-registration stations.

MALLEE

Located 12km south-east of Mildura on the banks of the Murray River. Access via Eleventh Street, east of Mildura. Conventional vehicle access in dry weather only. Some tracks may be closed due to seasonal flooding. Reserve protects natural floodplain ecosystem and magnificent river red gum forest. View Psyches Bend Pump Station.

Kings Billabong bush camping

FURTHER Information

> **Parks Vic Info Line**
> **Tel:** 13 19 63

Dispersed bush camping along banks of Murray River. From Mildura head east along Eleventh Street, signposted off highway. Turn right onto Cureton Avenue and then left into Psyche Bend Road. Access roads to bush campsites leave from this road. Numerous access roads from the pump station also lead to bush campsites. Toilet facilities are located on the western side of the billabong near the pump station.
Psyche Bend Pumps – **GPS** S:34 15.254
E:142 13.910
MR: Map 1 I2

Located 14km north of Rainbow. Access via Hopetoun-Rainbow Road. Conventional vehicle access to camping areas. Lake fills and empties in 20 year cycles. Last filled in 1974 — empty since 1984. Use of gas/fuel stove preferred. Activities include fishing, boating (when lake is full), bushwalking, four-wheel drive touring.

Western Beach camping area

Located on west side of lake. Access via Western Beach Road off Albacutya Road. Limited water supply, bring drinking water.
MR: Map 2 G5

Yaapeet Beach camping area

Located on east side of lake. Access from Yaapeet. Limited water supply, bring drinking water.
MR: Map 2 H5

MALLEE

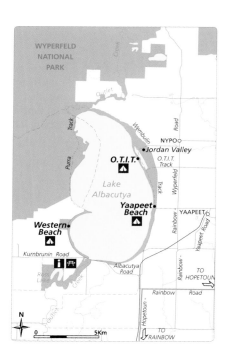

OTIT camping area

Located on east side of lake. Access via OTIT Track off Wembulin Track. Conventional vehicle access in dry weather only. Bring drinking water.
MR: Map 2 H5

FURTHER Information

> **Parks Vic Info Line**
> **Tel:** 13 19 63

105 Lake Cullulleraine

Located 58km west of Mildura. Access via Sturt Highway. Natural lake filled from Lock 9 on the Murray River. Watersport activities can be undertaken on lake.

Bushmans Rest Caravan Park

Access via Bushman Road, Cullulleraine.
MR: Map 1 E2

FURTHER Information

> **Bushmans Rest Caravan Park**
> **Tel:** 03 5028 2252. Bookings recommended, Easter and Christmas.
> **Camping fees:** Unpowered from $17.00 per site/night for 2 people. Powered from $19.90 per site/night for 2 people.

Lake Cullulleraine Holiday Park

Signposted access off Sturt Highway in Cullulleraine.
MR: Map 1 E2

FURTHER Information

> **Lake Cullulleraine Holiday Park**
> **Tel:** 03 5028 2226. Bookings required at peak times.
> **Camping fees:** Unpowered from $15.00 per site/night for 2 people. Powered from $20.00 per site/night for 2 people.

MALLEE

Lake Hindmarsh was named by explorer Edmund John Eyre when he discovered the lake in 1838. The lake is Victoria's largest natural freshwater lake and is surrounded by River Red Gum forests. The lake and its forests are home to numerous bird species. When full the lake is popular for water based activities including water skiing. Lake Hindmarsh is located west of Jeparit, which is on the C227 road, 22km north of Dimboola. Access also from Nhill via the Nhill-Jeparit Road.

Schulzes Beach camping area

Located on western shores of Lake Hindmarsh. Signposted access via Schulzes Beach Road off the Nhill-Rainbow Road. Bring drinking water and firewood.
MR: Map 2 G7

Williamsons Beach camping area

Located on the northern shores of Lake Hindmarsh. Access track is off the Nhill-Rainbow Road, east of the Amy Johnson Highway. Dry weather access only. Bring drinking water and firewood.
MR: Map 2 G6

The Wattles camping area

Located on the northern shores of Lake Hindmarsh. Access track is off the Nhill-Rainbow Road east of the Outlet Creek crossing. Dry weather access only. Bring drinking water and firewood.
MR: Map 2 G6

Picnic Point Beach camping area

Located on the south-eastern shores of Lake Hindmarsh and north of the Wimmera River crossing. Access track is off the unsealed Lake Road, which runs parallel with the lake's eastern shore, and is accessed off the Nhill-Jeparit Road. Dry weather access only. Bring drinking water and firewood.
MR: Map 2 G7

FURTHER Information

Parks Vic Info Line
Tel: 13 19 63

Four Mile Beach camping ground

Located 5km west of Jeparit, with access signposted along the Nhill-Jeparit Road. Limited tank water. Bring drinking water and firewood. Powered sites available. Coin operated hot showers.
MR: Map 2 G7

FURTHER Information

> **Hindmarsh Shire Council, Nhill**
> **Tel:** 03 5391 1811
> **Camping fees:** Four Mile Beach Camping Ground from $8.00 per site/night. Fees payable at council office: Town Hall, Roy Street, Jeparit, tel: 03 5397 2070, open Monday, Tuesday and Thursday.

107 Merbein Common—Horseshoe Bend

Located 10km north-west of Mildura on the banks of the Murray River at Horseshoe Bend near Merbein. Access via signposted Old Wentworth Road. Conventional vehicle access in dry weather only. Some tracks may be closed due to seasonal flooding.

Horseshoe Bend bush camping

Access via Old Wentworth Road off River Avenue in Merbein. Old Wentworth Road is near racecourse and winery entrances.
MR: Map 1 H2

FURTHER Information

> **Parks Vic Info Line**
> **Tel:** 13 19 63

MALLEE

Located between Robinvale and Swan Hill on the banks of the Murray River. Many signposted access roads off Murray Valley Highway. Conventional vehicle access in dry weather only. Check road conditions first. Some tracks may be closed due to seasonal flooding. Activities include bushwalking, fishing, swimming and canoeing.

MURRUMBIDGEE JUNCTION & NYAH STATE FOREST

Passage Camp camping area

Dispersed bush camping beside Murray River. Located 45km south-east of Robinvale. Access via Boundary Bend. Signposted access off the main road. Bring drinking water.
MR: Map 5 C2

Wakool Junction camping area

Dispersed bush camping beside Murray River. Located 7km east of Piambie. Signposted access off Murray Valley Highway. Site of Major Mitchell's 'Australia Felix' camp. Bring drinking water.
MR: Map 5 D2

Nyah bush camping

Dispersed bush camping beside Murray River, adjacent to Nyah township. Signposted access off Murray Valley Highway. Bring drinking water.
MR: Map 5 D5

VINIFERA MURRAY RIVER RESERVE

Vinifera bush camping

Dispersed bush camping beside Murray River. Located 20km north of Swan Hill near Vinifera. Signposted access off Murray Valley Highway. Bring drinking water.
MR: Map 5 D5

FURTHER Information

> **Parks Vic Info Line**
> **Tel:** 13 19 63
> **DSE Customer Service Centre**
> **Tel:** 13 61 86

MALLEE

Murray-Kulkyne Regional Park consists of two sections along the Murray River and is located east of Hattah-Kulkyne National Park. Access through the park is along the River Track. From the north River Track can be accessed from Kulkyne Way from Colignan, the park entrance is 7km south of Colignan. Kulkyne Way can be reached via Boonoonar Road which is signposted off the Calder Highway 8km south of Carwarp. From the south River Track is signposted along the Robinvale Road, 22.5km east of Hattah on the Calder Highway. Swim, fish and canoe along the Murray or go walking and wildlife watching.

Murray-Kulkyne bush camping areas

Numerous bush camping areas beside the Murray River. Access to sites is signposted along River Track. Camping is only permitted between River Track and the river. Caravans check road conditions first. Bring drinking water and firewood.

Emmerts Bend: Accessed via track from the park entrance and information board, which is 7km south of Colignan.
Park entrance **GPS** S:34 34.257 E:142 24.550
MR: Map 1 J5

Tarpaulin Bend: Signposted access along River Track 4.2km south of park entrance and information board. Then in 3.7km to river.
GPS S:34 35.043 E:142 27.382
MR: Map 1 J5

Britt Bend: Signposted access along River Track 4.2km south of park entrance and information board. Then in 3.1km to next signposted access track which leads a further 400m to the river.
GPS S:34 35.353 E:142 27.545
MR: Map 1 J5

Deep Bend: Signposted access along River Track 6.5km south of Tarpaulin and Britt Bend access track. Then in 300m to river.
GPS S:34 38.417 E:142 28.313
MR: Map 1 J5

Retail Bend A: Signposted access along River Track 4.4km south of Deep Bend access track. Then in 700m to river.
GPS S:34 40.333 E:142 29.590
MR: Map 1 J5

Retail Bend B: Access via the signposted track to Firemans Bend (which is in Hattah-Kulkyne National Park), which is 1.9km south of Retail Bend A access track. Follow this track east for 500m then take the signposted access to the north for 1.6km to the river.
GPS S:34 40.250 E:142 29.865
MR: Map 1 J5

The Boiler: Signposted access along River Track, 8km south of Firemans Bend access track and 3.4km north of southern entrance and information board. Then in 500m to river.
GPS S:34 44.985 E:142 30.479
MR: Map 1 J6

The Paddlewheel: Accessed along track which is 1.1km south of The Boiler access track and 2.3km north of southern entrance and information board.
MR: Map 1 K6

FURTHER Information

> **Parks Vic Info Line**
> **Tel:** 13 19 63

MALLEE

Mopoke Hut camping area

Murray-Sunset National Park is located 40km south-west of Mildura. Main access via Mallee Highway in the south and Millewa Road in the north. Conventional vehicle access to main camping areas only, others require 4WD. Activities include fishing and boating on the Murray River in the northern section of the park; bushwalking near Pink Lakes and four-wheel drive touring in remote sections of the park.

Lake Crosbie camping area

13km north of Mallee Highway on south side of Pink Lakes. Signposted access off highway, 10km west of Underbool via Pink Lakes Road. Bring drinking water. Gas/fuel stove preferred.
GPS S:35 03.346 E:141 43.829
MR: Map 1 F8

Lake Becking camping area

16km north of Mallee Highway on east side of Lake Becking. Signposted access 2km north of Lake Crosbie. Small area with two sites. Bring drinking water. Gas/fuel stove preferred.
GPS S:35 02.360 E:141 42.939
MR: Map 1 F7

Mount Crozier camping area

16km north of Mallee Highway on east side of Lake Becking. Signposted access 2km north of Lake Crosbie. Small area with two sites. Bring drinking water. Gas/fuel stove preferred.

Signposted access on Mt Crozier Track, 23km north of Lake Becking. 4WD access, suitable for off-road camper trailer. Mt Crozier Track has soft, sandy sections. Bring drinking water. Gas/fuel stove preferred.
GPS S:34 54.569 E:141 42.318
MR: Map 1 F7

Mopoke Hut camping area

Access via Mopoke Hut Track. Mopoke Hut Track is signposted off Last Hope Track. Located 4km south of Last Hope Track. 4WD access, suitable for off-road camper trailer. Bring drinking water. Gas/fuel stove preferred.
GPS S:34 48.634 E:141 45.573
MR: Map 1 F6

Large Tank camping area

Access via Mt Crozier Track, 10km west of Mt Crozier. 4WD access, suitable for off-road camper trailer. Mt Crozier Track has soft, sandy sections. Small site. Bring drinking water. Gas/fuel stove preferred.
MR: Map 1 E7

Cattleyards camping area

Located at intersection of Underbool & Grub Tracks. 4WD vehicle access recommended. Bring drinking water. Gas/fuel stove preferred.
MR: Map 1 E7

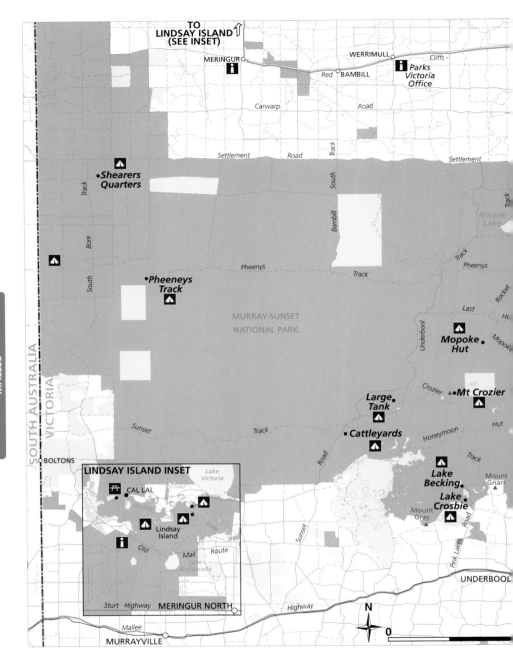

TO
LINDSAY ISLAND
(SEE INSET)

MERINGUR ℹ

WERRIMULL

BAMBILL
Red

Cliffs –

ℹ Parks
Victoria
Office

Carwarp   Road

Settlement   Road   Track   Settlement

△
•Shearers
Quarters

Track

Bore

South

Rocket
Lake

South   Bambill

Track

Pheenys   Track

△

•Pheeneys
Track

MURRAY-SUNSET

NATIONAL PARK

Pheenys

Last   Rocket

Ho

Mopoke

△
Mopoke
Hut   •

Underbool

Track

Crozier   ▲ •Mt Crozier

△

•
Large
Tank

△

• Cattleyards

△

Honeymoon   Track   Hut

Sunset   Track

Road

△
Lake
Becking •

Mount
Gnarr
▲

BOLTONS

LINDSAY ISLAND INSET

Lake
Victoria

Mount
Gray
▲

Lake
Crosbie •

△

Pink Lakes   Road

🛒 CAL LAL
•

△

△
Lindsay
Island

ℹ

Old   Mail   Route

Lake
Wallpolla

Sunset

Sturt   Highway   MERINGUR NORTH

Highway

UNDERBOOL

N

Mallee

MURRAYVILLE

0

SOUTH AUSTRALIA

VICTORIA

Rocket Lake camping area

Access via Rocket Lake Track from Pink Lakes or Nowingi Line Track from Nowingi on Calder Highway. 4WD vehicle access recommended. Bring drinking water. Gas/fuel stove preferred.
GPS S:34 38.293 E:141 49.905
MR: Map 1 G5

Pheenys Track camping area

Located on west end of Pheenys Track. 4WD vehicle access recommended. Bring drinking water. Gas/fuel stove preferred.
MR: Map 1 B5

Lindsay Island camping areas

Dispersed bush camping on Lindsay Island on banks of Murray River. Signposted access from Sturt Highway west of Meringur North. Bring drinking water. Gas/fuel stove preferred.
MR: Map 1 B1/C1/D1

The Shearers' Quarters (hut accommodation)

Historic iron hut, sleeps up to 14. Access via North-South Settlement Road from Sturt Highway. 4WD access recommended. Bring drinking water. Some firewood supplied. Bring gas/fuel stove.
MR: Map 1 B4

FURTHER Information

Parks Vic Info Line
Tel: 13 19 63. Advance bookings essential for Shearer's Quarters.
Bookings: Parks Vic Weerimul
Tel: 03 5028 1212
Accommodation fees: Contact office for current hire rates.

MALLEE

Located 20km south-east of Mildura between Nangiloc and Colignan on the banks of the Murray River. Access via signposted C253 (Kulkyne Way) off the Calder Highway 3km south of Red Cliffs. Dry weather access only. Some tracks may be closed due to seasonal flooding. Scenic stretch of river characterised by sharp bends, rock shelves and sandbars.

Nangiloc-Colignan bush camping

Numerous bush camping areas beside the Murray River. Access to the river bends are signposted off the C253 (Kulkyne Way) south to Murray-Kulkyne Regional Park. Alternative access from the south is via Boonoonar Road, which is signposted off the Calder Highway 9km south of Carwarp and leads 16km east to Kulkyne Way, 1.8km north of the signposted access to Mansells Bend. Bring drinking water and firewood.

Spences Bend: Signposted access off C253, 24.1km south-east of the Calder Way and 2km north of Nangiloc. Then in 200m to river.
Access track **GPS** S:34 27.794 E:142 21.187
MR: Map 1 J4

Police Bend: Signposted access off C253 at southern end of Nangiloc village. Then in 1.1km to river.
Access track **GPS** S:34 28.802 E:142 21.730
MR: Map 1 J4

Buxtons Bend: Signposted access via Hewitts Track off C253, 3.3km south of Police Bend access track. Then in 400m to river.
Access track **GPS** S:34 30.416 E:142 22.041
MR: Map 1 J4

Graces Bend: Signposted access via Briggs Lane off C253, 1.4km south of Buxtons Bend access track and 1.2km north of Colignan. Then in 1.2km to river.
Access track **GPS** S:34 31.048 E:142 22.515
MR: Map 1 J4

Watts Bend: Signposted access off C253, 1km south of Colignan and 800m north of signposted Boonoonar Road. Built boat ramp at this location.
Access track **GPS** S:34 32.119 E:142 22.247
MR: Map 1 J4

Mansells Bend: Signposted access off C253, 1.8km south Boonoonar Road and 3.3km north of entrance to Murray-Kulkyne Regional Park. Then in 150m to river.
Access track **GPS** S:34 32.989 E:142 23.553
MR: Map 1 J4

FURTHER Information

> **Parks Vic Info Line**
> **Tel:** 13 19 63

MALLEE

Located 15km south-west of Murrayville at Ngallo. Access via Ngallo South Road off the Mallee Highway west of Murrayville. At site of old tennis courts. Close to Big Desert Wilderness.

Ngallo Park camping

Located 2.6km south of the Mallee Highway on eastern side of Ngallo South Road. Limited tank water. Bring firewood.
GPS S:35 16.358 E:141 04.187
MR: Map 2 B2

FURTHER Information

Murrayville Newsagency
Tel: 03 5095 2181

113 Underbool

The small, friendly village of Underbool is situated on the Mallee Highway, 60km east of Murrayville and 21km west of Walpeup. From here it is possible to make day trips to Murray-Sunset National Park or Wyperfeld National Park.

Underbool Recreational Reserve

Recreational reserve is located on Gnarr Road on north side of the railway line. Tennis courts, bowls green, football oval and playground located here.
MR: Map 2 G1

FURTHER Information

> **Underbool General Store**
> **Tel:** 03 5094 6270
> **Camping fees:** Fee details at site. Payable at on-site honesty box.

114 Wallpolla Island State Forest

Located 25km west of Merbein on the banks of the Murray River. Access via Old Mail Road. Dry weather access only. Some tracks may be seasonally flooded.

Wallpolla Island bush camping

Dispersed bush camping along banks of Murray River. Signposted access via Old Mail Road. Bring firewood.
MR: Map 1 F1

FURTHER Information

> **DSE Customer Service Centre**
> **Tel:** 13 61 86
> **NB:** Camp fires are permitted and must be contained as per DSE fire regulations or risk a fine.

115 Walpeup Lake

Located 14km south-east of Walpeup at Timberoo South. Signposted access via Hopetoun-Walpeup Road.

Walpeup Lake camping area

Signposted access via Hopetoun-Walpeup Road. Lakeside location. Suitable for overnight stop. Bring drinking water and firewood.
MR: Map 2 H1

FURTHER Information

> **Parks Vic Speed**
> **Tel:** 03 5082 4276

Wyperfeld National Park is located to the west of Hopetoun. Main access via Yaapeet in the south and Patchewollock in the east. Western section of park is only suitable for 4WD vehicles. Wyperfeld is Victoria's third largest national park and protects large areas of undisturbed mallee vegetation. Explore the park by taking the Eastern Lookout Nature Drive or by walking or cycling.

Wonga camping area

Located on Park Entrance Road, 25km north of Yaapeet near Lake Brimin. Gas/fuel stove preferred.
MR: Map 2 H4

Casuarina camping area

Located 7km along Meridian Road west of Patchewollock. From Patchewollock take the road to Baring in a westerly direction, then proceed along Pine Plains Road to the signposted access to park, and then proceed south along Meridian Road. Conventional vehicle access. Bring drinking water. Gas/fuel stove preferred.
MR: Map 2 H3

Remote Camp camping area

Walk-in campsite at the end of Meridian Road. Access through management gate 3km south of Casuarina Campground, then walk-in 400m. Limited tank water, bring drinking water. Gas/fuel stove preferred.
MR: Map 2 H3

FURTHER Information

Parks Vic Info Line
Tel: 13 19 63
Camping fees: Wonga camping area: From $11.80 per site/night up to 6 people. Fees payable at self-registration stations.

MALLEE

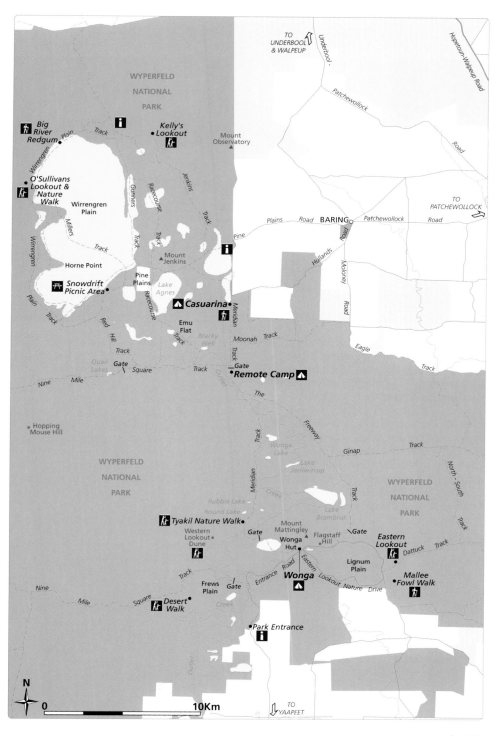

WYPERFELD
NATIONAL
PARK

Big River Redgum

Kelly's Lookout

Mount Observatory

O'Sullivans Lookout & Nature Walk

Wirrengren Plain

Horne Point

Snowdrift Picnic Area

Pine Plains

Mount Jenkins

Lake Agnes

Casuarina

Emu Flat

Bracky Well

Quail Lakes

Gate

Square

Track

Moonah

Track

Gate

Remote Camp

The

Hopping Mouse Hill

Nine Mile

WYPERFELD
NATIONAL
PARK

Wonga Lake

Lake Jerriwirrup

Ginap

Track

Rubble Lake

Round Lake

Lake Brambruk

WYPERFELD
NATIONAL
PARK

Tyakil Nature Walk

Western Lookout Dune

Gate

Mount Mattingley

Wonga Hut

Flagstaff Hill

Gate

Eastern Lookout

Dattuck

Lignum Plain

Mallee Fowl Walk

Nine Mile

Square

Desert Walk

Frews Plain

Gate

Wonga

Entrance Road

Eastern Lookout Nature Drive

Park Entrance

Outlet

TO UNDERBOOL & WALPEUP

Underbool

Hopetoun-Walpeup Road

Patchewollock

Road

TO PATCHEWOLLOCK

Plains Road

BARING

Patchewollock Road

Hillands

Moloney

Road

Eagle

Track

North-South Track

Track

N

0   10Km

TO YAAPEET

MALLEE

Camping GUIDE TO VICTORIA | 137

Central Murray

THE CENTRAL MURRAY REGION STRETCHES from the Murray River town of Swan Hill, east to the wine growing area of Rutherglen, and south towards historic Castlemaine. Apart from being centred around Australia's most famous river, this region also includes some wonderful historic areas which have long associations with Aboriginal occupation, European settlement and gold rush history. Areas such as Castlemaine Diggings National Heritage Park, Greater Bendigo National Park, Heathcote-Graytown National Park and Whroo Historic Reserve can all be enjoyed in this picturesque region of Victoria.

In the north the majestic river red gum forests along the mighty Murray River provide some top notch campsites, car touring, boating and fishing opportunities. These forests and reserves have a plethora of campsites along the river's banks, many of which have only basic or no facilities. During the summer holidays people flock to the banks of the Murray River to camp, so if you're after some seclusion pick another time to visit.

Greater Bendigo National Park is a large park just north of the regional centre of Bendigo and encompasses what was previously Kamarooka and Whipstick State Parks. Five campsites are scattered throughout the park providing access to scenic sites, walking and prospecting areas.

In the east of the region you can set up camp in the Strathbogie or Warby Ranges where the Kelly Gang once took refuge while on the run from police. These camping areas are good bases while exploring the ranges on foot.

Although summer is the prime time to visit this region, it is also the busiest, especially along the Murray River. Spring and autumn are pleasant with less crowds.

BEST Campsites!

The Camp camping area
Warby Range State Park

Christies Beach camping area
Echuca Regional Park

Gulf camping area
Barmah State Forest

Gunbower Island bush camping
Gunbower Island State Forest

Greens campground
Whroo Historic Reserve

Located 10km north-east of Barmah township on the banks of the Murray River. Access via Picola North Road from Picola. Dry weather access only. Some tracks may be closed due to seasonal flooding. Large river red gum forest. Fishing and canoeing in river.

The Gulf camping area

Access is via Gulf Road, which is accessed through Murrays Mill Gate. Access road is signposted off Picola North Road as Gulf Rd/Murray Mills Road. On entering the forest through Murrays Mill Gate, Gulf Road leads 11km to the camping area with dispersed bush camping on banks of Murray River. Bring drinking water.
The Gulf CA – **GPS** S:35 50.524 E:145 09.140
Murrays Mill Gate –**GPS** S:35 55.749 E:145 06.814
MR: Map 9 B1

Carters Beach camping area

Access is via Ulupna Bridge Road north of Strathmerton. From Strathmerton take the signposted Bourchiers Road north for 6km then turn left into road signposted 4km Ulupna Island, follow this for 1.6km then turn right into road signposted Ulupna Bridge Road. Follow Ulupna Bridge Road for 4.8km to entrance to forest. On entering the forest the road leads 1.5km to Carters Beach. Good beach access to the river. Bring drinking water.
GPS S:35 49.308 E:145 27.214
MR: Map 9 C1

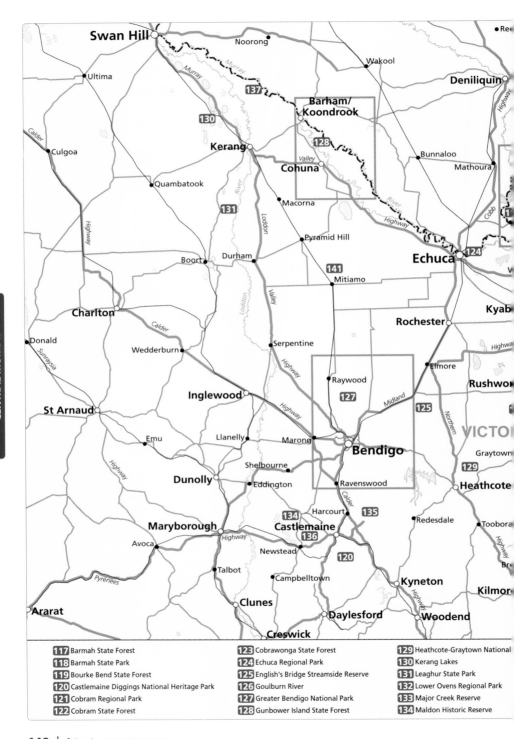

CENTRAL MURRAY

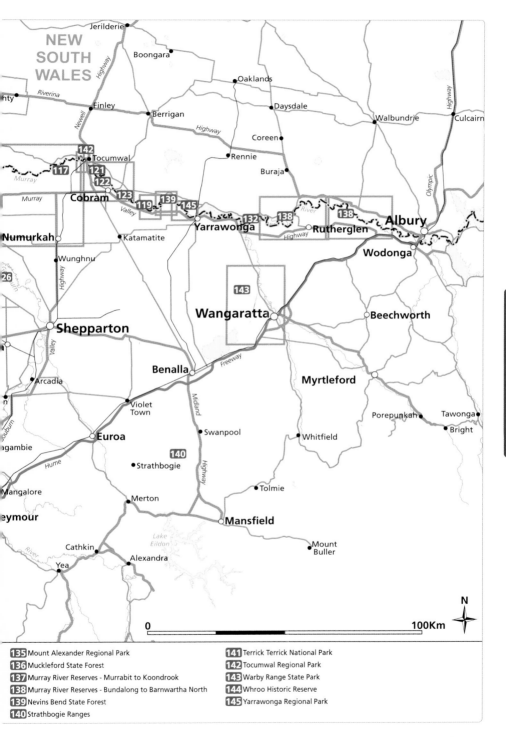

NEW SOUTH WALES

Jerilderie
Boongara
Oaklands
Daysdale
Finley
Berrigan
Coreen
Walbundrie
Culcairn
Tocumwal
Rennie
Buraja
Cobram
Yarrawonga
Rutherglen
Albury
Numurkah
Katamatite
Wodonga
Wunghnu
Wangaratta
Beechworth
Shepparton
Myrtleford
Benalla
Arcadia
Violet Town
Porepunkah
Tawonga
Bright
Euroa
Swanpool
Whitfield
Strathbogie
Tolmie
Mangalore
Merton
Seymour
Mansfield
Cathkin
Yea
Alexandra
Mount Buller

Murray
Riverina Highway
Newell
Highway
Valley
Olympic Highway
Freeway
Midland Highway
Hume
Lake Eildon
River

0   100Km

N

135 Mount Alexander Regional Park	**141** Terrick Terrick National Park
136 Muckleford State Forest	**142** Tocumwal Regional Park
137 Murray River Reserves - Murrabit to Koondrook	**143** Warby Range State Park
138 Murray River Reserves - Bundalong to Barnwartha North	**144** Whroo Historic Reserve
139 Nevins Bend State Forest	**145** Yarrawonga Regional Park
140 Strathbogie Ranges	

Doctors Bend camping area

Access is via Ulupna Bridge Road north of Strathmerton. From Strathmerton take the signposted Bourchiers Road north for 6km then turn left into road signposted 4km Ulupna Island. Follow this for 1.6km then turn right into road signposted Ulupna Bridge Road. Follow Ulupna Bridge Road for 4.7km and turn right (this turn is 100m prior to forest entrance). Follow this road for 1.7km to enter the forest and then continue for a further 100m to the camping area. Bring drinking water.
GPS S:35 49.040 E:145 28.178
MR: Map 9 C10

Barmah bush camping

Dispersed bush camping on banks of Murray River. Bring drinking water. Numerous access tracks to the forests east of Barmah and west of Strathmerton. From Barmah take the Picola Road and at 7km turn left (north) on the signposted Trickeys Lane. Trickeys Lane leads north for 3.2km to Vales Road on the right, which proceeds east and has numerous access roads to the forest and river.
Trickeys Gate, access track is on the left 200m north of Vales Road, then in 1.1km to entrance
– **GPS** S:35 58.030 E:145 01.153
Gowers Gate, access is via Corrys Mill Rd which is 2.2km along Vales Road, then in 3.1km to entrance
– **GPS** S:35 56.401 E:145 03.408
Eddys Gate, access is via Edwards Lane, which is 2.5km east of Corrys Mill Road, then in 2.4km to entrance
– **GPS** S:35 56.410 E:145 05.029
Murrays Mill Gate, see The Gulf CA above.
Hughes Gate, access is via signposted Hughes Lane off Lancaster Road, 3.3km north-east of Picola North Road, then in 700m to entrance
– **GPS** S:35 54.105 E:145 10.508
Thorpes Gate, access is via signposted Thorpes Lane off Lancaster Road 1.9km east of Hughes Lane, then in 2.4km to entrance
– **GPS** S:35 52.622 E:145 11.330
Darlows Gate, access is via signposted Darlows Lane off Lancaster Road 1.9km east of Thorpes Lane, then in 1.1km to entrance
– **GPS** S:35 52.616 E:145 12.635
Tipperary Gate, gate is off Lancaster Road 2.6km east of Darlows Lane
– **GPS** S:35 53.198 E:145 15.534

FURTHER Information

> **DSE Nathalia**
> **Tel:** 03 5866 2702

Early Morning on the Murray River

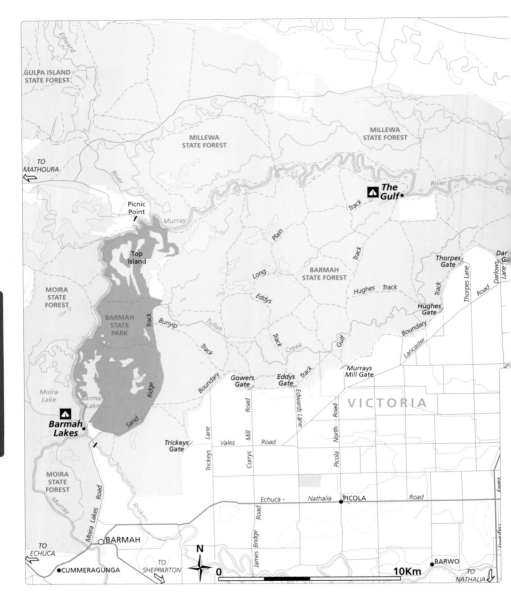

118 Barmah State Park

Made up of two sections along the banks of the Murray River. Section 1 includes the Barmah Lakes section (the western area) and is located north of Barmah. The Dharnya Centre is located in this section. Section 2 includes Ulupna Island, (the north-east area) and is north of the Murray Valley Highway. Many

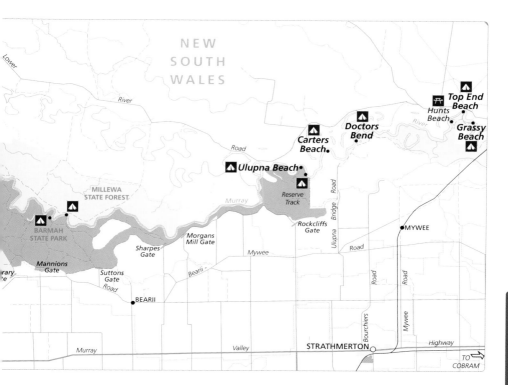

access roads off Murray Valley Highway and from Barmah. Dry weather access only. Some tracks may be closed due to seasonal flooding. Large river red gum forest. Fishing and canoeing.

Barmah Lakes camping area

Located within section 1 of the state park. Access road is signposted Maloney St/Dharnya Centre 14km east of the Cobb Highway. Enter state park 6.2km along this road, then at a further 400m is signposted access to camping area, which leads 600m into camping area. A very large attractive area with dispersed camping beside the river among river red gum forest. Bring drinking water.
GPS S:35 57.389 E:144 57.565
MR: Map 9 A2

Ulupna Beach camping area

Located within section 2 of the state park, north of Strathmerton. From Strathmerton take the signposted Bourchiers Road north for 6km then turn left into road signposted 4km Ulupna Island. Follow this for 1.6km then turn right into road signposted Ulupna Bridge Road. Follow Ulupna Bridge Road for 3km to road on left which leads 1.1km into state park and information board. Follow past the information board for 700m then turn left into signposted Reserve Track which leads to Ulupna Beach. Bring drinking water.
GPS S:35 49.795 E:145 26.163
MR: Map 9 C1

Barmah State Park bush camping

Dispersed bush camping on banks of Murray River between Barmah State Forest and section 2 of the state park. Bring drinking water. Access can be made via Mannions Gate and Suttons Gate, which are accessed off Lancaster Road, which is north of the Murray Valley Highway and signposted off the Picola North Road. Access can also be made through Sharps Gate, Morgans Mill Gate and Rockliffs Gate, which are accessed off the Bearii-Mywee Road, which is north of the Murray Valley Highway and is west of Ulupna Bridge Road.

Mannions Gate – **GPS** S:35 52.955 E:145 16.580
Suttons Gate – **GPS** S:35 52.883 E:145 18.738
MR: Map 9 C1

FURTHER Information

Parks Vic Info Line
Tel: 13 19 63

CAMPING UNDER
River red Gums

Although the majestic river red gums that line our inland rivers make delightful, shady campsites, do not make your camp directly under these trees. River red gums are notorious for dropping large branches at any time - without warning!

119 Bourke Bend State Forest

Forest situated along the Murray River. Access is off the Murray Valley Highway 19km south-east of Cobram and 17km north-west of Yarrawonga, via a road behind a signposted roadside picnic area. Follow the road north for 100m to entrance of forest and information board. Bush camping beside the Murray River. Dry weather access only. Some tracks may be closed due to seasonal flooding. Activities include bushwalking, fishing, swimming, canoeing, power boating and water-skiing in some areas.

Bourkes No 1 Beach camping area

Dispersed bush camping on banks of Murray River. Once at forest entrance gate, proceed in a northerly direction along Bourkes Bend Track for 1.8km to junction with Murray Track on the right (east). From here proceed north for a further 400m to a junction passing the track on the left (west) and at a further 900m reach camping area. Bring drinking water.

GPS S:35 58.612 E:145 50.091
MR: Map 9 F2

CENTRAL MURRAY

Bourkes No 2 Beach camping area

Dispersed bush camping on banks of Murray River. Once at forest entrance gate, proceed in a northerly direction along Bourkes Bend Track for 1.8km to junction with Murray Track on the right (east). From here proceed north for a further 400m to a junction and turn left (west). Follow this track for 600m to a track on the right (north), turn here and proceed north for 300m to camping area. Bring drinking water.
GPS S:35 58.546 E:145 49.652
MR: Map 9 F2

Bourkes No 3 Beach camping area

Dispersed bush camping on banks of Murray River. Once at forest entrance gate, proceed in a northerly direction along Bourkes Bend Track for 1.8km to junction with Murray Track on the right (east). From here proceed north for a further 400m to a junction and turn left (west). Follow this track for 900m to camping area, passing the access track at 600m to Bourkes No 2 Beach. Bring drinking water.
GPS S:35 58.742 E:145 49.599
MR: Map 9 F2

Bourke Bend State Forest bush camping

Dispersed bush camping on banks of Murray River throughout forest. Access to forest is via road behind a signposted roadside picnic area on the highway 19km south-east of Cobram and 17km north-west of Yarrawonga. Then proceed north for 100m to entrance to forest. Once in forest tracks lead to various parts of the forest and to the river. Self sufficient campers. Bring drinking water.
Forest entrance – **GPS** S:35 59.821 E:145 49.523
MR: Map 9 F2

FURTHER *Information*

> **Parks Vic Info Line**
> **Tel:** 13 19 63
> **Cobram Barooga Visitor Information Centre**
> **Tel:** 03 5872 2132 or 1800 607 607

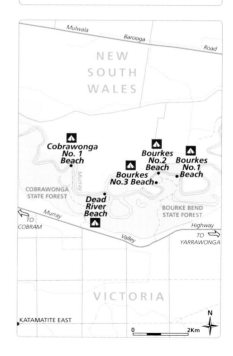

Castlemaine Diggings National Heritage Park is located 10km south Castlemaine. Access via the signposted Vaughan Springs Road off the Midland Highway at Yapeen south of Castlemaine. The area has many historic mining sites and mineral springs. Activities include bushwalking, cycling, fishing and picnicking. Visit the 22m Garfield Water Wheel, Spring Gully and Eureka Reef. Colourful wildflowers in spring. Fish for trout in the Loddon River.

Castlemaine Diggings camping area

Signposted access along Vaughan Springs Road, 5.5km south-east of the Midland Highway, and 1.6km west of the Vaughan Drummond Road. Then in 200m to open camping area with little shade. Camping area is located above the picnic area, where all facilities are located. NB: Dogs are permitted in the camping area but not permitted in the picnic or springs area.
GPS S:37 09.602 E:144 12.854
MR: Map 7 H3

Warburton Bridge bush camping

Located on the southern bank of the Loddon River along the Vaughan-Drummond Road 1.6km south of its junction with the Vaughan Springs Road. Grassed, long area on the river flat. Bring drinking water and firewood.
GPS S:37 10.201 E:144 14.279
MR: Map 7 H3

Chokem Flat campground

Located 1.3km north-west of Irishtown along Fryers Road which is off the Vaughan-Chewtown Road 1.1km north of Vaughan Springs Road. Signpost is set back from the road. This is on the Irishtown side of the crossing of Fryers Creek. Dispersed bush camping for self sufficient campers along the banks of Fryers Creek (normally dry), some grassed areas and some good shade. Bring drinking water and firewood.
GPS S:37 08.434 E:144 13.518
MR: Map 7 H3

FURTHER Information

> **Parks Vic Info Line**
> **Tel:** 13 19 63

Warburton Bridge bush camping

CENTRAL MURRAY

Cobram Regional Park is located beside the Murray River to the north and south of Cobram. The park has a number of beached areas where camping is permitted. To access the northern section of the park, take the signposted Wondah Street off the C370 (Mookarii Street) and proceed north for 1.1km to the park's entrance gate and information board. To access the southern section of the park, take the signposted River Road off the C370 (Mookarii Street), just prior to the bridge over the Murray River, then follow this to the signposted access tracks to the various beaches. Dry weather access only. Some tracks may be closed due to seasonal flooding. Activities include bushwalking, fishing, swimming, canoeing, power boating and water-skiing in some areas. The beach areas act as a natural boat launch.

Little Toms Beach camping area

Located north of the park entrance. Once at the park's entrance via Wondah Street, continue straight ahead for 1.2km to Little Toms Beach. Alternatively take the centre track for 800m then turn right (east) for 400m. Natural boat launch. Bring drinking water.
GPS S:35 54.035 E:145 39.319
MR: Map 9 E2

Big Toms Beach camping area

Located north-west of the park entrance. Once at the park's entrance via Wondah Street proceed in a north-westerly direction along the centre track for 1.7km to Big Toms.
GPS S:35 53.604 E:145 38.813
MR: Map 9 E2

Scotts Beach camping area

Located in southern section of the park. Take the signposted River Road off the C370 and proceed south for 1.3km to park's entrance and information board. In park at 200m is a junction where

the track on left leads 100m into the camping area. Attractive well grassed site beside the river, and very popular. Bring drinking water.
GPS S:35 55.633 E:145 40.539
MR: Map 9 E2

Horseshoe Beach camping area

Located in the southern section of the park and east of Scotts Beach. From Scotts Beach entrance off River Road, proceed along River Road for a further 1.7km to signposted entrance and information board. Once in forest proceed along signposted Horseshoe Track for 1.5km to Horseshoe Beach and camping area. Bring drinking water.
GPS S:35 55.765 E:145 41.790
MR: Map 9 E2

FURTHER Information

Parks Vic Info Line
Tel: 13 19 63
Cobram Barooga Visitor Information Centre
Tel: 03 5872 2132 or 1800 607 607

Scotts Beach camping area

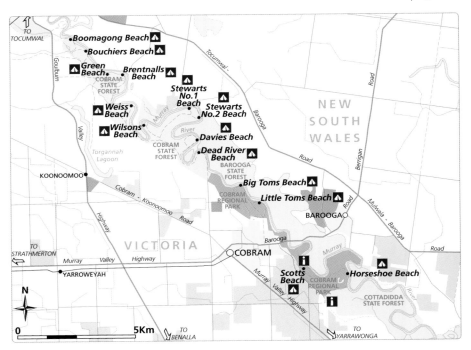

State forest area stretched along the Murray River north-west of Cobram towards Tocumwal, where dispersed bush camping is permitted. Access from Cobram to the southern section of the forests is via Racecourse Road, which is signposted off the Cobram-Koonoomoo Road. Follow Racecourse Road for 2.4km to enter the forest, then once in the forest follow Cobram Track which will lead to all the access tracks to the camping areas. Access to the northern section of the forest and the northern start of Cobram Track is via Green Lane which is signposted off the Goulburn Valley Highway 6km south of the bridge over the Murray River, and leads 1.3km into the forest entrance. Dry weather access only. Some tracks may be closed due to seasonal flooding. Activities include bushwalking, fishing, swimming, canoeing, power boating and water-skiing in some areas. The beach areas act as a natural boat launch.

Dead River Beach camping area

Enter the forest 2.4km north of the Cobram-Koonoomoo Road via the signposted Racecourse Road. Then proceed north for 500m to meet with Dead River Track on the right. Follow Dead River Track around the river for 800m to reach the camping area. Bring drinking water.
GPS S:35 52.830 E:145 37.660
MR: Map 9 E2

Davies Beach camping area

From Dead River Beach follow the track around to the west for 300m to meet again with Cobram Track. Then follow Cobram Track in north-westerly direction for 400m to Davies Beach Track on the right, which leads 1.1km to camping area. Bring drinking water.
GPS S:35 52.536 E:145 37.664
MR: Map 9 E2

CENTRAL MURRAY

Wilsons Beach camping area

From Davies Beach Track continue along Cobram Track in westerly direction for 1.1km to large junction with signage to Stewarts. Turn right (north) here and at 100m there is a track on the left, which leads 900m to Wilsons Beach. Bring drinking water.

GPS S:35 52.154 E:145 36.106
MR: Map 9 D1

Stewarts No 1 Beach camping area

Located north-east of Wilsons Beach. From the Wilsons Beach turn off follow the main track towards Stewarts for 1.8km to a track on left which leads north for 300m to Stewarts No 1 Beach. Bring drinking water.

GPS S:35 51.766 E:145 37.436
MR: Map 9 D1

Stewarts No 2 Beach camping area

Located south of Stewarts No 1 Beach. From the turn off to Stewarts No 1 Beach continue on the main track for 500m in an easterly direction to Stewarts No 2 Beach. Bring drinking water.

GPS S:35 52.017 E:145 37.730
MR: Map 9 D1

Weiss Beach camping area

Located north of Wilsons Beach. From the Stewarts turn off on Cobram Track, continue on Cobram Track in westerly direction for 1.7km to track on the right (north-east) which is Weiss Track. Weiss Track leads 900m in a northerly direction to Weiss Beach and camping area. Bring drinking water.

GPS S:35 51.665 E:145 35.776
MR: Map 9 D1

Brentnalls Beach camping area

Located north of Weiss Beach. From the Weiss Beach turn off, continue along Cobram Track for 1.7km to reach Brentnalls Track on the right (north-east). Brentnalls Track leads 800m to a track junction, at this junction continue north for 300m to Brentnalls Beach. Bring drinking water.

GPS S:35 50.957 E:145 35.547
MR: Map 9 D1

Green Beach camping area

Located west of Brentnalls Beach. Access can be made from Brentnalls Beach by turning west at the junction 300m south of Brentnalls Beach, this is Brentnalls Track and continues for 900m to meet with a track which leads north for 200m to Green Beach. Access can also be made from the Goulburn Valley Highway by taking the signposted Green Lane which is 6km south of the bridge over Murray River, and leads 1.3km to the forest entrance. At entrance continue east along Green Lane for 600m to camping area. This route is not recommended for caravans. Bring drinking water.

GPS S:35 50.936 E:145 35.107
MR: Map 9 D1

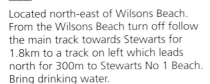

CENTRAL MURRAY

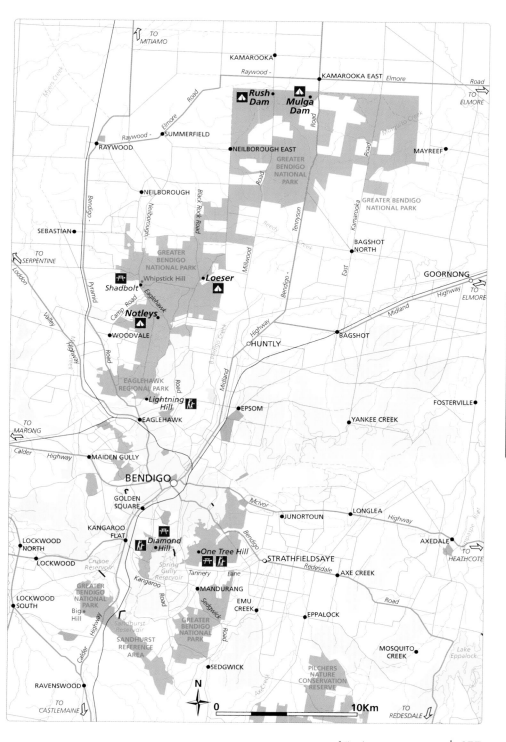

TO
MITIAMO

KAMAROOKA

Raywood -   KAMAROOKA EAST   Elmore

Road

TO
ELMORE

🏕 Rush
Dam

🏕 Mulga
Dam

Elmore

SUMMERFIELD

Raywood -

RAYWOOD

NEILBOROUGH EAST

GREATER
BENDIGO
NATIONAL
PARK

MAYREEF

Road

Black Rock Road

NEILBOROUGH

Neilborough -

Road

GREATER BENDIGO
NATIONAL PARK

SEBASTIAN

Bendigo -

Millwood

Bendigo -

Tennyson

Reedy

Kamarooka

BAGSHOT
NORTH

TO
SERPENTINE

GREATER
BENDIGO
NATIONAL
PARK

Whipstick Hill

Pyramid

Eaglehawk

🎯 Shadbolt
Camp Road

• Loeser
🏕

East

GOORNONG

Highway

Midland

TO
ELMORE

🏕 Notleys

WOODVALE

Road

BAGSHOT

Highway

HUNTLY

Midland

Loddon

Valley

Highway

Myers Creek

EAGLEHAWK
REGIONAL PARK

Road

🚶 Lightning
Hill

EAGLEHAWK

EPSOM

YANKEE CREEK

FOSTERVILLE

TO
MARONG

Calder
Highway

MAIDEN GULLY

Bendigo

BENDIGO

GOLDEN
SQUARE

Mclvor

JUNORTOUN

LONGLEA
Highway

AXEDALE

TO
HEATHCOTE

KANGAROO
FLAT

🚶 🎯 Diamond
Hill

LOCKWOOD
NORTH

Crusoe
Reservoir

LOCKWOOD

Kangaroo

Spring
Gully
Reservoir

🎯 🚶 • One Tree Hill

Tannery

Lane

Redesdale

STRATHFIELDSAYE

AXE CREEK

Road

LOCKWOOD
SOUTH

GREATER
BENDIGO
NATIONAL
PARK

Big
Hill

Road

• MANDURANG

Sedgwick

EMU
CREEK

EPPALOCK

Calder

Highway

Sandhurst
Reservoir

SANDHURST
REFERENCE
AREA

GREATER
BENDIGO
NATIONAL
PARK

Road

MOSQUITO
CREEK

Lake
Eppalock

RAVENSWOOD

TO
CASTLEMAINE

N

• SEDGWICK

PILCHERS
NATURE
CONSERVATION
RESERVE

Axe Creek

TO
REDESDALE

0   10Km

Rush Dam picnic and camping area

Located beside small dam along Camp Road. From the Bendigo-Tennyson Road, continue west along the Raywood Road for 3.1km to the signposted Millwood Road, this is 14.5km east of Raywood on the Bendigo-Pyramid Road. Millwood Road leads south for 1.6km to the signposted crossroads of Camp Road. Road on right leads 700m to camping area with dispersed bush camping in vicinity of dam. Bring drinking water and firewood.
GPS S:36 29.876 E:144 20.651
MR: Map 6 I6

Loeser bush camping area

Large bush camping area in the centre of the park at the junction of Loeser Road and Black Rock Road at site of an old distillery, there is an old boiler and dam at this location. Self sufficient campers. Bring drinking water and firewood.
GPS S:36 37.406 E:144 17.550
MR: Map 6 I7

FURTHER Information

> **Parks Vic Info Line**
> **Tel:** 13 19 63

128 Gunbower Island State Forest

This large island is between the Murray River and Gunbower Creek and stretches from Koondrook in the north for 50km to Torrumbarry in the south. There are numerous access roads off the Murray Valley Highway between these two villages. From Koondrook take the signposted Bridge Road just south of town and access the forests via Condidorios Bridge; from Torrumbarry take the signposted Headworks Road which leads north to campsite number 1 in the forests. Once in the forests follow River Track which follows the Murray River and Koondrook Track which follows Gunbower Creek. Off these main tracks there are numerous access tracks which lead to campsites, many are signposted with numbered posts. Dry weather access. Tracks may be closed due to seasonal flooding. Fishing and watersports on river.

Gunbower Island bush camping

Numerous dispersed bush camping (over 100 sites) on the island along the banks of the Murray River and Gunbower Creek. Some sites have facilities. NB: Disabled toilet located near Twin Bridges via Koondrook access. Caravan access depends on road conditions. Bring drinking water.
Condidoris Bridge
– **GPS** S:35 39.016 E:144 08.014
Headworks Road
– **GPS** S:36 01.710 E:144 30.816

Graham's Hut
– **GPS** S:35 44.768 E:144 16.491
MR: Map 5 H8 & Map 6 H1/I1/I2/J3

FURTHER Information

> **DSE Cohuna**
> **Tel:** 03 5456 2266

CENTRAL MURRAY

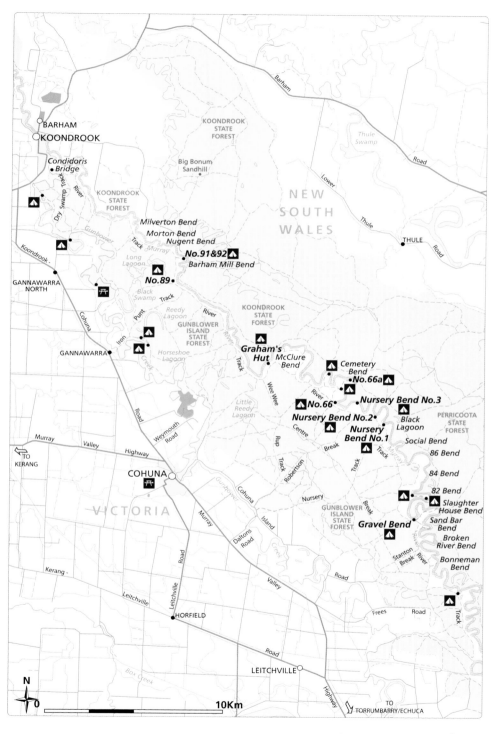

BARHAM
KOONDROOK

Condidoris
Bridge

KOONDROOK
STATE
FOREST

Big Bonum
Sandhill

Thule
Swamp

NEW
SOUTH
WALES

Lower

Thule

Road

THULE

Road

KOONDROOK
STATE
FOREST

Gunbower

River

Dry Swamp Track

Koondrook -

GANNAWARRA
NORTH

Milverton Bend
Morton Bend
Nugent Bend

No.91&92

Barham Mill Bend

No.89

Long
Lagoon

Murray

Track

Black
Swamp

Track

Reedy
Lagoon

River

Punt

Iron

Cohuna

GANNAWARRA

GUNBLOWER
ISLAND
STATE
FOREST

Horseshoe
Lagoon

Creek

KOONDROOK
STATE
FOREST

Graham's
Hut

McClure
Bend

River

Track

Wee Wee

Little
Reedy
Lagoon

Cemetery
Bend

No.66a

Nursery Bend No.3

No.66

Nursery Bend No.2

Nursery
Bend No.1

Black
Lagoon

PERRICOOTA
STATE
FOREST

Social Bend

86 Bend

84 Bend

82 Bend

Slaughter
House Bend

Sand Bar
Bend

Broken
River Bend

Bonneman
Bend

Centre

Rup

Break

Track

Murray

Murray

Valley

Highway

TO
KERANG

COHUNA

VICTORIA

Weymouth
Road

Road

Gunbower

Cohuna

Island

Robertson

Track

Nursery

Break

GUNBLOWER
ISLAND
STATE
FOREST

Gravel Bend

Stanton
Break

River

Murray

Daltons

Road

Valley

Kerang -

Leitchville

Road

HORFIELD

Frees

Road

Track

Box Creek

Road

LEITCHVILLE

TO
TORRUMBARRY/ECHUCA

N

0   10Km

Gunbower Island bush camping

129 Heathcote—Graytown National Park

Heathcote-Graytown National Park is home to wonderful forests of Red Ironbark, Grey and Yellow Box and an amazing array of wildlife and birdlife. Historically the park provided food and tools for local Aboriginal tribes; was once home to thousands of gold diggers during the gold rush; and a prisoner-of-war camp during World War II. The park is located 40km east of Bendigo and just north of Heathcote, access from Heathcote via Heathcote-North Costerfield Road and Heathcote-Nagambie Road.

Dargile camping and picnic area

Signposted access 600m along Plantation Track which is signposted off Plantation Road 3.9km north of the Heathcote-North Costerfield Road. From Heathcote take the signposted Chauncey Street to the signposted Plantation Road. Located at historic school site. Bring drinking water.
GPS S:36 51.092 E:144 44.563
MR: Map 7 K1

Spring Creek camping area

At western end of Graytown locality, which is 30km north-east of Heathcote on the Heathcote-Ngambie Road, take the signposted Graytown-Rushworth Rd/Rushworth 27km. Follow this north for 2km then turn left into signposted Boundary Road. Follow Boundary Road for 400m and then turn left into track which leads to an open grassed camping area surrounded by woodland forest. Bush camping, for self sufficient campers, no facilities. Bring drinking water and firewood.
GPS S:36 47.864 E:144 56.582
MR: Map 7 L1

FURTHER Information

Parks Vic Info Line
Tel: 13 19 63

Spring Creek camping area

Kerang Lakes is a cluster of lakes to the north-west and south of Kerang township. Access via Murray Valley Highway. These lakes are an important wetland area and home to a large number of birds. Picnic, bird watch or camp. NB: The Kerang Lakes System is subject to potentially toxic Blue-Green Algae blooms from time to time. Please observe any warning signs that may be posted.

Lake Bael Bael camping areas

Located west of Kerang. Dispersed camping on north-west side of lake. Access via Fairley Road off Murray Valley Highway.
MR: Map 5 F8

Middle Reedy Lake camping area

Located north of Kerang. Dispersed camping around lake. Access via Pratt Road off Murray Valley Highway.
MR: Map 5 F8

The Marshes camping areas

Located west of Lake Charm. Dispersed camping around marsh system. Access via Bael Bael-Boga Road. 4WD recommended.
MR: Map 5 F8

FURTHER Information

> **Parks Vic Kerang**
> **Tel:** 03 5452 1266

Lake Boga Caravan Park

Situated on Murray Valley Highway in Lake Boga, a short walk to all town facilities. Three camping areas around lake, all sites have lake frontage. Camp kitchen. Laundry facilities.
MR: Map 5 E7

FURTHER Information

> **Lake Boga Caravan Park**
> **Tel:** 03 5037 2386. Bookings essential during Christmas and New Year holiday period.
> **Camping fees:** Unpowered from $18.00 per site/night for 2 people. Powered from $21.00 per site/night for 2 people.

CENTRAL MURRAY

Leaghur State Park is located 25km south of Kerang, with the main access signposted along the Kerang-Boort Road. Dry weather access only. The park preserves black box woodlands and wetlands. Recreational activities include bushwalking, cycling, picnicking, driving the scenic route and bird and wildlife watching.

Lake Meran picnic and camping

Located at southern end of lake. Access via Vallance Track off Lake Meran Track, the scenic route. Bring drinking water and firewood. Gas/fuel stove preferred.
MR: Map 6 F2

Park Entrance picnic and area camping area

Located near main park entrance. Access off Kerang-Boort Road. Bring drinking water and firewood. Gas/fuel stove preferred.
MR: Map 6 F2

FURTHER Information

> **Parks Vic Info Line**
> **Tel:** 13 19 63

132 Lower Ovens Regional Park

Located 20km east of Yarrawonga at the junction of Ovens and Murray Rivers. Access via Murray Valley Highway. Dry weather access only. Some tracks may be seasonally flooded. Fishing and canoeing in river.

Parolas Track bush camping areas

Signposted access to Lower Ovens Regional Park off Murray Valley Highway on the eastern side of bridge over Lower Ovens River. This turnoff is 2.3km east of the Murray Valley Highway and Yarrawonga-Wangaratta Road junction. Then in 400m to Parolas Track which leads for 2.8km with dispersed bush camping along the river. Some sites well shaded and grassed. No facilities, self sufficient campers. Bring drinking water.
GPS S:36 03.681 E:146 11.884
MR: Map 9 H3

CAMPING With Your Dog

> If you own a well behaved and well socialised dog you may wish to take your 'best friend' along camping with you. Dogs are usually welcome in state forests and some reserves, but are not permitted in national parks. Each listing in this guide indicates whether you can bring your dog with you.

CENTRAL MURRAY

Camerons Track bush camping areas

Camerons Track is signposted off the Murray Valley Highway on the western side of bridge over Lower Ovens River, and is 400m west of the main signposted access to park. Camerons Track leads 200m south to bush campsites on the western shore of river. Alternative access is via the signposted Chapel Lane off the Yarrawonga-Wangaratta Road, this turn off is 1.3km south of the Murray Valley Highway. Chapel Lane then leads 600m into park entrance and then becomes Camerons Track and leads 1.1km to camping area and boat ramp. No facilities, self sufficient campers. Bring drinking water.
GPS S:36 04.319 E:146 11.938
MR: Map 9 H3

Lower Ovens bush camping

Access via Playfair Road which is an unsignposted gravel road off the Murray Valley Highway, 2.6km east of Bundalong which is 15km east of Yarrawonga. Playfair Road leads 400m north to an area with dispersed bush camping on the western shores of Ovens River. No facilities, self sufficient campers. Bring drinking water.
GPS S:36 02.910 E:146 11.856
MR: Map 9 H3

FURTHER Information

> **Parks Vic Info Line**
> **Tel:** 13 19 63

133 Major Creek Reserve

Located 29km north of Seymour beside Major Creek. From the Goulburn Valley Highway 21km north of Seymour take the signposted road west to Mitchellstown and follow for 8km to reserve. Fishing and canoeing in river.

Major Creek Reserve camping area

Located at junction of Mitchellstown Road and Wattle Vales Road, 8km west of the Goulburn Valley Highway. Shaded sites beside creek along the Major Mitchell Trail. Bring drinking water and firewood.
GPS S:36 51.261 E:145 04.013
MR: Map 9 B8

FURTHER Information

> **Parks Vic Info Line**
> **Tel:** 13 19 63

Located adjacent to Maldon township. The reserve protects many historical features from the gold rush era. Take one of the walking tracks to explore mining relics such as a 'puddler'. Please stay on marked tracks for safety due to old mine shafts.

Butt's Reserve camping area

From Maldon take the signposted Mt Tarrengower Road and follow for 900m to attractive camping area with good shade and some grass at the base of the hill to Mt Tarrengower. Bring drinking water and firewood.
GPS S:36 59.191 E:144 03.222
MR: Map 7 G2

FURTHER Information

> **Parks Vic Info Line**
> **Tel:** 13 19 63

Located east of Harcourt, which is at the junction of the Midland and Calder highways. Access is via the Faraday-Sutton Gorge Road, which leaves the Calder Highway 6km south of Harcourt. The park has walking trails, panoramic lookouts and a koala park.

Leanganook picnic area and bush camping

FURTHER Information

> **Parks Vic Info Line**
> **Tel:** 13 19 63

Signposted access 2km along Joseph Young Drive, which is signposted off the Faraday-Sutton Gorge Road 3km north-east of Faraday. Dispersed bush camping located behind the day use/picnic area where all facilities are located. Bring drinking water.
GPS S:37 01.123 E:144 18.469
MR: Map 7 H2

CENTRAL MURRAY

136 Muckleford State Forest

Muckleford State Forest is located to the west of Castlemaine and east of Maldon. The forest is mainly ironbark, however grey box and red box also grow here. Gold mining occurred in the forests from the late 1850s through to 1915. A 5km walk leads through the forest visiting the historic mining sites; grab a copy of the walk brochure from DSE or the local tourist information centres. To access the forest take the road from Castlemaine to Maldon and at a total of 4.1km west of Castlemaine turn into the signposted Muckleford School Road, and follow for 3.9km to enter the forest. From Maldon take the road towards Castlemaine and at 8.2km take the signposted Butchers Road and follow to the signposted junction with Muckleford School Road and turn right. Be cautious around old mine workings as there are unmarked shafts.

Red, White and Blue Mine camping area

Located 1.4km along Bells Lane Track at its junction with Red, White and Blue Track. Bells Lane Track is signposted off Muckleford School Road at entrance to forest as described in introduction above. Bring drinking water.
GPS S:37 03.557 E:144 06.461
MR: Map 7 G2

FURTHER Information

DSE Castlemaine
Tel: 03 5472 1110

CENTRAL MURRAY

137 Murray River Reserves — Murrabit to Koondrook

Numerous dispersed bush campsites along the Murray River between Murrabit to Koondrook. Main access via River Track from Murrabit or Koondrook. Dry weather access only. Some tracks may be closed due to seasonal flooding. Fishing and watersports.

Benwell State Forest bush camping

Dispersed bush camping on banks of Murray River. Access via Murray Road from Murrabit or via Hall Lane or Watsons Lane from Murrabit-Koondrook Road. Bring drinking water.
MR: Map 7 G8

Guttrum State Forest bush camping

Dispersed bush camping on banks of Murray River. Access via River Track off Cassidys Lane from Koondrook. Bring drinking water.
MR: Map 7 H8

FURTHER Information

> **Parks Vic Kerang**
> **Tel:** 03 5450 3951

138 Murray River Reserves — Bundalong to Barnawartha North

Numerous dispersed bush campsites along the Murray River between Bundalong and Barnawartha North. Access roads are off the Murray Valley Highway. Dry weather access only. Some tracks may be closed due to seasonal flooding. Activities include bushwalking, fishing, swimming, canoeing, power boating and water-skiing in some areas.

Taylors Bend camping area

Accessed via Brimin Road which is signposted off the Murray Valley Highway 18km west of Rutherglen and 8km east of the highway's junction with the

Yarrawonga-Wangaratta Road. Follow Brimin Road north for 4.1km to the signposted Clarke Lane on the east. Follow Clarke Lane for 1.7km to enter forest and follow track around for a further 700m to the grassed camping area. No facilities. Bring drinking water.
GPS S:36 02.144 E:146 17.483
MR: Map 9 H2

CENTRAL MURRAY

Lumbys Bend camping area

Accessed via Raitts Road which is signposted off the Murray Valley Highway 4km east of Brimin Road and 14km west of Rutherglen. Follow Raitts Road for 3.4km to enter forest. Once in forest continue on main track for 1.6km to attractive grassed sites beside the river. Bring drinking water.
GPS S:36 02.202 E:146 18.054
MR: Map 9 H2

Lumbys Bend bush camping area

Accessed via Raitts Road which is signposted off the Murray Valley Highway 4km east of Brimin Road and 14km west of Rutherglen. Follow Raitts Road for 3.4km to enter forest. Once in forest continue on main track for 300m to track on left (west) which leads into some dispersed bush camping areas. Bring drinking water.
GPS S:36 02.831 E:146 17.810
MR: Map 9 H2

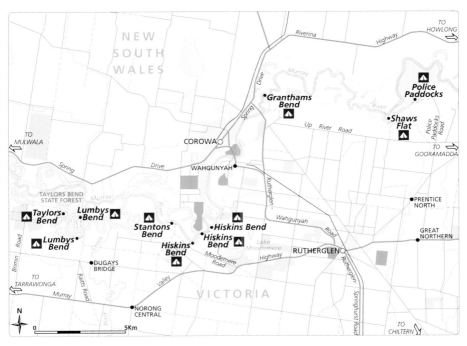

CENTRAL MURRAY

Hiskins Bend camping area

Accessed via Moodemere Road which is signposted off the Murray Valley Highway 8.6km east of Raitts Road and 5.4km west of Rutherglen. Follow Moodemere Road for 2.9km to the signposted Hiskins Road. Turn into Hiskins Road and follow for 200m to river and entrance grid. Track continues on for 800m to a nice camping area and a further 600m to more sites. Bring drinking water.

Entrance – **GPS** S:36 03.094 E:146 22.026
MR: Map 9 I3

Stantons Bend camping area

Accessed via Moodemere Road which is signposted off the Murray Valley Highway 8.6km east of Raitts Road and 5.4km west of Rutherglen. Follow Moodemere Road 4km to entrance. Follow the main track which loops around the river with dispersed bush camping along the river. Bring drinking water.

Entrance – **GPS** S:36 02.718 E:146 21.450
MR: Map 9 I3

Granthams Bend camping area

Located 10km north of Rutherglen. From Rutherglen take the C376 road north towards Corowa and at 9.8km, just prior to the bridge over the river, take the turn off to the right (east) signposted Granthams Bend Reserve. This access road proceeds 300m to enter the forests with dispersed bush camping along the river. Bring drinking water.

Entrance – **GPS** S:35 59.114 E:146 24.862
MR: Map 9 I2

Shaws Flat camping area

Located north of Rutherglen with access off Up River Road. From Rutherglen take the C376 road towards Corowa and at 9.3km turn right (east) into the signposted Up River Road. Follow Up River Road for 6.3km to the signposted Shaws Flat Road. Follow Shaws Flat Road north for 800m to the entrance to Shaws Flat. Once in reserve track leads for 900m along the river with dispersed bush camping with flat grassy sites. Bring drinking water.

GPS S:35 39.463 E:146 29.447
MR: Map 9 J2

Police Paddocks camping area

Situated within Gooramadda State Forest. Located north of Rutherglen with access off Up River Road. From Rutherglen take the C376 road towards Corowa and at 9.3km turn right (east) into the signposted Up River Road. Follow Up River Road for 8.8km to the signposted Police Paddocks Road (this is 2.5km east of Shaws Flat Rd). Coming from the east off the Howlong Road take the Gooramadda Road and follow this west for 7.3km to the signposted Up River Road, and continue west for 2.2km to Police Paddocks Road. Follow Police Paddocks Road north for 500m to entrance to Gooramadda State Forest with attractive grassed and well shaded campsites along the river. Natural boat launch here. Bring drinking water.

GPS S:35 58.735 E:146 30.615
MR: Map 9 J2

CENTRAL MURRAY

Weidners Road camping area

Small bush camping area beside river along Weidners Road. Weidners Road is to the west of the C378 (Howlong Road) and is signposted just prior to the bridge over the river. Weidners Road leads in 200m to a small reserve which would be suitable for an overnight stop. Bring drinking water.
GPS S:35 59.802 E:146 36.953
MR: Map 9 J2

Doolans Bend camping area

Signposted access off the Barnawartha-Howlong Road 3.8km north-west of its junction with the Murray Valley Highway and 2.6km east of the C381 to Chiltern. Access is signposted as River Access then in 100m to signpost Doolans Bend/Murray River Reserve. Follow access track to the left and over the creek crossing to a lovely grassed site, well shaded on the river with a natural boat launch. There are other dispersed sites at the creek crossing. Bring drinking water.
Entrance – **GPS** S:36 01.779 E:146 39.147
MR: Map 9 J2

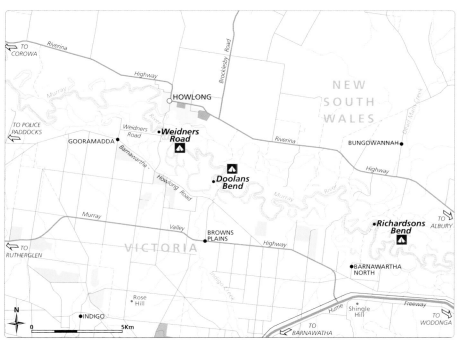

Richardsons Bend camping area

Accessed off the Old Barnawartha Road which is signposted 18km west of Wodonga off the Murray Valley Highway, just north of the Hume Freeway. Follow Old Barnwartha Road then at 1.1km turn into road signposted Kings Road/River Access, then follow all River Access signage for a total of 2.6km to the signposted entrance to the river reserve which is located along Moss Road. Dispersed bush campsites beside the river, some open sites with little shade and others grassed and shaded. Natural boat launch here.

Entrance – **GPS** S:36 03.249 E:146 44.561
MR: Map 9 K3

FURTHER Information

Parks Vic Info Line
Tel: 13 19 63

Granthams Bend camping area

CENTRAL MURRAY

State forest located along the Murray River 23.5km south-east of Cobram and 12km north-west of Yarrawonga. Access to the forest is via the signposted Thoms Road off the Murray Valley Highway and then proceed north for 2.5km to forest entrance gate and a further 200m to the information board. Bush camping beside the Murray River. Dry weather access only. Some tracks may be closed due to seasonal flooding. Activities include bushwalking, fishing, swimming, canoeing, power boating and water-skiing in some areas.

Nevins West Beach camping area

Dispersed bush camping on banks of Murray River. Once at forest information board, proceed on track on left (north-west) onto Nevins West Track for a total of 2.3km to junction with track on right (north) which is Harris Track. From this junction continue in a westerly direction for 400m to camping area. Bring drinking water.
GPS S:35 58.135 E:145 50.940
MR: Map 9 F2

Redbank Beach camping areas

Dispersed bush camping on banks of Murray River. Follow directions to Nevins West Beach and turn right (north) onto Harris Track and follow this for 900m to junction, then turn left (west) for 200m to the camping area. Bring drinking water.
GPS S:35 57.722 E:145 51.171
MR: Map 9 F2

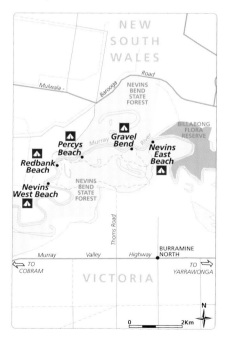

CENTRAL MURRAY

Percys Beach camping areas

Dispersed bush camping on banks of Murray River. Located 200m north of Harris Track. From forest information board continue north along the main track and then turn left (west) into Harris Track. Follow Harris Track for 1.2km to access track on the right (north) and proceed north for 200m to camping area. Bring drinking water.
GPS S:35 57.528 E:145 51.812
MR: Map 9 F2

Gravel Bend camping areas

Dispersed bush camping on banks of Murray River. From forest information board continue north along the main track and then turn right (east) into Buchanans Track. Follow Buchanans Track for 2.2km and then turn left (north) into Gravel Bend Track. This leads 1.1km to the camping area. Bring drinking water.
GPS S:35 57.361 E:145 53.066
MR: Map 9 F2

Nevins East Beach camping areas

Dispersed bush camping on banks of Murray River. From forest information board turn right (east) into Collins Lane and follow for 1.4km, then turn left (north) into Nevins Track. Follow Nevins Track for 1.1km to track on left (north – this is 400m north of Buchanans Track) which leads 500m north to the camping area. Bring drinking water.
GPS S:35 57.266 E:145 53.563
MR: Map 9 F2

Nevins Bend State Forest bush camping

Dispersed bush camping on banks of Murray River throughout forest. Access to forest is via signposted Thoms Road off the Murray Valley Highway 23.5km south-east of Cobram and 12km north-west of Yarrawonga, then proceed north for 2.5km to forest entrance gate. Once in forest tracks lead to various parts of the forest and to the river. Self sufficient campers. Bring drinking water.
Forest entrance – **GPS** S:35 58.177 E:145 52.544
MR: Map 9 F2

FURTHER Information

> **Parks Vic Info Line**
> **Tel:** 13 19 63
> **Cobram Barooga Visitor Information Centre**
> **Tel:** 03 5872 2132 or 1800 607 607

CENTRAL MURRAY

The large area of the Strathbogie Ranges are located 25km north-west of Mansfield and bounded by Benalla, Euroa and Bonnie Doon. Main access is from the Midland Highway south of Benalla and north of Mansfield via Lima East. The area was once used by the Kelly Gang as a hide out. Activities include cycling, bushwalking, four-wheel driving and horse riding.

James' Reserve

From the Midland Highway take the road signposted Lima East, this is 600m south of the signposted Swanpool Road and 20km south of Benalla and 43km north of Mansfield. Follow the road to Lima East for 1.4km then turn left following the road signposted Lima East, then at a total of 10.8km arrive at the signposted reserve. This is a spacious open area with limited shade. Horse yards located here. Water from creek, boil or treat first.
GPS S:36 50.197 E:145 56.827
MR: Map 9 F8

White Gum bush camping

Located within the forests along the A11 Road, just north of the signposted junction of the A11 and B2 roads. From the Midland Highway take the road signposted Lima 5, which is 18km south of Benalla and 45km north of Mansfield. Follow this road as it becomes Ethel Road and then the A Road for a total of 10km. Follow the A Road for a further 6km to its junction with the A11 Road, which leads 2.8km to the camping area. This is a large cleared bush camping area beside a creek with tall shady white gums, for self sufficient campers. Popular area with trail bike riders. Bring drinking water.
GPS S:36 47.810 E:145 53.820
MR: Map 9 F8

FURTHER Information

> **DSE Benalla**
> **Tel:** 03 5761 1611

CENTRAL MURRAY

Terrick Terrick National Park is located 4km north of Mitiamo and 60km north of Bendigo. Access from Mitiamo is via the signposted Haig Street, dry weather access only. In spring the park has wonderful wildflower displays. Take in the views from Mount Terrick Terrick. With abundant wildlife it is an ideal place for wildlife spotting.

Mt Terrick Terrick camping area

From Mitiamo on the C334 road, take the road signposted Haig Street and proceed north for 4.3km to the signposted Cemetery Track. Follow Cemetery Track for 1.7km to the signposted access track to the campground which leads 200m to the small camping area with limited level sites, situated below the picnic area. All facilities are located in the picnic area. Bring drinking water. Gas/fuel stove only.

GPS S:36 10.125 E:144 14.540
MR: Map 6 H4

FURTHER Information

> **Parks Vic Info Line**
> **Tel:** 13 19 63
> **Parks Vic Kerang**
> **Tel:** 03 5450 3951. It is requested that the ranger is advised of your stay in the park.

CENTRAL MURRAY

The park is situated on the western and eastern side of the Goulburn Valley Highway and is located adjacent to the New South Wales town of Tocumwal on the Victorian banks of the Murray River. Access to the park is off the Goulburn Valley Highway south of the bridge over the Murray. Dry weather access only.

Apex Beach camping area

Located on the western side of the Goulburn Valley Highway. Take the signposted Bridge Street at southern end of bridge over Murray River and at 200m is park entrance and information board. From information board proceed west for 300m to track on right signposted Apex Beach. This leads 500m to camping area beside the river with a good beach and good access to the river. Bring drinking water.
GPS S:35 48 806 E:145 32.824
MR: Map 9 D1

Grassy Beach camping area

Located on the western side of the Goulburn Valley Highway. Proceed west past Apex Beach turn off and follow the river for 3.3km to Grassy Beach with dispersed bush camping on banks of river. Bring drinking water.
GPS S:35 48.516 E:145 32.435
MR: Map 9 D1

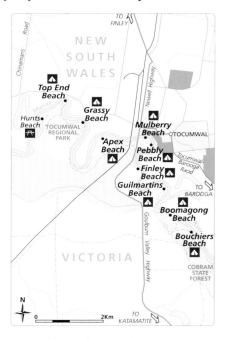

Top End Beach camping area

Located on the western side of the Goulburn Valley Highway. Proceed past Grassy Beach access track for 800m then turn right (north) into track which leads 500m to Top End Beach with dispersed bush camping on banks of river. Bring drinking water.
GPS S:35 48.144 E:145 32.115
MR: Map 9 D1

Mulberry Beach camping area

Located on the eastern side of the Goulburn Valley Highway. Take the track just south of the bridge over Murray River, which is 200m north of the signposted Bridge Street on the west. Follow this track in to information boards and then keep left at junction and at total of 300m reach camping area with dispersed bush camping among forest set back from the river opposite Tocumwal. Bring drinking water.
GPS S:35 48.798 E:145 33.646
MR: Map 9 D1

Pebbly Beach camping area

Located on the eastern side of the Goulburn Valley Highway and south of Mulberry Beach. Take the track just south of the bridge over Murray River, which is 200m north of the signposted Bridge Street on the west. Follow this track in to information boards and then keep right at the junction and at total of 400m reach camping area with dispersed bush camping along banks of river. Bring drinking water.
GPS S:35 48.917 E:145 33.789
MR: Map 9 D1

Finley Beach camping area

Located on the eastern side of the Goulburn Valley Highway. Take the road signposted Tocumwal, this is 1km south of the bridge over Murray River and 400m south of the signposted Bridge Street on the western side of the highway. Track leads in 100m to information boards and then a further 300m to the camping area beside the river. Bring drinking water.
GPS S:35 49.303 E:145 33.507
MR: Map 9 D1

Guilmartins Beach camping area

Located on the eastern side of the Goulburn Valley Highway. From highway take the road that is signposted State Forest/Guilmartins Bend 2.7km south of the bridge over the Murray River and 1.7km south of Finley Beach access road. Then proceed in 900m to area beside the river with dispersed bush camping. Bring drinking water.
GPS S:35 49.627 E:145 34.007
MR: Map 9 D1

FURTHER Information

> **Parks Vic Info Line**
> **Tel:** 13 19 63

Ned Kelly and his gang used The Warby's as a refuge during the late 1800s. Warby Range State Park is located 15km west of Wangaratta and accessed via Wangandary Road from Wangaratta. The park has many walking tracks to explore.

Wenhams Campsite

From Wangaratta city centre take the signposted Booths Road and follow it north on to the Wangaratta-Yarrawonga Road. At a total of 3.8km turn left into the signposted Wangandary Road and follow this for 10.5km, then turn into the signposted Gerrett Road/Wenham. Then at 1.5km turn into signposted Booths Road/Wenhams, then at 2.8km turn into road signposted Wenhams Campsite. This access road leads 200m to the open camping area on the edge of a large clearing. Bring drinking water. Groups contact ranger first.
GPS S:36 20.472 E:146 12.244
MR: Map 9 H4

The Camp camping area

From Wangaratta city centre take the signposted Booths Road and follow it north on to the Wangaratta-Yarrawonga Road. At a total of 13km take the road on west signposted Boweya 13 (this is 9.3km north of the Wangandary Road which leads to Wenhams campsite). Follow the Boweya road west for 5.9km and take the track on the right signposted Killawarra Forest. This leads 200m to the entrance of the signposted Warby Range State Park, and a further 2.3km to The Camp camping area which has individually bollarded campsites surrounded by ironbark forest. Best suited for tent based camping or campervans, only 2 sites suitable for camper trailer or smaller caravans. Bring drinking water.
GPS S:36 13.311 E:146 10.739
MR: Map 9 H4

Bush camping
Bush camping is permitted in the park. Contact ranger for details.

FURTHER Information

> **Parks Vic Info Line**
> **Tel:** 13 19 63

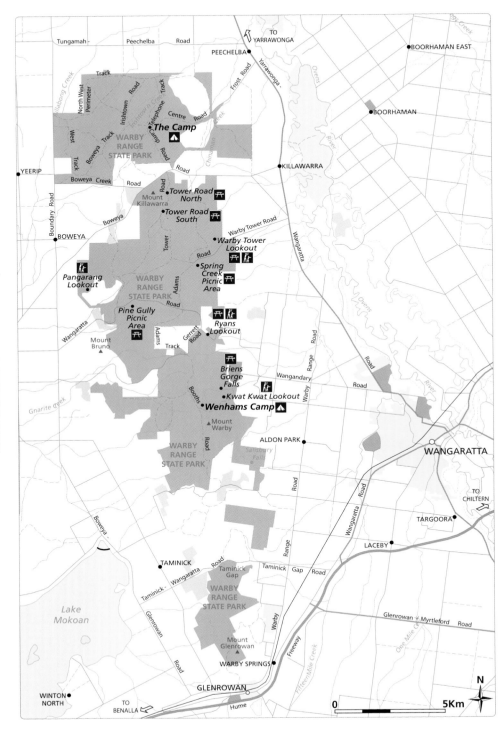

Tungamah - Peechelba Road

PEECHELBA

TO YARRAWONGA

BOORHAMAN EAST

BOORHAMAN

North West Perimeter Track

Irishtown Road

Telephone Track

Centre Road

West Track

Boweya Track

The Camp

WARBY RANGE STATE PARK

Chinaman Creek

KILLAWARRA

YEERIP

Boweya Creek Road

Boundary Road

Mount Killawarra

Tower Road North

Tower Road South

Warby Tower Road

Boweya

BOWEYA

Tower Road

Warby Tower Lookout

Spring Creek Picnic Area

Pangarang Lookout

WARBY RANGE STATE PARK

Adams Road

Pine Gully Picnic Area

Wangaratta

Adams Track

Mount Bruno

Gerrett Road

Ryans Lookout

Briens Gorge Falls

Wangandary Road

Kwat Kwat Lookout

Booths Road

Wenhams Camp

Mount Warby

Gnarite Creek

ALDON PARK

Salisbury Falls

WANGARATTA

WARBY RANGE STATE PARK

Warby Range Road

Wangaratta Road

TO CHILTERN

TARGOORA

LACEBY

Boweya - Wangaratta

TAMINICK

Taminick - Wangaratta Road

Taminick Gap

Taminick Gap Road

Lake Mokoan

WARBY RANGE STATE PARK

Glenrowan Road

Warby Range Road

Glenrowan - Myrtleford Road

Mount Glenrowan

WARBY SPRINGS

Freeway

WINTON NORTH

GLENROWAN

TO BENALLA

Hume

Fifteenmile Creek

One Mile Creek

Ovens River

N

0   5Km

144 Whroo Historic Reserve

This historic reserve was part of the 1850s gold rush when gold was found in 1853. Explore the ruins of the historic township and cemetery which has some 400 grave sites, walk through the tunnel and view the old mining sites. Wildflowers bloom in spring adding colour to the region. The reserve is situated 7km south of Rushworth. Access is along the Rushworth-Nagambie Road.

Greens campground

Located on Greens Road which is signposted off the Rushworth-Nagambie (Reedy Lake) Road 100m south of the Whroo information and picnic area, which is 6km south of Rushworth and 25km north of Nagambie. Alternatively from Murchison follow the C345 west towards Rushworth, then take the signposted Old Whroo Road. Camping area is set among ironbark and box trees. Walk to the reserve's historic and mine sites. Bring drinking water.

GPS S:36 38.817 E:145 01.962
MR: Map 9 A7

FURTHER Information

> **Parks Vic Info Line**
> **Tel:** 13 19 63

CENTRAL MURRAY

Yarrawonga Regional Park is located to the north-west of Yarrawonga on the Murray River. The park offers dispersed bush camping along the Murray River. Access to the park is via signposted access roads off the Murray Valley Highway west of Yarrawonga. These include: Brears Road at 2.8km west; Forges Pump Lane at 6.9km north-west and Bruces Road at 7.4km north-west. These access roads lead into an entrance gate and information boards. Dry weather access only. Some tracks may be closed due to seasonal flooding. Activities include bushwalking, fishing, swimming, canoeing, power boating and water-skiing in some areas.

Green Bank camping area

Accessed via Brears Road 2.8km west of Yarrawonga. Follow Brears Road north for 600m to park entrance. Proceed through entrance gate and at 500m pass Loop Track on right (east) and then at a further 300m arrive at camping area. NB: The camping area is the area set back from the water's edge – the area close to the water is the day use only area, only camp in the designated area. Bring drinking water.
GPS S:36 00.574 E:145 58.646
MR: Map 9 G2

Chinamans Bend camping area

Accessed via Brears Road 2.8km west of Yarrawonga. Follow Brears Road north for 600m to park entrance. At entrance turn left (west) and pass through another gate, this is Chinamans Track and passes in front of private property. Follow Chinamans Track for 900m to reach the signposted Chinamans Loop Track which is 1.4km loop along the Murray River, where dispersed bush camping is possible. Bring drinking water.
GPS S:36 00.324 E145 58.201
MR: Map 9 F2

Forges No 1 Beach camping area

Accessed via Forges Pump Lane 6.9km north-west of Yarrawonga. Follow Forges Pump Lane east for 1.5km to park entrance. At entrance continue into forest for 100m to junction. At junction take the track on right (east), this is Forges Bend Track, for 800m to camping area. Bring drinking water.
GPS S:35 59.770 E:145 57.767
MR: Map 9 F2

Forges No 2 Beach camping area

Accessed via Forges Pump Lane 6.9km north-west of Yarrawonga. Follow Forges Pump Lane east for 1.5km to park entrance. At entrance continue into forest for 100m to junction. At junction take the centre track which leads 500m to the camping area. Bring drinking water.
GPS S:35 59.586 E:145 57.347
MR: Map 9 F2

CENTRAL MURRAY

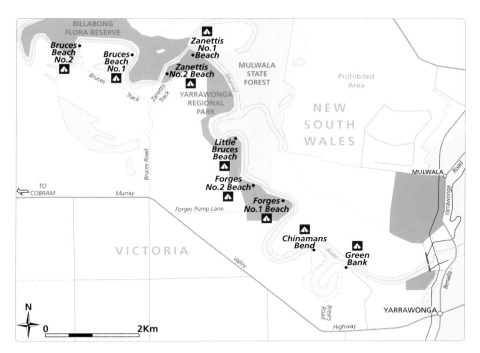

Little Bruces Beach camping area

Accessed via Forges Pump Lane 6.9km north-west of Yarrawonga. Follow Forges Pump Lane east for 1.5km to park entrance. At entrance continue into forest for 100m to junction. At junction take the track on left (north), this is Little Bruces Track and leads 1.6km to the camping area. Bring drinking water.
GPS S:35 59.042 E:145 57.117
MR: Map 9 F2

Zanettis No 2 Beach camping areas

Accessed via Bruces Road 7.4km north-west of Yarrawonga. Follow Bruces Road north for 1.1km to the park entrance. At entrance continue north for 800m to track junction. At junction take track on right (east), this is Zanettis Track which leads 700m to track on left (north) which leads 200m to the camping area. Bring drinking water.
GPS S:35 58.240 E:145 56.128
MR: Map 9 F2

Zanettis No 1 Beach camping areas

Accessed via Bruces Road 7.4km north-west of Yarrawonga. Follow Bruces Road north for 1.1km to the park entrance. At entrance continue north for 800m to track junction. At junction take track on right (east), this is Zanettis Track which leads 700m to track on left (north) which leads to Zanettis No 2. Continue past this access track for a further 600m to track that leads north for 300m to the camping area. Bring drinking water.
GPS S:35 58.017 E:145 56.500
MR: Map 9 F2

Bruces No 1 Beach camping areas

Accessed via Bruces Road 7.4km north-west of Yarrawonga. Follow Bruces Road north for 1.1km to the park entrance. At entrance continue north for 800m to track junction. At junction take track on left (west) which is Bruces Track and follow this for 900m to track on right (north), this is signposted as Bruces Bend 1. This track leads 1km to the camping area. Bring drinking water.
GPS S:35 58.012 E:145 55.713
MR: Map 9 F2

Bruces No 2 Beach camping areas

Accessed via Bruces Road 7.4km north-west of Yarrawonga. Follow Bruces Road north for 1.1km to the park entrance. Follow directions to Bruces No 1 Beach, follow past no 1 Beach access track for a further 700m, then take track on right (north) which leads 400m to the camping area. Bring drinking water.
GPS S:35 57.893 E:145 54.887
MR: Map 9 F2

Yarrawonga Regional Park bush camping

Dispersed bush camping on banks of Murray River throughout park. Access via the signposted roads off the Murray Valley Highway west of Yarrawonga: Brears Road at 2.8km west; Forges Pump Lane at 6.9km north-west and Bruces Road at 7.4km north-west. Once in the regional park tracks lead to various parts of the forest and to the river. Self sufficient campers. Bring drinking water.
MR: Map 9 F2

FURTHER Information

> **Parks Vic Info Line**
> **Tel:** 13 19 63

East Gippsland

ONE OF OUR FAVOURITE VICTORIAN destinations, the East Gippsland region stretches along the coastline from Lakes Entrance to the New South Wales border and west to the High Country. Its beautiful coastal beaches and lakes attract surfers and boaters while its magnificent inland rivers are a drawcard for fisherfolk and canoeists.

Croajingolong National Park offers a range of camping from the large and popular

BEST Campsites!

Delegate River camping area
Baldwin Spencer Trail

Buchan Caves Campground
Buchan Caves Reserve

Mueller Inlet camping area
Croajingolong National Park

Ada River camping area
Errinundra National Park

Snowy River camping area
Snowy River National Park

Thurra River camping area to smaller sites on Mueller Inlet. The beaches and waterways of this park are ideal for canoeing, boating and fishing. Walkers can amble to hidden lakes, explore large sand dunes and visit Point Hicks Lighthouse; its headland location offering fabulous coastal vistas.

To the north of the Princes Highway are the magnificent old growth forests of Errinundra National Park. The Ada River camping area is an attractive site and an ideal base camp whilst exploring the park. Or a little further north near Bendoc is the delightful Delegate River camping area, located along the Baldwin Spencer Trail.

McKillops Bridge and the Snowy River offer scenic surrounds within the Snowy River National Park. Here, in the northern section of the park, are numerous campsites beside the river and close to the historic bridge, and in the southern section are a number of small camping areas beside the river. The Snowy is popular with canoeists and rafters.

Buchan Caves Reserve has a beautiful camping ground and tours of the spectacular limestone caves.

The warmer months of the year offer the best weather for camping in this part of Victoria.

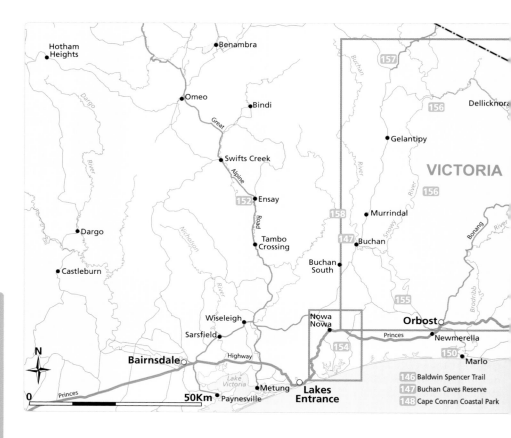

146 Baldwin Spencer Trail

A 262km driving trail following the route of Baldwin Spencer's 1889 expedition to East Gippsland. This circular route from Orbost takes in the Cann Valley Highway and Errinundra Plateau. Activities include vehicle touring, walking trails and camping.

Delegate River camping area

Located 8km south-west of Bendoc beside Delegate River. Access via Gap Road from Bendoc. Water from river, boil or treat first.
GPS S:37 11.750 E:148 49.658
MR: Map 13 K1

Goongerah camping area

Signposted access along the Bonang-Orbost Road at Goongerah, 24km south of Bonang and 78km north of Orbost. Sealed road from Orbost. Bring drinking water and firewood.
GPS S:37 20.581 E:148 42.040
MR: Map 13 J2

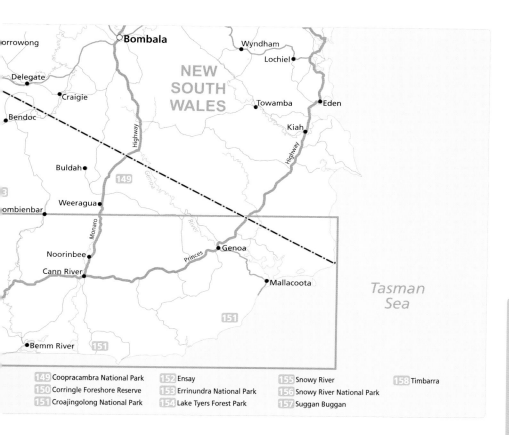

149 Coopracambra National Park	152 Ensay
150 Corringle Foreshore Reserve	153 Errinundra National Park
151 Croajingolong National Park	154 Lake Tyers Forest Park

155 Snowy River	158 Timbarra
156 Snowy River National Park	
157 Suggan Buggan	

EAST GIPPSLAND

FURTHER Information

DSE Bendoc
Tel: 02 6458 1456

Delegate River camping area

Located adjacent to Buchan township with access signposted off Buchan Road. The caves contain some of the most spectacular limestone formations found in Australia. Activities include cave tours, walking trails and camping. Abundant wildlife in the reserve.

Buchan Caves Campground

Located at Buchan Caves in Buchan. Signposted access via Caves Road off Buchan Road. Other accommodation also available.
GPS S:37 29.748 E:148 09.778
MR: Map 13 G3

FURTHER Information

Parks Vic Info Line
Tel: 13 19 63. Bookings essential at peak times (Victorian school and public holidays).
Bookings: Parks Vic Buchan
Tel: 03 5162 1900 or
online at www.parkstay.vic.gov.au
Camping fees: Unpowered from $13.50 per site/night for 2 people. Powered from $18.50 per site/night for 2 people.

EAST GIPPSLAND

Located 19km east of Marlo. Access from Marlo via the Cape Conran Road, alternatively take the signposted access off the Princes Highway at Cabbage Tree Creek, 30km east of Orbost. Enjoy the spectacular coastal scenery, amazing bird and wildlife, beaches, walking, surfing, fishing and swimming.

Banksia Bluff camping area

Access from the west via Marlo along the Cape Conran Road, or from the Princes Highway via the Cabbage Tree Creek-Cape Conran Road. Bring drinking water and firewood.
MR: Map 13 J5

FURTHER Information

Cape Conran Coastal Park
Tel: 03 5154 8438. Bookings essential at peak times. Ballot system applies for December/January and Easter.
Web: www.conran.net.au
Camping fees: From $16.50 per site/night up to 4 people.
Cabin accommodation available.

Located 30km north of Cann River. Main access via Monaro Highway. Conventional vehicle access to Beehive Falls. All other roads only suitable for 4WD vehicles or walkers. The park is one of the most remote and least disturbed in Victoria. Activities include 4WD touring and bushwalking.

Coopracambra bush camping

Dispersed bush camping, no facilities, for self-sufficient campers. Walk-in or 4WD access only.
Beehive Falls – **GPS** S:37 20.188 E:149 13 499
MR: Map 14 A2

FURTHER Information

Parks Vic Info Line
Tel: 13 19 63

Located 18km south of Newmerella near the mouth of the Snowy River estuary. Access via Corringle Road from Newmerella on the Princes Highway. Located in a natural bush setting close to the beach. Activities include swimming, boating, canoeing, fishing and walking.

EAST GIPPSLAND

Corringle Slips camping area

Access via Corringle Road which is signposted off the Princes Highway. Limited tank water available. Bring drinking water and firewood.
MR: Map 13 I5

FURTHER Information

> **Parks Vic Orbost**
> **Tel:** 03 5161 1222. Advance bookings via ballot system for peak periods (Victorian school and public holidays).
> **Camping fees:** Off-peak: From $14.00 per site/night. Fees payable at self-registration station outside peak periods.

151 Croajingolong National Park

This large national park stretches for over 100km along Victoria's far eastern coastline from the eastern shore of Sydenham Inlet to the NSW border. Main access routes into the park are from Mallacoota in the north-east section and the south-western section of the park from Cann River. Access is also possible from numerous access tracks off the Princes Highway. Conventional vehicle access is generally OK, however check road conditions after rain. Some internal tracks are closed seasonally. Explore unspoilt beaches, tranquil waterways and observe abundant birdlife. Activities include swimming, boating, canoeing, fishing and walking.

Shipwreck Creek campground

Located near the mouth of Shipwreck Creek. From Mallacoota follow the signposted Maurice Avenue for 6.7km to road junction and then take the road signposted to Shipwreck Creek via Centre Track. Follow signage to Shipwreck Creek for 8km to the camping area. A small area in tall forest with five sites beside the creek. Communal fireplaces and picnic tables. Limited firewood supplied.
GPS S:37 38.669 E:149 41.882
MR: Map 14 D4

Wingan Inlet campground

Located on the western side of Wingan Inlet in the centre of the park. Access is via West Wingan Road off the Princes Highway, east of Cann River. 24 sites. Communal fireplaces and picnic tables. Limited firewood supplied.
GPS S:37 44.459 E:149 29.874
MR: Map 14 C5

EAST GIPPSLAND

Canoeing Croajingolong National Park

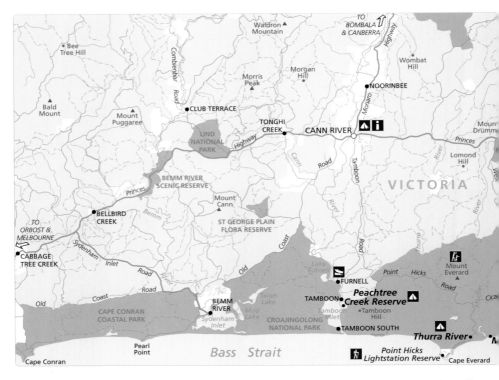

Peach Tree Creek campground

Located beside Cann River near Tamboon Inlet. From Cann River follow the signposted Tamboon Road south for 21km then turn into road on right signposted Fishermans Track. This leads 6km to the campground with two separate areas with a total of 12 sites. Caravan access with care. Natural boat launch. Limited firewood supplied.
GPS S:37 44.498 E:149 08.295
MR: Map 14 A5

Mueller Inlet campground

Located on the western shore of Mueller Inlet along Bald Hills Track. From Cann River follow the signposted Tamboon Road south for 21km where the road becomes Point Hicks Road. Follow this for a further 19.4km to the signposted Bald Hills Track, which leads 1.6km to the campground. Picturesque camping area beside the inlet with eight individual sites. Sites 1-3 are walk-in only and 4-8 area vehicle-based sites located on the water's edge. Bring drinking water. Gas/fuel stove only.
GPS S:37 46.661 E:149 19.426
MR: Map 14 B5

Thurra River camping area

Located near the mouth of the Thurra River. From Cann River follow the signposted Tamboon Road south for

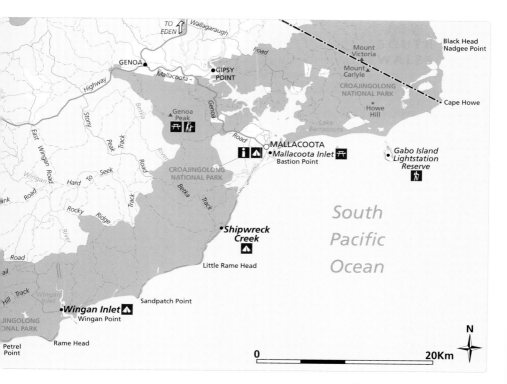

21km where the road becomes Point Hicks Road. Follow this for a further 20.3km to the entrance of the camping area on the south side of bridge over Thurra River. 46 sites. Small vans only. Communal fireplaces and picnic tables. Water from river, boil or treat first. Bring drinking water and firewood or purchase firewood on site.
GPS S:37 46.753 E:149 18.437
MR: Map 14 B5

Tamboon Inlet boat-based camping areas

Nine boat accessible camping areas around shores of Tamboon Inlet. Bush camping, no facilities, for self sufficient campers. Use of portable toilets preferred. Bring drinking water and firewood.
MR: Map 14 A5

FURTHER Information

Parks Vic Info Line
Tel: 13 19 63. Bookings are recommended at all times and essential at peak times. A ballot system applies to all sites for Christmas/New Year and Easter. Minimum period is one week.
Parks Vic Cann River
Tel: 03 5158 6351 or
Parks Vic Mallacoota
Tel: 03 5161 9500
Bookings: Thurra River and Mueller Inlet Campground: contact Point Hicks Lighthouse **Tel:** 03 5158 4268 Shipwreck Creek, Wingan Inlet, Peach Tree Creek and Tamboon Inlet: contact Parks Vic Cann River **Tel:** 03 5158 6351
Camping fees: Fees apply and change annually. Contact Parks Vic Info Line or Cann River for current fee schedule.

The town of Ensay is situated on the Great Alpine Road, 53km north of Bruthen and 17km south of Swifts Creek. From here it is possible to explore the old mining areas along Haunted Stream and the forested areas to the east of the village.

Ensay Recreation Ground

Situated near the Tambo River on the Ensay-Doctors Flat Road, on western side of the Great Alpine Road. Walk from recreation ground to store and pub. Bring firewood.
MR: Map 13 E2

FURTHER Information

Ensay General Store
Tel: 03 5157 3244
Camping fees: From $10.00 per site/night for 2 people. Powered from $20.00 per site/night for 2 people. Fees payable to and collect keys for amenities block from Ensay General Store.

153 Errinundra National Park

Located 70km north-east of Orbost near Goongerah. Access via Bonang Highway from Orbost or Combienbar Road from Club Terrace. Conventional vehicle access in dry weather only. The park protects large areas of cool temperate rainforest and 'old growth' eucalypt forest. Use of fuel/gas stove preferred. Activities include vehicle touring (part of the Baldwin Spencer Trail) and bushwalking.

Ada River campsite

Shaded site beside Ada River along Errindundra Road. From the south Errinundra Road is signposted off the Club Terrace-Combienbar Road, then 12km north-west to the camping area. From the north the camping area is 25km south of the Errinundra Road and Gunmark Road junction. Water from river, boil or treat first.
GPS S:37 24.259 E:148 53.640
MR: Map 13 K3

EAST GIPPSLAND

Frosty Hollow camping area

Signposted access on Coast Range Road. From Bendoc take signposted Jamieson Street which becomes Clarkeville Road, and follow in a southerly direction for 17.8km then turn into signposted Hensleighs Crk Road and follow 10.8km to track junction. Keep right into road signposted To Coast Range Rd/To Frosty Hollow. Follow for 2.1km and turn into signposted Coast Range Road, then follow for 2.5km to the track signposted Frosty Hollow Camping Area. This leads 300m to the grassed, bush camping area. NB: Hensleighs Creek Road has seasonal closures. Bring drinking water and firewood.

GPS S:37 17.913 E:148 57.784
MR: Map 13 K2

FURTHER Information

> **Parks Vic Info Line**
> **Tel:** 13 19 63

ACCESS to campsites in wet weather

> During wet weather or after heavy rain access may be difficult, if not sometimes impossible to some of the camping areas listed in this guide. It is always best to phone ahead and get up-to-date information as to whether roads are passable. Driving on wet roads not only causes damage to the road surface but may leave you stranded until they dry out.

154 Lake Tyers Forest Park

Surrounding the large waterway of Lake Tyers the western section of the park can be accessed via the signposted Burnt Bridge Road off the Princes Highway, south-west of Nowa Nowa and north-east of Lakes Entrance; this section of the park has numerous picnic areas, walking tracks and good access to the lake. The eastern section of the park is accessed off the Princes Highway via the signposted Tyers House Road 6km east of Nowa Nowa. This section of the park provides bush camping along with good access to the waters of Nowa Nowa Arm and the lake. All access roads are unsealed and recommended for dry weather access only. The use of portable toilets is encouraged in the bush camping areas. Activities include picnicking, camping, fishing, canoeing and boating.

Cameron Arm camping area

Located 2km along Camerons Arm No.1 Track, which is signposted off Tyers House Road 5.1km south of the Princes Highway. Bush camping area set high above the river, walk to river and carry canoe. Bring drinking water. Gas/fuel stove preferred.

GPS S:37 46.825 E:148 08.148
MR: Map 13 G5

Trident Arm camping area

Located 1.7km along Trident Arm Track, which is signposted off Tyers House Road 5.1km south of Camerons Arm No.1 Track. Terraced camping area set high above the river, walk to river and carry canoe. Bring drinking water. Gas/fuel stove preferred.

GPS S:37 49.441 E:148 08.125
MR: Map 13 G5

Lake Tyers near The Glasshouse camping area

The Glasshouse camping area

Located at end of Tyers House Road, 5.2km south of Trident Arm Track. Very large grassed area with dispersed bush camping, some sites are well shaded and protected. Very scenic site with good access to the water. NB: Camp at least 50 metres from the water. No facilities. Bring drinking water. Gas/fuel stove preferred.

GPS S:37 50.767 E:148 06.508
MR: Map 13 G6

FURTHER *Information*

> **Parks Vic Info Line**
> **Tel:** 13 19 63

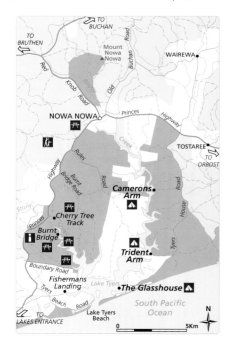

The Snowy River flows over 500 kilometres from Mount Kosciuszko to Marlo where it enters the Tasman Sea. This once mighty river was once an Aboriginal trade route between the mountains and the coast. It is now a popular canoeing and rafting river and is well known for its fishing in the lower reaches. To the north-west of Orbost camping is possible beside the Snowy River in state forest.

Woods Point camping ground

From Orbost take the signposted McLeod Street, which becomes B road and follow for 10km to cross a grid where the road now becomes the signposted Garnett Track. Continue on Garnett Track for a further 6.4km to the signposted access track to Woods Point Camping Ground. This track leads in a westerly direction for 4km to the camping area; a scenic, grassed area set on a large sandy beach on a bend in the river. NB: Camp only in the signposted camping area, not the picnic area. Space for 2 or 3 sites. Suitable for camper trailers with 4WD tow vehicle. Beach boat launch. Horseyards. Bring drinking water and firewood.

GPS S:37 38.523 E:148 19.230
MR: Map 13 H4

FURTHER Information

DSE Orbost
Tel: 03 5161 1222

EAST GIPPSLAND

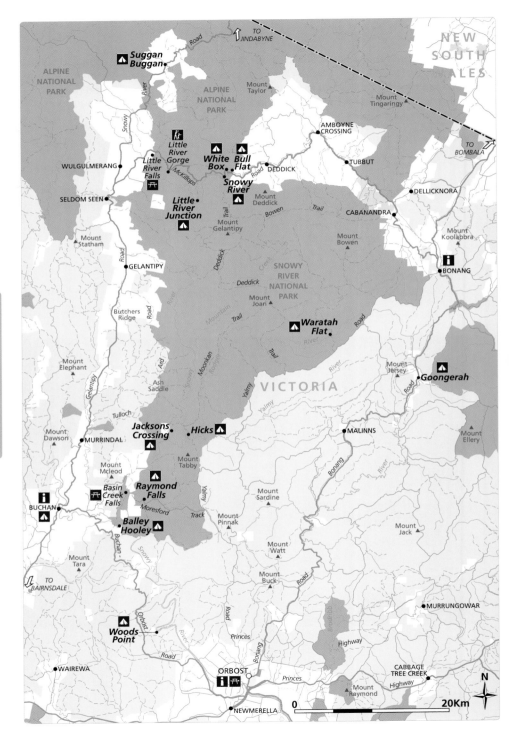

The Snowy River National Park stretches from near Buchan to the Deddick River/ Snowy River junction. Main access into the park is via the Bonang-Gelantipy Road (McKillops Road) off the Buchan Road or from Bonang. Main areas accessible by conventional vehicle, other roads and tracks only suitable for 4WD vehicles. This spectacular park takes in the unspoilt scenery of the mighty Snowy River, inviting sandy river beaches and towering craggy peaks. Activities include bushwalking, canoeing, rafting, 4WD touring, horse riding and fishing.

NORTHERN SECTION

Waratah Flat camping area

Located close to the Rodger River along Waratah Flat Road. From the Bonang-Orbost Road take the signposted Rising Sun Road, which is 1.9km south of the Bonang Store. Follow this road for 1.6km then veer onto the signposted Yalmy Road and follow for 23km to the signposted Waratah Flat Road, which leads 2.9km to the camping area. 7 shaded sites. Suitable for off-road caravans. Bring drinking water.
GPS S:37 17.188 E:148 34.342
MR: Map 13 I2

Bull Flat camping area

Signposted access along McKillops Road 700m east of McKillops Bridge. Then in 200m to camping area with individual bollarded sites. Carry gear in. Bring drinking water and firewood.
GPS S:37 04.954 E:148 25.454
MR: Map 12 H8

EAST GIPPSLAND

Waratah Flat camping area

White Box camping area

White Box camping area

Signposted access along McKillops Road 200m east of McKillops Bridge. Then in 100m to camping area with bollarded sites. Some carry gear in sites. Bring drinking water and firewood.
GPS S:37 04.920 E:148 24.978
MR: Map 12 H8

Snowy River camping area

Signposted access along McKillops Road 500m west of McKillops Bridge. Very large area beside the road, situated back from the river among shady box trees. Camper trailer and caravan access with care from Bonang, check road conditions first.
GPS S:37 05.469 E:148 24.773
MR: Map 12 H8

Little River Junction camping area

Located 3.3km along Little River Track which is signposted off McKillops Road (the Bonang-Gelantipy Road) 7km west of McKillops Bridge. Large area among tall shady trees set high above the junction of Little and Snowy rivers. Sites well spread out, some suitable for camper trailers, others carry gear over bollards to sites. Seasonal closures apply to Little River Track.
GPS S:37 07.294 E:148 22.348
MR: Map 12 H8

Snowy River

SOUTHERN SECTION

Balley Hooley camping area

Located near Snowy River east of Buchan. From Buchan take the signposted road to Orbost and proceed east, then at 4.7km turn left into the signposted Basin Road (which becomes Old Basin Road after 3.2km). Follow Basin/Old Basin Road for a total of 6km to a five way junction then turn right into track signposted Balley Hooley/To Snowy River. This track leads 4.6km to the camping area which has two vehicle based campsites and four walk-in tent based sites. Bring drinking water and firewood.
GPS S:37 31.078 E:148 15.818
MR: Map 13 H3

Raymond Falls camping area

Located beside Raymond Creek north of Orbost. From Orbost take the signposted Scott Street and proceed in a westerly direction for 2.6km, then turn right into the signposted Yalmy Road. Continue along Yalmy Road for 25.5km to the signposted Moresford Rd, which leads 8.9km to the camping area with four individual shaded sites. Walk to the falls. Bring drinking water and firewood.
GPS S:37 29.113 E:148 18.453
MR: Map 13 H3

Hicks camping area

Located beside Yalmy River north of Orbost. From Orbost take the signposted Scott Street and proceed in a westerly direction for 2.6km, then turn right into the signposted Yalmy Road. Continue along Yalmy Road for 25.8km then veer

into track signposted Varney's Track (this is 6.4km north of Raymond Falls CA access road). Then at 6.5km is signposted access track which leads in 700m to the large open grassed camping area beside the river. Water from river, boil or treat first. Bring drinking water.
GPS S:37 24.794 E:148 21.561
MR: Map 13 H3

Jacksons Crossing camping area

Located beside Snowy River north of Orbost. Signposted access along Varney's Track 4.1km west of Hicks CA access track and 100m east of the Snowy River crossing. Access track leads 900m and a further 700m to campsites along the river. Bring drinking water. NB: it is possible to bush camp on the western side of the river crossing.
GPS S:37 23.626 E:148 20.078
MR: Map 13 H3

FURTHER *Information*

Parks Vic Info Line
Tel: 13 19 63

EAST GIPPSLAND

Located 75km north of Buchan. Signposted access along Snowy River Road. Bush camping at the town reserve. Walk to the historic school.

Suggan Buggan Town Reserve

Located 23km north of McKillops Road, which is signposted off Snowy River Road 56km north of Buchan. Bush campsite beside road on western side of road at locality of Suggan Buggan, beside Suggan Buggan River. Bring drinking water and firewood.
GPS S:36 57.176 E:148 19.476
MR: Map 12 H7

FURTHER Information

Parks Vic Buchan
Tel: 03 5162 1900

EAST GIPPSLAND

Located 23km north-west of Buchan on the Timbarra River. Access via Timbarra Road off Buchan Road. Excellent trout fishing.

Timbarra Bridge camping area

From Buchan proceed in a southerly direction along Buchan Road towards Bruthen. At 4.1km turn into signposted Timbarra Road and follow for 24km to bridge over Timbarra River. Camping on both sides of bridge. Bring drinking water.
Bridge – **GPS** S:37 22.870 E:148 05.786
MR: Map 13 F3

Timbarra bush camping areas

From Timbarra Bridge CA proceed a further 5.6km along Timbarra Road to dispersed bush campsites along the road beside the river, prior to the locality of Timbarra. Suitable for self sufficient campers. Bring drinking water.
Bush campsite – **GPS** S:37 20.928 E:148 04.167
MR: Map 13 F3

FURTHER Information

> **Parks Vic Buchan**
> **Tel:** 03 5162 1900

Timbarra Bridge camping area

EAST GIPPSLAND

Gippsland

GIPPSLAND HAS MANY SCENIC HIGHLIGHTS, from the lofty peak of Mount Baw Baw through to the waterways of the Gippsland Lakes, beautiful forests and beaches of Wilsons Promontory and the historic town of Walhalla, just to name a few.

The Gippsland region has a good choice of destinations for campers to visit. Wilsons Promontory National Park, on the southernmost tip of mainland Australia, has superb beaches dotted with rugged

headlands. The main camping area, Tidal River, has an excellent range of facilities and is popular during the holiday periods. Remote campsites are also located within the park and are accessible by walkers only.

Situated in the historic goldmining village of Walhalla is the North Gardens camping area. This popular campsite is an ideal base for exploring the town and the region. Surrounding Walhalla are a number of state forests which are popular four-wheel drive touring destinations. These forests also provide camping opportunities, although many of these only offer basic facilities.

To the north of Yarram within Won Wron State Forest is the scenic White Womans Waterhole camping area. Here there is an information board depicting the legend of a white woman found living with an Aboriginal tribe in the area in the mid 1800s. This region is a popular summer destination with its seemingly endless stretches of coastline and rugged mountain ranges providing an ideal destination for a summer camping break.

Spring, summer and autumn are without doubt the best seasons to experience this region.

BEST Campsites!

Tidal River camping area
Wilsons Promontory National Park

North Gardens camping ground
Walhalla Historic Area

Reeves Beach camping area
Woodside Area

O'Tooles camping area
Thomson State Forest

Bear Gully camping area
Cape Liptrap Coastal Park

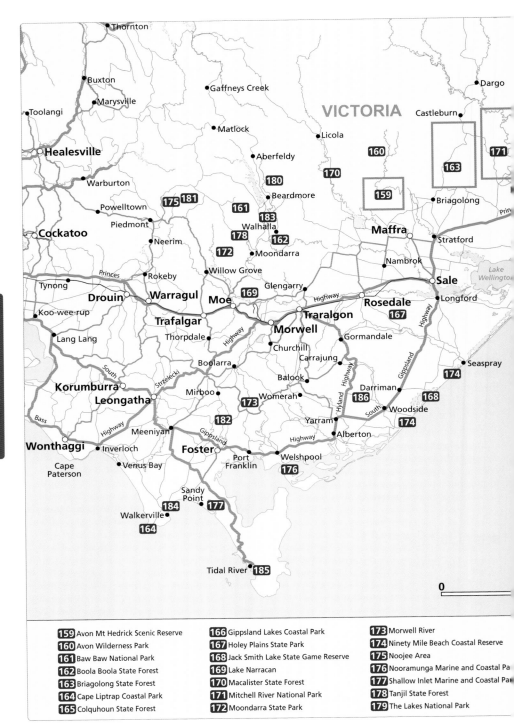

Thornton

Buxton
Marysville
Toolangi

Gaffneys Creek

VICTORIA

Dargo

Castleburn

Healesville

Matlock

Warburton

Aberfeldy

Licola

Briagolong

Prin

Powelltown

Piedmont

Neerim

Cockatoo

Walhalla

Beardmore

Moondarra

Maffra

Stratford

Nambrok

Lake Wellington

Princes
Rokeby
Willow Grove

Tynong

Drouin

Warragul

Moe

Glengarry

Sale

Koo-wee-rup

Trafalgar

Thorpdale

Highway

Morwell

Traralgon

Rosedale

Longford

Lang Lang

Churchill

Gormandale

Boolarra

Carrajung

Balook

Seaspray

Korumburra

Strzelecki

Mirboo

Womerah

Darriman

Leongatha

Bass

Meeniyan

Gippsland

Yarram

Woodside

Wonthaggi

Inverloch

Highway

Foster

Port
Franklin

Welshpool

Alberton

Cape
Paterson

Venus Bay

Sandy
Point

Walkerville

Tidal River

GIPPSLAND

159 Avon Mt Hedrick Scenic Reserve	**166** Gippsland Lakes Coastal Park	**173** Morwell River
160 Avon Wilderness Park	**167** Holey Plains State Park	**174** Ninety Mile Beach Coastal Reserve
161 Baw Baw National Park	**168** Jack Smith Lake State Game Reserve	**175** Noojee Area
162 Boola Boola State Forest	**169** Lake Narracan	**176** Nooramunga Marine and Coastal Pa
163 Briagolong State Forest	**170** Macalister State Forest	**177** Shallow Inlet Marine and Coastal Pa
164 Cape Liptrap Coastal Park	**171** Mitchell River National Park	**178** Tanjil State Forest
165 Colquhoun State Forest	**172** Moondarra State Park	**179** The Lakes National Park

UNDER Cover

Your choice of camping accommodation, be it a tent, camper trailer, caravan, swag or roof top tent really depends on things such as the time you'll spend using it, your budget, available vehicle space (whether it is to be stowed in the vehicle, on a roof rack or towed), the number of people to accommodate and the environment it will be used in.

Camper trailers are gaining in popularity at an amazing pace, especially the more rugged off-road units and are often favoured by long term travellers and families who camp out regularly. Advantages include extra storage space, comfortable sleeping area and often extra shade and weather cover from awnings. Remember though that some destinations are out of bounds or just not practical if you are towing a trailer. Becoming increasingly more common are the number of national park campsites throughout the state which aren't trailer friendly. These sites are ringed by bollards, providing a small vehicle parking space. You carry your camping gear over these to the grassed campsite.

GIPPSLAND

180 Thomson State Forest
181 Toorongo Falls Reserve
182 Turtons Creek Reserve
183 Walhalla Historic Area
184 Walkerville Foreshore Reserve
185 Wilson Promontory National Park
186 Won Wron State Forest

Located 20km north-west of Maffra on the Avon River. A number of access roads run off the Newry-Glenmaggie Road. Conventional vehicle access to some areas, others require four-wheel drive vehicle. Walk to summit of Mt Hedrick. Fishing, swimming, walking and four-wheel drive touring.

Dermodys Camp camping area

Located beside the Avon River at the end of Dermody Road. From Maffra travel north to Boisdale. From Boisdale continue north for 3km to turn left (west) into Luckmans Road, then follow this to turn right (north) into Warrigal - Toms Creek Road. From Warrigal - Toms Creek Road take Boundary Track to the west into the reserve then turn onto Dermody Road. Conventional vehicle access in dry weather only.
MR: Map 10 L7

Wombat Crossing camping area

Located beside Avon River along O'Keefe Road, which is accessed off Back Wombat Road, which is off Luckmans Road from Boisdale. River crossing requires 4WD.
MR: Map 10 L7

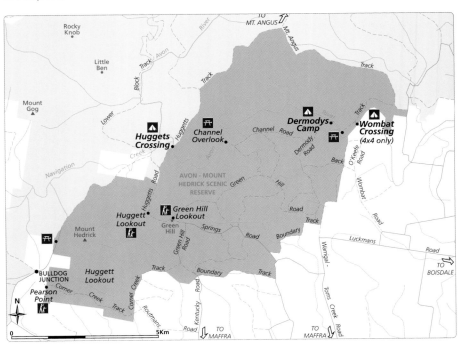

GIPPSLAND

Huggetts Crossing camping area

Located beside Avon River on Huggetts Track. From Maffra travel north-west towards Newry to join the Newry-Boisdale Road. From this road, north of Newry, take the Horstmans Road to the west and follow this towards Maffra West Upper then take Kentucky Road, which proceeds north and enters the reserve. Once in the reserve take Green Hill Road off Kentucky Road and follow to the lookout, then take Huggetts Road to the west and follow this north as it becomes Huggetts Track. Huggetts Track is 4WD only.

MR: Map 10 K7

FURTHER Information

> **DSE Heyfield**
> **Tel:** 03 5139 7777

160 Avon Wilderness Park

Located 40km north of Heyfield near Licola. Vehicle access to edge of park only. Access via Mt Margaret Track from Licola Road and Mt Wellington Track from Moroka Road via Arbuckle Junction. Walkers to register with ranger.

Avon Wilderness bush camping

Dispersed bush camping for self-sufficient walkers. Gas/fuel stove preferred. Contact ranger for details.

MR: Map 10 K6

FURTHER Information

> **Parks Vic Info Line**
> **Tel:** 13 19 63

161 Baw Baw National Park

Located 40km north of Moe near Rawson. Access via Thomson Valley Road from Rawson. Popular bushwalking and cross-country skiing area. Australian Alps Walking Track passes through the park.

Aberfeldy River camping area

Located beside Aberfeldy River, 17km north of Walhalla. Signposted access via Walhalla-Aberfeldy Road. Water from river; boil or treat first. Bring drinking water. Many 4WD touring tracks nearby.

MR: Map 10 I7

Eastern Tyers camping area

Located on Australian Alps Walking Track, west of Walhalla. Walk-in access only. Bring drinking water. Gas/fuel stove preferred.

MR: Map 10 I7

Baw Baw Plateau bush camping

Walk-in access to dispersed bush camping on the plateau accessed via the Australian Alps Walking Track. Bring drinking water. Gas/fuel stove only. Limit of 2 nights stay. Contact ranger for further details.
MR: Map 10 I7

FURTHER Information

> **Parks Vic Info Line**
> **Tel:** 13 19 63

162 Boola Boola State Forest

Located south-east of Rawson. Access via Walhalla Road off Tyers-Thomson Valley Road. Explore historic mining areas.

Thomson Bridge camping area

Small area beside the road at bridge over Thomson River, south of Walhalla on the Walhalla Road.
MR: Map 10 I8

Coopers Creek camping area

Conventional vehicle access via signposted Coopers Creek Track off Walhalla Road, south-west of Walhalla, or via Coopers Creek Track off the Rawson-Tyers Road, south of the Walhalla Road.
MR: Map 10 I8

Bruntons Bridge camping area

Located beside Thomson River at Bruntons Bridge, 12km south-east of Walhalla. Access to Bruntons Bridge is signposted from Walhalla. Campsites on the western side of the river can be accessed from Walhalla. Large cleared area on the eastern side of the river is best accessed via Bruntons Bridge Road which is off the Cowwarr-Walhalla Road west of Cowwarr. 4WD is required to cross the wide Thomson River crossing.
Thomson River – **GPS** S:37 59.877 E:146 28.360
MR: Map 10 J8

FURTHER Information

> **Parks Vic Erica**
> **Tel:** 03 5165 2200

GIPPSLAND

Located 15km north of Stratford with numerous campsites beside Freestone Creek. From Briagolong proceed north along signposted Forbes Street, which then becomes Freestone Creek Road and is sealed up to The Blue Pool. Freestone Creek Road is also signposted off the Bairnsdale-Dargo road, 32km from Dargo and 56km from Bairnsdale – this access is a very scenic route, however it is narrow and winding and not suitable for trailers or vans. Camping is also possible beside Valencia Creek north-west of Briagolong. From Briagolong take signposted Forbes Street north for 2.1km, then follow the signposted road to Valencia Creek. Popular area for swimming and gold panning, don't forget your fossickers licence.

Quarry Reserve camping area

Located 3km north of Briagolong. From Briagolong take signposted Forbes Street towards Dargo and travel north for 2.7km to the signposted access to reserve. Drive in 300m to large shaded area situated above the river. Childrens playground area. Bring firewood.
GPS S:37 48.785 E:147 05.354
MR: Map 13 A5

The Blue Pool camping area

Signposted access along the sealed Freestone Creek Road, 5.6km north of Quarry Reserve. Large camping area set back from the road above the river, shaded sites with some grassed areas. Bring drinking water and firewood.
GPS S:37 46.841 E:147 06.760
MR: Map 13 A5

Froam picnic and camping area

Signposted access along Freestone Creek Road, 700m north of The Blue Pool, then in short distance to open area with three campsites. Bring drinking water and firewood.
GPS S:37 46.529 E:147 06.850
MR: Map 13 A5

McKinnons Point camping area

Signposted access along Freestone Creek Road, 1.5km north of Froam picnic area. Then in 200m to open camping area above the creek with two sites. Bring drinking water and firewood.
GPS S:37 45.730 E:147 06.393
MR: Map 13 A5

Carneys campsite

Signposted access along Freestone Creek Road, 2.4km north of McKinnons Point. Small area with two small sites. Bring drinking water and firewood.
GPS S:37 44.999 E:147 06.807
MR: Map 13 A5

GIPPSLAND

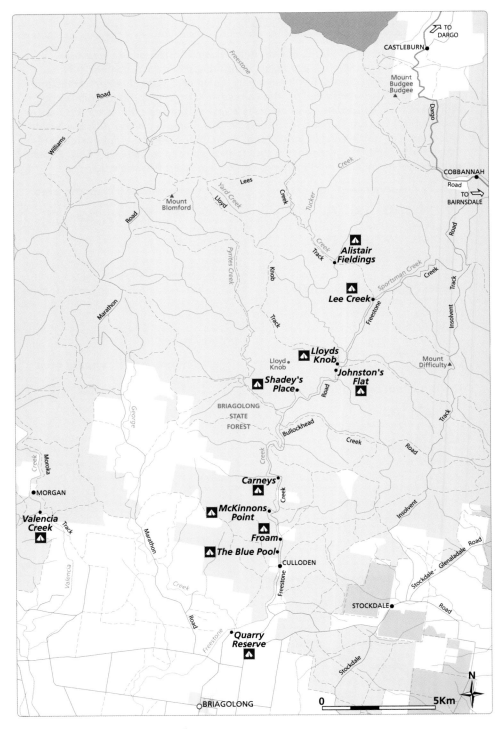

TO
DARGO

CASTLEBURN

Mount
Budgee
Budgee

COBBANNAH

TO
BAIRNSDALE

Williams

Road

Road

Freestone

Lees

Lloyd

Creek

Mount
Blomford

Yard Creek

Pyrites Creek

Tucker

Creek

Creek

Road

Knob

Track

Marathon

Track

🏕 Alistair
Fieldings

🏕 Lee Creek

Sportsman Creek

Creek

Track

Freestone

Insolvent

🏕 Lloyds
Knob

Lloyd
Knob

🏕 Johnston's
Flat

Mount
Difficulty

🏕 Shadey's
Place

Road

BRIAGOLONG
STATE
FOREST

George

Bullockhead

Creek

Track

Road

Moroka

Creek

Creek

🏕 Carneys

MORGAN

🏕 McKinnons
Point

Valencia
Creek
🏕

Track

Marathon

Creek

🏕 Froam

🏕 The Blue Pool

CULLODEN

Freestone

Insolvent

Stockdale - Glenaladale Road

STOCKDALE

Road

Valencia

Road

🏕 Quarry
Reserve

Freestone

Creek

Stockdale

N

BRIAGOLONG

0   5Km

Holey Plains State Park is 30km south-west of Sale and south-east of Rosedale. From Rosedale take the road off the Princes Highway signposted towards Willung. A scenic drive can be taken through the park via West Boundary, Long Ridge and Wildflower Tracks. Take in the views of the surrounding forests and farmland from Holey Hill (the highest point in the park), walk along one of the park's walking tracks or enjoy the spectacular wildflower displays.

Harriers Swamp camping area

From Rosedale take the road south towards Willung for 1.5km to the signposted Rosedale-Stradbroke Road. Turn left (west) into the Rosedale-Stradbroke Road and follow it for 6.1km to the signposted West Boundary Track. Turn right (south), then at 700m take the signposted Long Ridge Track to the east which leads 900m to the camping area. The camping area is an attractive site situated opposite Harriers Swamp. Horseyards. Bring drinking water and firewood.
GPS S:38 12.512 E:146 50.745
MR: Map 11 K2

Holey Hill camping area

Access is off the Rosedale-Stradbroke Road. Follow directions from Rosedale as for Harriers Swamp CA to West Boundary Track. Continue on the Rosedale-Stradbroke Road, passing West Boundary Track, for a further 6km to the signposted Holey Hill Track. Turn left (east) into Holey Hill Track and follow this for 4.4km to the camping area, a small area adjacent to the picnic area surrounded by banksia and eucalypt forest. Bring drinking water and firewood.
GPS S:38 13.899 E:146 56.333
MR: Map 11 L2

FURTHER Information

> **Parks Vic Info Line**
> **Tel:** 13 19 63

GIPPSLAND

Holey Hill camping area

168 Jack Smith Lake State Game Reserve

Located 25km east of Yarram near Woodside. Access via Giffard Road off South Gippsland Highway or Stringy Bark Lane from Woodside. Main feature of park is Jack Smith Lake.

Jack Smith bush camping

Access via Kuchs Road from Giffard Road off South Gippsland Highway north of Woodside. Dispersed bush camping, no facilities. Most sites are open with little shade. Bring drinking water.
MR: Map 11 L4

FURTHER Information

> **Parks Vic Info Line**
> **Tel:** 13 19 63

169 Lake Narracan

Located 5km north-east of Moe and north of Newborough. Access via South Shore Road. Watersports venue.

Lake Narracan Caravan Park

Signposted access along South Shore Road.
MR: Map 11 H1

FURTHER Information

> **Lake Narracan Caravan Park**
> **Tel:** 03 5127 8724. Bookings required for Christmas and Easter.
> **Camping fees:** Unpowered tent site from $10.00 per adult/night. Powered sites from $30.00 per site/night.

170 Macalister State Forest

Forest located to the west of the Licola-Heyfield Road, south of Licola and north of Glenmaggie. The forest provides car, 4WD and trail bike touring as well as fishing in the rivers and creeks.

Cheynes Bridge campground

Located along the Licola-Heyfield Road at the bridged crossing of the Macalister River, 32km north of Heyfield.
MR: Map 10 J7

FURTHER Information

> **DSE Heyfield**
> **Tel:** 03 5139 7777

This rugged park with remote gorges, rainforests and rivers is located 45km north-west of Bairnsdale. Access to the western sections of the park is off the Dargo Road. The park offers some first rate canoeing, walking trails, rock climbing and four-wheel drive touring.

Angusvale camping area

Beside the Mitchell River on Mitchell Dam Road. Mitchell Dam Road is signposted off the Dargo Road, then 16km north-east into the camping area which has 15 sites. Bring drinking water and firewood.
MR: Map 13 C4

Rock Creek Track camping area

Situated beside Mitchell River. Located at the end of the 4WD Angusvale Track and along the Rock Creek Walking Track. Angusvale Track is off the 4WD only Mitchell Road, which can be accessed from the north off Mitchell Dam Road or from the south off Billy Goat Bend Road. 4WD vehicle, walk-in or river access. 2 sites. Bring drinking water. Gas/fuel stove only.
MR: Map 13 C4

Billy Goat Bend camping area

Located at the end of Billy Goat Bend Road, which can be accessed off Waller Road or off the Dargo Road south of Mitchell Dam Road and north of Waller Road. Mitchell River Walking Track passes through. 6 sites. Bring drinking water and firewood.
MR: Map 13 C4

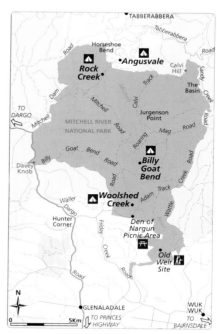

Woolshed Creek camping area

Located along the Mitchell River Walking Track north of the Den of Nargun Picnic Area. Walk-in or river access only. 4 sites. Bring drinking water. Gas/fuel stove only.
MR: Map 13 C4

FURTHER Information

Parks Vic Info Line
Tel: 13 19 63

172 Moondarra State Park

Located 13km north of Moe. Conventional vehicle access is via Seninis Track off the Moe-Erica Road. The park is home to a variety of wildlife including koalas. Scenic drives, bushwalking, swimming, mountain biking and nature study.

Seninis Recreation Area

Located along Seninis (sometimes spelt Sennis) Track which is signposted off the Moe-Erica Road. Alternative access from the west is via the Tanjil Bren Road off the Moe-Erica Road and follow this in a north-westerly direction, then take Seninis Track to the east and follow to the Tyers River and the camping area. This route is suitable for 4WD vehicles only.

MR: Map 11 I1

FURTHER Information

> **Parks Vic Info Line**
> **Tel:** 13 19 63
> **NB:** At the time of research the conventional vehicle access route of Seninis Track off the Moe-Erica Road was closed due to flood damage, therefore access to the camping area was only possible via the western route via 4WD vehicle. Check with Parks Vic, Erica tel: 03 5165 3204 for up-to-date access details.

173 Morwell River

The Morwell River commences in the Strzelecki Ranges and joins with the Latrobe River at Yallourn. To the south of the town of Boolarra the river hosts a number of bush campsites.

Morwell River camping areas

From Boolarra village take the signposted C456 road towards Churchill and Morwell. At 700m veer right into Morwell River Road and proceed in a southerly direction. Follow Morwell River Road for 8km and from here a number of tracks lead off Morwell River Road to cleared bush campsites beside the river.

GPS S:38 25.649 E:146 18.550
MR: Map 11 H3

FURTHER Information

> **Parks Vic Foster**
> **Tel:** 03 5683 9000

GIPPSLAND

174 Ninety Mile Beach Coastal Reserve

Ninety Mile Beach is located south of Seaspray and is accessed off the South Gippsland Highway near Woodside. The beach is unprotected and is adjacent to the waters of Ninety Mile Beach Marine National Park which offers diving, snorkelling and fishing opportunities within the marine national park regulations.

McGaurans Beach camping area

Located 21km north-east of Woodside. Take signposted Giffard Road off the South Gippsland Highway north of Woodside. Travel along Giffard Road for 8.7km to the signposted, unsealed, McGaurans Beach Road. Camping area at end of McGaurans Beach Road. Bring drinking water.
MR: Map 13 F8

Reeves Beach camping area

Located 13km south-east of Woodside at end of Reeves Beach Road, which is 3.7km along Balloong Road, which leaves Woodside Beach Road 4.6km east of Woodside village. Bring drinking water.
MR: Map 11 L4

FURTHER Information

> **Parks Vic Info Line**
> **Tel:** 13 19 63

175 Noojee Area

Noojee is situated to the east of Yarra Junction and west of Mt Baw Baw. The village was originally settled in the mid 1860s by gold prospectors and is located beside the Latrobe River. It is surrounded by forest and offers excellent visitor facilities for walkers and vehicle touring, as well as historic sites and picturesque waterfalls.

Loch Valley camping area

Located 7km north of Noojee. Access via Henty Street off the Powelltown Road at junction with Bennett Street. Conventional vehicle access. Dispersed camping beside Loch River. NB: Log trucks use this road.
MR: Map 10 G7

Hawthorn Bridge camping area

Located 25km north-east of Neerim South on Latrobe River Road. Access via Neerim East Road from Nerrim South then Latrobe River Road. Conventional vehicle access. Dispersed camping on both sides of bridge beside Latrobe River.
MR: Map 10 G8

FURTHER Information

> **DSE Customer Service Centre**
> **Tel:** 13 61 86

Stretching from Port Welshpool north-east to the southern end of Ninety Mile Beach, activities in the park include bushwalking, picnicking, swimming, fishing and nature study. Camping is permitted on Snake and Little Snake islands, south of Port Welshpool. Boat access only to islands. Boat charter operators can provide access to islands.

Snake Island camping areas – Swashway Jetty, Gulf and The Huts

Dispersed bush camping at the three designated areas: Swashway Jetty camping area at the north-eastern tip of the island; Gulf camping area located on the eastern side of the island north of The Gulf Gutter; The Huts located on the western side of the island north of Bentley Point. Boat access only. Toilets and water at The Huts. Bring drinking water. Gas/fuel stove preferred.
MR: Map 11 I5

Little Snake Island camping areas

Located offshore from Port Welshpool. Boat access only. Dispersed bush camping on island at The Bluff on south-west side of island. Bring drinking water. Gas/fuel stove preferred.
MR: Map 11 I5

FURTHER Information

Parks Vic Info Line
Tel: 13 19 63
Camping permit: Permit required. Contact Parks Vic Forster ph 03 5683 9000.

ISLAND Retreat

If you are after a secluded island camping holiday then why not check out Snake Island. The largest sand island in Victoria, Snake Island is only accessible by boat. If you don't have your own boat (check with locals or Parks Vic Yarram for advice as navigation in the channels surrounding the islands can be tricky) then there are charter operators who provide a taxi service from Port Welshpool. Contact the visitor information centre at Yarram on 03 5182 6533 for details.

Apart from the camping, there are plenty of walking tracks criss-crossing the island for the more energetic and the fishing is reported to be pretty good. Snapper, Flathead and King George Whiting can be had from the island's ocean beach.

GIPPSLAND

177 Shallow Inlet Marine and Coastal Park

Located 28km south of Fish Creek near Yanakie. Access to the western side of Shallow Inlet is via Sandy Point and access to the eastern side is off the Wilsons Promontory Road. The park has picnicking facilities at Western Beach on Sandy Point Road, while on the eastern side there is the short Hourigan Camp Lane walking track. The waters of Shallow Inlet are popular for boating and fishing. Camping is not permitted in the park however camping is possible at the camping ground on the eastern shores of Shallow Inlet.

Shallow Inlet camping ground

From Foster on South Gippsland Highway, take the road signposted to Wilsons Promontory. At 18.8km take the signposted Lester Road/Shallow Inlet, which leads 3.6km south to the camping ground. Dispersed camping among vegetation beside the inlet, some sites are private and secluded. Gas/fuel stove only.
GPS S:38 49.211 E:146 10.296
MR: Map 11 H6

FURTHER Information

> **Shallow Inlet Camping Ground**
> **Tel:** 03 5687 1365
> **Camping fees:** Camping ground open November 1 to end of Easter. Contact office for current fee structure.

GIPPSLAND

178 Tanjil State Forest

Located 10km west of Rawson. Access via Telbit Road off Moe-Rawson Road south of Erica. Activities include bushwalking, fishing and four-wheel drive touring.

Western Tyers camping area

Located beside Tyers River West Branch. Signposted access via Western Tyers Road off Telbit Road.
MR: Map 10 H8

Dispersed bush camping

Dispersed bush camping is possible throughout the forest, adhering to DSE camping codes. Contact DSE Erica for details.

FURTHER Information

> **DSE Erica**
> **Tel:** 03 5165 2200

179 The Lakes National Park

Located 60km east of Sale near Loch Sport. Access via Longford-Loch Sport Road from Longford. Also boat access from Paynesville. Activities include boating, walking, fishing and birdwatching.

Emu Bight camping area

Located 5km east of Loch Sport on shores of Lake Victoria. Access via Lake Victoria Track.
MR: Map 13 D7

Rotamah Island

Booked group camping only. Contact Parks Vic Loch Sport for details.

FURTHER Information

> **Parks Vic Info Line**
> **Tel:** 13 19 63
> **Parks Vic Loch Sport**
> **Tel:** 03 5146 0278
> **Camping fees:** From $10.50 per site/night. Peak periods of Christmas, Easter and Victorian school holidays from $15.50 per site/night. Permit and bookings required contact Parks Vic Sale Tel: 03 5143 8200.

GIPPSLAND

Located 40km north of Walhalla. Access is via the narrow and winding Walhalla Road. Popular area for fishing and four-wheel drive touring. Many historic gold mining sites to explore.

Andersons campground

Located beside Aberfeldy River on southern bank, 5.8km south of the locality of Aberfeldy, 27km south of Woods Point along the Walhalla Road. Small area with two separate sites.
GPS S:37 43.441 E:146 23.395
MR: Map 10 I6

Junction campground

Beside Aberfeldy River with access signposted along Junction Track. From Andersons campground continue in a south-easterly direction, this is along Donnelly Ck Rd, for 6.5km to the signposted Junction Tk. Follow Junction Tk for 1.2km to the signposted access track, which leads in 100m to the open area beside the river. Bring drinking water and firewood.
GPS S:37 45.514 E:146 24.063
MR: Map 10 I6

Merringtons camping area

Located beside Aberfeldy River along Merringtons Tk. From Junction campground proceed in south-westerly direction along Junction Tk for 900m, then take the signposted Merringtons Tk, which leads 800m to a large open camping area with little shade. Bring drinking water and firewood.
GPS S:37 45.661 E:146 24.079
MR: Map 10 I7

Jorgenson Flat camping area

Beside Donnelly Creek along Donnelly Creek Track. From Andersons campground continue in a south-easterly direction (this is Donnelly Ck Rd) for 6.5km to the signposted junction of Donnelly Ck Rd and Junction Tk. Continue on Donnelly Ck Rd for 900m to a T-junction, where the track on right is signposted Jorgenson. This track leads a short distance to the camping area in the vicinity of a private hut. Bring drinking water and firewood.
GPS S:37 44.895 E:146 24.731
MR: Map 10 I7

Little O'Tooles camping area

Seasonal closure access. Located beside Donnelly Creek, with access signposted along Donnelly Creek Track. From the T-junction to Jorgenson Flat cross Donnelly Creek and continue on Donnelly Creek Track for 3km to the signposted access track, which leads 200m to a cleared circular space surrounded by trees. This access track is 700m west of O'Tooles access track. Bring drinking water and firewood.
GPS S:37 44.857 E:146 26.411
MR: Map 10 I6

GIPPSLAND

Morning Star Waterwheel Thomson State Forest

O'Tooles camping area

Seasonal closure access. Located beside Donnelly Creek, with access signposted along Donnelly Creek Track, 700m east of Little O'Tooles CA. To access from the east from Walhalla proceed in a northerly direction towards Aberfeldy and Woods Point, then at 10.2km veer right (north-east) into the signposted Binns Rd and follow this for 13km to then turn left (north) onto signposted McEvoy's Tk. Follow McEvoy's Tk north for 10.6km to the signposted Donnelly's Tk. Turn into Donnelly's Tk and follow this for 15km to the signposted access track to O'Tooles CA. Bring drinking water and firewood.
GPS S:37 44.873 E:146 26.561
MR: Map 10 I6

Bush camping

Dispersed bush camping is possible throughout the forest in accordance with the DSE bush camping code. Along McEvoy's Trk is The Springs, which is 1.8km south of Donnelly's Tk (GPS S:37 45.546 E:146 32.954). Sites along Donnelly's Tk include: Edwards Hill at 3.4km along Donnelly's Tk (GPS S:37 45.584 E:146 31.479); at 7.6km along Donnelly's Track (GPS S:37 45.330 E:146 30.197); at Store Point 7.7km along Donnelly's Track (GPS S:37 45.264 E:146 30.097); beside Donnelly Creek, which is accessed along Morning Star Tk, 100m west of Store Point (GPS S:37 45.242 E:146 30.007). Bring drinking water and firewood.

FURTHER Information

DSE Erica
Tel: 03 5165 2200

O'Tooles camping area

181 Toorongo Falls Reserve

Located 8km north-east of Noojee. Access via Toorongo Falls Road from Baw Baw Tourist Road. Main features of park are Toorongo Falls and tall mountain forests.

Toorongo Falls camping area

Located beside Toorongo River. Access via Toorongo Falls Road off Mt Baw Baw Tourist Road from Noojee. Not suitable for large caravans. Walk to falls.
MR: Map 10 G7

FURTHER Information

DSE Customer Service Centre
Tel: 13 61 86

182 Turtons Creek Reserve

Located north of Forster along Turtons Creek Road, the reserve has beautiful eucalypt forest, fern glades and waterfalls. From the South Gippsland Highway 3km east of Forster, take the signposted Boolarra Road north for 1.8km, then turn into signposted road to Turtons Creek and follow signage. From the north access is via Mirboo-Foster Road off Grand Ridge Road, 7km south-east of Mirboo North. Follow Mirboo-Foster Road south for 6.8km to the signposted Turtons Creek Road, which leads 7.3km to the camping area.

Turtons Creek camping area

Take the Boolarra Road off the South Gippsland Highway, east of Forster. Travel north for 1.8km, then turn left into the road signposted Turtons Creek. Follow this for 6km to junction and turn left into road signposted Turtons Creek/Mirboo North. Follow this road for 1.7km to the signposted Turtons Creek Road and turn right. Then at a further 1.2km is another junction, turn right into the signposted Turtons Creek Road. Follow Turtons Creek Road for 6.2km to the signposted access to the camping area, which leads 100m to an open grassed flat area beside the creek. Dispersed camping along the creek. Bring drinking water and firewood.
GPS S:38 32.044 E:146 15.022
MR: Map 11 H4

FURTHER Information

Parks Vic Foster
Tel: 03 5683 9000

GIPPSLAND

Includes the township and surrounding area of historic Walhalla. Access via Walhalla Road from Rawson in the south or Matlock/Aberfeldy to the north. Explore the town and surrounds. Many gold mining sites. Activities include sightseeing, four-wheel drive touring and horse riding. NB: Phytophthora (root rot) kills plants, and is prevalent here. Please observe signage and take steps to help combat the spread of this disease to other areas. Further information is available from DSE and Parks Vic.

North Gardens camping ground

Located beside Stringer Creek in Walhalla township. Access via Walhalla Road. Limited space for small vans and camper trailers.
GPS S:37 55.952 E:146 26.908
MR: Map 10 I8

FURTHER Information

Parks Vic Info Line
Tel: 13 19 63

GIPPSLAND

184 Walkerville Foreshore Reserve

Located 30km south-west of Foster. Access via Walkerville-Fish Creek Road. Fronts Waratah Bay.

Walkerville Camping Reserve

Located at Walkerville North on Bayside Drive, access signposted. Store.
GPS S:38 50.447 E:146 00.029
MR: Map 11 G6

FURTHER Information

Walkerville Foreshore Reserve
Tel: 03 5663 2224
Camping fees: Off-Peak: Unpowered from $20.10 per site/night for 2 people. Powered from $22.20 per site/night for 2 people.

185 Wilsons Promontory National Park

Located 200km south-east of Melbourne, The 'Prom' is the southern most tip of mainland Australia. Access via Wilsons Promontory Road, signposted off the South Gippsland Highway at Foster. Entrance gate to the park is 29km south of the highway, and the park's visitor centre and store at Tidal River is a further 29km. Stunning coastal scenery. Good level of facilities. Caters for people with limited mobility. Many walking tracks. Popular for watersports. Cabin and lighthouse accommodation available.

Tidal River

Tidal River camping area

Access via Wilsons Promontory Road.
480 sites. Gas/fuel stoves only.
GPS S:39 01.838 E:146 19.292
MR: Map 11 I7

Southern Walk-in camping areas – Sealers Cove, Refuge Cove, Little Waterloo Bay, Halfway Hut, Roaring Meg, Oberon Bay

Overnight camping/hiking permit required. Remote walk-in sites in southern section of the park. Walks commence/finish at Tidal River or Telegraph Saddle carpark. Boat based camping possible at Refuge Cove. Carry drinking water. Gas/fuel stove only. Contact Parks Vic for details.

Northern Walk-in camping areas – Barry Creek, Lower Barry Creek, Tin Mine Cove, Johnny Souey Cove, Five Mile Beach

Overnight camping/hiking permit required. Remote walk-in sites in northern section of the park. Walks commence/finish at Five Mile Road carpark. Boat based camping possible at Tin Mine Cove. Carry drinking water. Gas/fuel stove only. Contact Parks Vic for details.

FURTHER *Information*

Parks Vic Info Line
Tel: 13 19 63. Bookings are recommended. Campsite applications are required for long weekends of Melbourne Cup, Labour Day and Easter. Ballot system applies for Christmas period (mid December to end January).
Camping fees: Tidal River: Off-peak from $18.00 per site night includes 3 people and 1 vehicle. Peak from $22.50 per site/night includes 2 people and 1 vehicle.
Walk-in campsites: From $7.10 per person/night.

Tidal River camping area, Wilsons Promontory National Park

186 Won Wron State Forest

Located 15km north of Yarram. Access via Carrajung Road, 300 metres south of Woodside on South Gippsland Highway then Won Wron Road. Access also via Won Wron Road on the Hyland Highway from Won Wron.

White Womans Waterhole picnic and camping area

Signposted access along Napier Road (Won Wron Road). From South Gippsland Highway take Carrajung Road south of Woodside. Travel for 6km then take the gravel signposted Won Wron Road. White Womans Waterhole is located a further 5km along this road. Large shady area near small creek.

MR: Map 11 K3

FURTHER Information

DSE Yarram
Tel: 03 5183 9100

High Country

VICTORIA'S MAGNIFICENT HIGH COUNTRY contains some of the state's most beautiful and unspoiled countryside. Enjoyable year round, this alpine destination is frequented by downhill and cross-country skiers during the winter and for the rest of the year is popular for bushwalking, fishing, mountain bike riding, vehicle touring, sightseeing, horse riding and camping.

The majority of camping in this region is situated within the large and scenic Alpine National Park. When it comes to camping, this park has it all: remote walk-in sites, four-wheel drive only sites in hidden valleys, sites beside crystal clear mountain streams and camping nearby to historic cattlemen's huts. Also in this region you can visit old goldmining towns, cemeteries and mining sites where rusting relics of a more prosperous time can be seen. A number of these historic sites also cater for campers.

Close to Omeo, the camping area at Victoria Falls Historic Area is a scenic site just off the Great Alpine Road while near Mansfield, Howqua Hills has a number of camping sites stretched along the banks of the Howqua River. Frys Flat, located in Howqua Hills Historic Area, is where local bushman and High Country legend Fred Fry built his slab home.

Near Dargo, Grant Historic Area has some lovely shaded sites beside Crooked River. Other delightful camping areas include the sites stretched along Upper Dargo Road, the Buckland Valley and Buffalo River state forests near Bright, Murray River Reserves and the sites along the Mansfield-Woods Point Road within the Upper Goulburn Historic Area.

Late spring through to autumn are the best times for a High Country camping sojourn, although winter offers back country adventurers opportunities for snow camping.

BEST Campsites!

 Wonnangatta Valley camping area
Alpine National Park

 Davies Plain Hut camping area
Alpine National Park

 Talbotville camping area
Grant Historic Area

 Italian Flat camping area
Dargo Area

 Bentleys Plain Reserve camping area
Nunniong State Forest

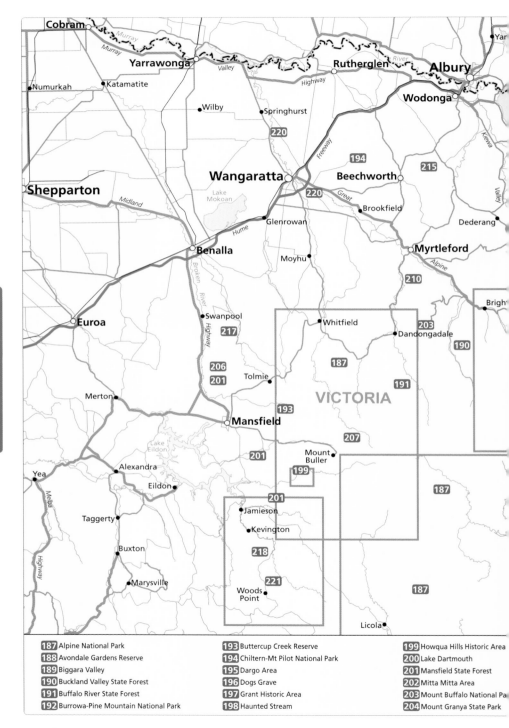

Cobram
Murray
Murray
Yarrawonga
Valley
Numurkah
Katamatite
Wilby
Springhurst
220
Rutherglen
Albury
Highway
Wodonga
Yar
Kiewa
Shepparton
Midland
Wangaratta
Lake
Mokoan
220
Great
Beechworth
194
Brookfield
Glenrowan
Hume
Benalla
Broken
River
Moyhu
215
Dederang
Myrtleford
Alpine
210
Euroa
Highway
Swanpool
217
Whitfield
Dandongadale
203
190
Brigh
206
201
Tolmie
VICTORIA
187
191
Merton
193
Mansfield
207
201
Lake
Eildon
Mount
Buller
199
187
Yea
Alexandra
Eildon
201
Melba
Jamieson
Taggerty
Kevington
187
Buxton
218
Highway
Marysville
221
Woods
Point
187
Licola

187 Alpine National Park	193 Buttercup Creek Reserve	199 Howqua Hills Historic Area
188 Avondale Gardens Reserve	194 Chiltern-Mt Pilot National Park	200 Lake Dartmouth
189 Biggara Valley	195 Dargo Area	201 Mansfield State Forest
190 Buckland Valley State Forest	196 Dogs Grave	202 Mitta Mitta Area
191 Buffalo River State Forest	197 Grant Historic Area	203 Mount Buffalo National Pa
192 Burrowa-Pine Mountain National Park	198 Haunted Stream	204 Mount Granya State Park

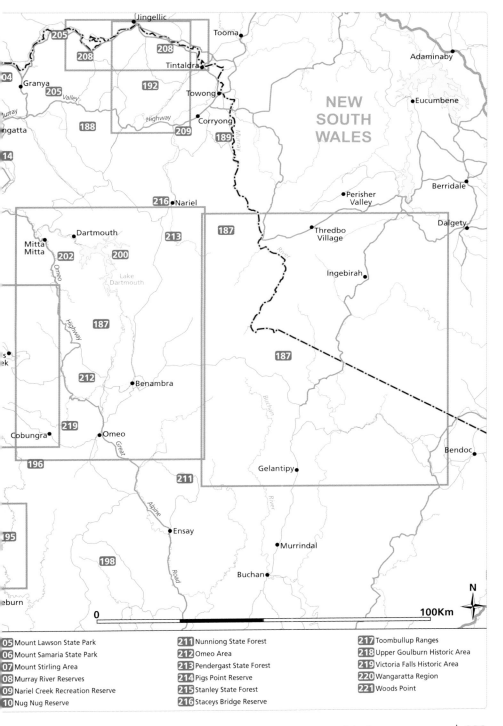

205 Mount Lawson State Park
206 Mount Samaria State Park
207 Mount Stirling Area
208 Murray River Reserves
209 Nariel Creek Recreation Reserve
210 Nug Nug Reserve

211 Nunniong State Forest
212 Omeo Area
213 Pendergast State Forest
214 Pigs Point Reserve
215 Stanley State Forest
216 Staceys Bridge Reserve

217 Toombullup Ranges
218 Upper Goulburn Historic Area
219 Victoria Falls Historic Area
220 Wangaratta Region
221 Woods Point

Alpine National Park stretches from the NSW border near Tom Groggin, south to Licola, and is Victoria's largest national park. Features the state's highest mountains; stunning alpine scenery; wildflower displays during summer. Discover historic cattlemen's huts. Popular destination for bushwalking, snow skiing, four-wheel drive touring, horse riding, fishing and mountain biking. Many roads pass through the park providing access. Conventional vehicle access to main areas. Some areas of the park only accessible by 4WD vehicle (seasonal closures apply). Some roads closed to all vehicles during winter. Be prepared for sudden changes in weather. Huts within Alpine National Park are refuge huts and should not be relied upon except in an emergency. Follow hut etiquette. NB: Horse riding season is December to April, permits are required.

BOGONG AREA

Located 365km north-east of Melbourne and 90km south-east of Wodonga. Access from south via Great Alpine Road or Bogong High Plains Road which is 41km north of Omeo via the Omeo Highway to reach Falls Creek. From north-west take Kiewa Valley Highway or Great Alpine Road. Use of gas/fuel stove preferred.

Wallace's Hut

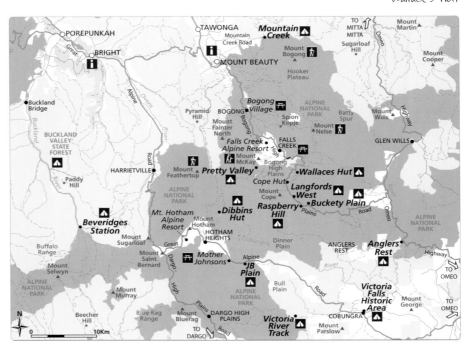

HIGH COUNTRY

Mountain Creek camping area

Located 11km along Mountain Creek Road, which is signposted off Kiewa Valley Highway, east of Tawonga. Water from creek, boil or treat first. Bring drinking water and firewood.
MR: Map 12 B6

Langfords West camping area

Located 16km south of Falls Creek. Signposted access along Bogong High Plains Road, 2.4km west of Raspberry Hill CA. Horseyards can be booked. Bring drinking water and firewood.
GPS S:36 55.727 E:147 18.264
MR: Map 12 B7

Raspberry Hill camping area

Located 18km south of Falls Creek, 2.4km east of Langfords West CA and 1.1km west of Buckety Plain CA. Signposted access along Bogong High Plains Road. Bring drinking water and firewood.
GPS S:36 56.567 E:147 19.059
MR: Map 12 B7

Buckety Plain camping area

Located 19km south of Falls Creek and 18.3km west of Omeo Highway. Signposted access along Bogong High Plains Road, then in 230m to camping area. NB: Hut is for emergency accommodation only. Bring drinking water and firewood.
GPS S:36 56.351 E:147 19.748
MR: Map 12 C7

JB Plain camping area

Walk-in site near hut. Located 11km south-east of Mt Hotham and west of Dinner Plain. Access carpark along Great Alpine Road. Bring drinking water.
MR: Map 12 B8

4WD & Walk-in bush camping

Numerous 4WD and walk-in only access campsites throughout the park, many in the vicinity of huts. Bush camping, no facilities. Follow Parks Vic Bush Camping regulations. Obtain large scale maps and contact Park Ranger for further details.

FURTHER Information

> **Parks Vic Info Line**
> **Tel:** 13 19 63

WONNANGATTA - MOROKA AREA

Located 200km east of Melbourne near Licola. Access from south via Tamboritha Road from Licola. From the west via Circuit Road from Mansfield, Myrtleford-Buffalo River Road from Myrtleford and the Buckland Valley Road from Bright in the north. From the east take Crooked River Road from Dargo. Remote area, be prepared. Use of gas/fuel stove preferred.

Whitfield Region

Bennies camping area

Located beside Rose River, 29km south of Whitfield on Upper Rose River Road, which is accessed off Rose River Road. Bring drinking water and firewood.
MR: Map 10 J1

Sandy Flat camping area

Dispersed camping beside King River, 9km south-east of Lake William Hovell picnic area. 4WD access via Sandy Flat Track from Lake William Hovell or signposted Sandy Flat Track off Basin Track which is off Cobbler Lake Road. Bring drinking water and firewood.
MR: Map 10 I1

Evans Creek Hut camping area

Located 8km south of Lake William Hovell. 4WD access via Evans Creek Track, which is 2.7km south of the Lake William Hovell picnic area, from Top Crossing Track.
MR: Map 10 I1

Top Crossing Hut camping area

Located beside King River, 13km south of Lake William Hovell picnic area. 4WD access via Top Crossing Track from Lake William Hovell.
MR: Map 10 J1

Lake Cobbler camping area

Located 47km south of Whitfield beside Lake Cobbler. Access via Cobbler Lake Road, which is a continuation of Upper Rose River Road, off Whitfield-Myrtleford Road. High clearance 2WD vehicles and off-road camper trailers from the north (Whitfield-Myrtleford Road). 4WD access from the south via Little Cobbler Track off Speculation Road from Circuit Road. Water from lake, boil or treat first. Near shelter hut. Bring firewood.
GPS S:37 02.978 E:146 37.573
MR: Map 10 J2

Lake Cobbler

King Hut camping area

Located 35km east of Mt Stirling on King Basin Road near King River. 4WD access via Speculation Road which is signposted off Circuit Road, 6km east of Craig's Hut turn off. Then 7km north to hut and camping in the hut's vicinity. Water from river, boil or treat first. Horseyards. Bring firewood.
GPS S:37 05.283 E:146 34.341
MR: Map 10 I2

Pineapple Flat camping area

Located 10km north of Mt Stirling beside the King River. 4WD access via King Basin Road off Circuit Road, west of Craig's Hut turn off. Signposted access off King Basin Road 10km north-east of Circuit Road. Then in 700m to large shaded camping area. Crossing of King River required. Water from river, boil or treat first. Bring firewood.
GPS S:37 03.953 E:146 29.955
MR: Map 10 I1

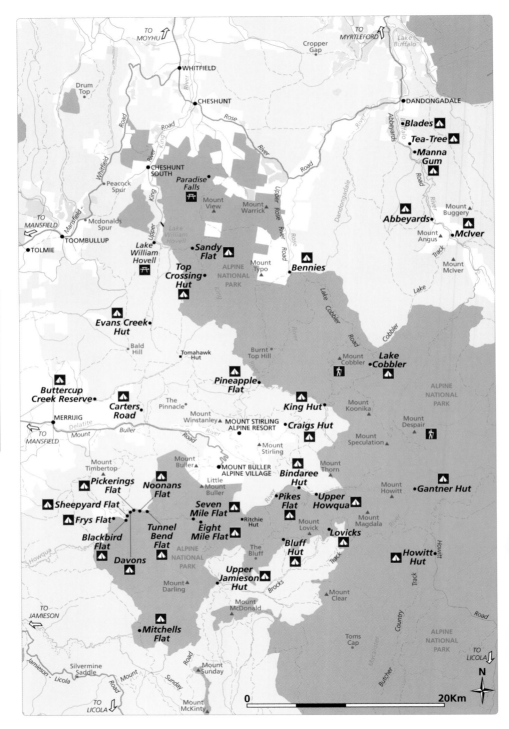

TO
MOYHU

TO
MYRTLEFORD

Lake
Buffalo

Cropper
Gap

WHITFIELD

Drum
Top

CHESHUNT

DANDONGADALE

Blades

Tea-Tree

Manna
Gum

CHESHUNT
SOUTH

Paradise
Falls

Peacock
Spur

Mount
View

Mount
Warrick

Abbeyards

Mount
Buggery

Mcdonalds
Spur

TO
MANSFIELD

TOOMBULLUP

Lake
William
Hovell

Mount
Angus

McIver

TOLMIE

Sandy
Flat

Mount
Typo

Bennies

Mount
McIver

Top
Crossing
Hut

ALPINE
NATIONAL
PARK

Evans Creek
Hut

Bald
Hill

Tomahawk
Hut

Burnt
Top Hill

Lake
Cobbler

ALPINE
NATIONAL
PARK

Mount
Cobbler

Lake
Cobbler

Buttercup
Creek Reserve

MERRIJIG

Carters
Road

The
Pinnacle

Pineapple
Flat

King Hut

Mount
Koonika

Mount
Despair

TO
MANSFIELD

Mount
Winstanley

MOUNT STIRLING
ALPINE RESORT

Craigs Hut

Mount
Speculation

Mount
Timbertop

Mount
Buller

Mount
Stirling

Bindaree
Hut

Mount
Thorn

Gantner Hut

Pickerings
Flat

Noonans
Flat

MOUNT BULLER
ALPINE VILLAGE

Little
Mount
Buller

Pikes
Flat

Upper
Howqua

Mount
Howitt

Sheepyard Flat

Seven
Mile Flat

Ritchie
Hut

Mount
Magdala

Frys Flat

Tunnel
Bend
Flat

Eight
Mile Flat

Mount
Lovick

Lovicks

Blackbird
Flat

ALPINE
NATIONAL
PARK

The
Bluff

Bluff
Hut

Howitt
Hut

Davons

Upper
Jamieson
Hut

Brocks

Mount
Darling

Mount
Clear

TO
JAMIESON

Mitchells
Flat

Mount
McDonald

ALPINE
NATIONAL
PARK

TO
LICOLA

Silvermine
Saddle

Mount
Sunday

Toms
Cap

TO
LICOLA

TO
LICOLA

Mount
McKinty

0   20Km

N

Mansfield Region

Seven Mile Flat camping area

Signposted access along Brocks Road and then in 500m to vehicle based camping area and a walk-in area beside Howqua River. From the Mansfield-Mount Buller Road take the signposted Howqua Track, 19km east of Mansfield and follow it for 16km to Sheepyard Flat. Continue along Howqua Track, which becomes Brocks Road, for 9.6km to the signposted access. 4WD vehicle recommended. Suitable for off-road camper trailer. Bring drinking water and firewood.
GPS S:37 11.695 E:146 25.332
MR: Map 10 I3

Eight Mile Flat camping area

Signposted access along Brocks Road, 1.3km east of Seven Mile Flat CA, and then in 500m to large grassed area beside Howqua River. Some shady sites. Small creek crossing to negotiate to access campsites. 4WD vehicle recommended. Suitable for off-road camper trailer. Bring drinking water and firewood.
GPS S:37 11.882 E:146 25.757
MR: Map 10 I3

Upper Jamieson Hut camping area

Access track is off Brocks Road (on a sharp bend), 6.7km south of Eight Mile Gap and 1.2km west of the signposted turnoff to Low Saddle Road on Brocks Road. Then in 800m to the historic hut. Camping in its vicinity. There is a deep crossing of the Jamieson River to access the hut and camping area which may be impassable after rain. Bring drinking water and firewood.
GPS S:37 15.462 E:146 26.863
MR: Map 10 I3

Bluff Hut camping area

Accessed 12.5km along Bluff Link Road, which is signposted off Brocks Road at Eight Mile Gap, 19.2km east of Sheepyard Flat on Howqua Road. Bush campsites located 300m north of the hut. Horseyards. Bring drinking water and firewood.
GPS S:37 12.959 E:146 31.441
MR: Map 10 I3

Lovicks camping area

Located 6.5km east of Bluff Hut along Bluff Track, which is 300m from the junction of Bluff Track and Cairn Creek Track. Horseyards. Bring drinking water and firewood.
GPS S:37 12.400 E:146 34.637
MR: Map 10 J3

Upper Howqua camping area

Signposted access 9.9km along Bindaree Road, which is signposted off Circuit Road, 9.8km south of the signposted Craig's Hut turn-off. Then in 300m to camping area with two large campsites beside the river. Bring drinking water and firewood.
GPS S:37 10.405 E:146 33.740
MR: Map 10 I3

Bindaree Hut camping area

Signposted access along Bindaree Road, 300m west of access track to Upper Howqua CA. Then in 1.4km to the hut and very large camping area along the river flats beside the Howqua River. Bring drinking water and firewood.
GPS S:37 10.028 E:146 32.623
MR: Map 10 I3

Bindaree Hut

Pikes Flat camping area

Situated beside Howqua River, north of Bluff Link Road. From Bindaree Road at the signposted access track to Bindaree Hut continue along Bluff Link Road for 11.5km to the signposted access track

to Pikes Flat, then proceed north to dispersed bush camping on the flats beside the river. Bring drinking water and firewood.
MR: Map 10 I3

Mitchells Flat camping area

Situated beside Mitchell Creek at site of old homestead. Access from the west from Jamieson via the Jamieson-Licola Road. At 31.6km west of Jamieson take the signposted Mt Sunday Road and follow this for 11.9km to Y-junction. Keep left here on track signposted Mitchells Ck and follow this for 8.4km to the information board at Mitchells Flat. Tracks on the left and right lead to campsites along Mitchells Creek.

From the north, access is via Mitchells Track; which is accessed via Tobbaco Flat south of Howqua Hills Historic Area. This route is dry weather only as access track is steep and clay based. Access is also available from Steiners Road, which is off Howqua River Road off the Mansfield-Jamieson Road. NB: Off-road camper trailer access via the Mt Sunday Road from Jamieson route. Bring drinking water and firewood.

GPS S:37 18.133 E:146 21.505
MR: Map 10 I3

Mitchells Flat camping area

4WD & Walk-in bush camping

Numerous 4WD and walk-in only access campsites throughout the park, many in the vicinity of huts. Bush camping, no facilities. Follow Parks Vic Bush Camping regulations. Obtain large scale maps and contact Park Ranger for further details.

Heyfield Region

Wellington River camping areas

Numerous sites beside the Wellington River along Tamboritha Road. Sites are noted by numbered posts along Tamboritha Road, starting at 9.4km north of Licola and running north for 12km to the Lake Tali Karng car park. Water from river, boil or treat first. Bring drinking water and firewood. Facilities vary from site to site. Horseyards.
MR: Map 10 J5

Horseyard Flat camping area

Located 78km north-east of Licola. Signposted access via Moroka Road from Arbuckle Junction, 46.9km north-east of Licola. Camping area is 31km east of Arbuckle Junction. Access track leads in 300m to hut, then a further 300m to the large camping area. Water from river, boil or treat first. Bring drinking water and firewood.
GPS S:37 28.975 E:146 58.884
MR: Map 10 L5

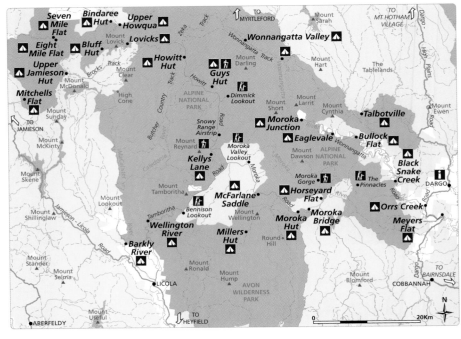

Moroka Bridge camping area

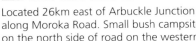

Located 26km east of Arbuckle Junction along Moroka Road. Small bush campsite on the north side of road on the western side of the river. Beside the road at

bridge over signposted Moroka River. Bush camping, no facilities. Bring drinking water.
Bridge **GPS** S:37 30.086 E:146 57.319
MR: Map 10 L5

HIGH COUNTRY

Moroka Hut

Moroka Hut camping area

Located 300m south of Moroka Road via walking track. Car park and signposted walk-in access is 24km east of Arbuckle Junction along Moroka Road. Large grassed camping area in vicinity of the hut. Bush camping, no facilities. Bring drinking water and firewood.
Car park **GPS** S:37 30.324 E:146 55.937
MR: Map 10 L5

McFarlane Saddle camping area

Located 12km east of Arbuckle Junction. Signposted access along Moroka Road. Bush camping, no facilities. Suitable for an overnight stop. Bring drinking water and firewood.
GPS S:37 28.476 E:146 50.963
MR: Map 10 K4

Millers Hut camping area

Located 5km south-west of Mt Wellington summit and 12.3km south-west of Moroka Road. Seasonal access/ 4WD access via Mt Wellington Track which is signposted off Moroka Road, 17km east of Arbuckle Junction. Bush camping in hut vicinity. No facilities. Bring drinking water.
GPS S:37 32.387 E:146 49.337
MR: Map 10 K5

Kellys Lane camping areas

Dispersed bush camping along Kellys Lane on edge of Holmes Plains. Kellys Lane is signposted along Howitt Road, 4.6km north-west of Arbuckle Junction.
MR: Map 10 K4

Guys Hut camping area

Walk-in access 1km along Bryce's Gorge Walk. Car park is signposted along Howitt Road, 18km north of Arbuckle Junction and 12km south of Howitt Hut. Bring drinking water. Gas/fuel stove preferred.
Car park **GPS** S:37 17.753 E:146 45.624
MR: Map 10 K3

Howitt Hut

Howitt Hut camping area

Signposted access along Howitt Road, 30km north of Arbuckle Junction. Located beside Caledonia River. Camping in hut vicinity. Bring drinking water and firewood. Horseyards.
GPS S:37 13.887 E:146 41.882
MR: Map 10 J3

Gantner Hut camping area

Walk-in access along Mt Howitt Walking Track. Car park is signposted along Howitt Road, 3.6km west of Howitt Hut. Camping in hut vicinity. Bring drinking water. Gas/fuel stove preferred.
Car park **GPS** S:37 12.303 E:146 40.813
MR: Map 10 J2

Lake Tali Karng camping area

Located near The Sentinels. Walk in access, 12km from McFarlane Saddle on Moroka Road, which is 12km east of Arbuckle Junction. Bring drinking water. Gas/fuel stove only.
MR: Map 10 K5

Barkly River camping area

Bush camping near bridge over Barkly River, 14.5km north-west of Licola. From Licola proceed in north-westerly direction towards Jamieson. At 8.8km veer right (east) into the signposted Link Road and follow for 5.7km to the river and camping area. Access road is narrow and steep. Suitable for camper trailers with 4WD tow vehicle. Bring drinking water and firewood.
GPS S:37 33.532 E:146 34.087
MR: Map 10 J5

HIGH COUNTRY

Bullock Flat camping area

Located 43km north-west of Dargo beside Wonnangatta River. From Black Snake CA (see page 244), continue along Crooked River Road (Wonnangatta Road) in a north-westerly direction for a further 22km to the signposted access. Bring drinking water and firewood.
GPS S:37 22.480 E:147 03.404
MR: Map 10 L4

Eaglevale camping area

Located 50km north-west of Dargo beside Wonnangatta River. Signposted access along the Wonnangatta Road (Crooked River Road) at the junction of signposted Eaglevale Track. Bring drinking water and firewood.
GPS S:37 22.126 E:147 00.454
MR: Map 10 L4

Moroka Junction camping area

Located 62km north-west of Dargo and west of Eaglevale CA along Moroka Junction Track, which is accessed off Wonnangatta Road (Crooked River Road). Situated beside Wonnangatta River, 1km east of its junction with Moroka River.
MR: Map 10 L4

Wonnangatta Valley camping area

Large secluded valley beside the Wonnangatta River with numerous riverside campsites. Located north-west of Dargo and east of Howitt Road. There are numerous access tracks into the valley. Popular routes include:

- From Howitt Road take Zeka Spur Track (steep, narrow track), which is signposted 2.2km north of Howitt Hut, this junction is 80km north of Licola.
- From Dargo proceed south towards Bairnsdale and at 5.9km take signposted Short Cut Road, which leads 2.2km to a T-intersection. Turn right here, this is Crooked River Road (Wonnangatta Road). Follow this for 41.8km and then veer into the signposted Eaglevale Tk. From Eaglevale Track take the signposted Wombat Range Track at 4.4km and follow this for 28.5km to the valley. It is also possible to access Wonnangatta Valley via Herne Spur Track off Eaglevale Track. Both Wombat Range Track and Herne Spur Track are steep.
- From Myrtleford proceed south along Buffalo River Road and Abbeyards Road for 54km to McIver CA and then continue in south-easterly direction along Abbeyards Road to East Buffalo Road and then Rileys Creek Track to Wonnangatta Valley, this is a total of 60km from McIver CA. NB: Drivers with limited 4WD experience and vehicles with off-road camper trailers should use this entrance route.

Bring drinking water and firewood.
GPS S:37 12.445 E:146 49.939
MR: Map 10 K3/L3

Wonnangatta Valley

HIGH COUNTRY

Bright Region

Beveridges Station camping area

Located beside Buckland River. Signposted access along Buckland Valley Road, 40km south of large roundabout on the Great Alpine Road at Porepunkah. Then in 200m to large grassed and well-shade camping area. Bring drinking water and firewood.
GPS S:36 59.128 E:146 57.402
MR: Map 10 L1

FURTHER Information

> **Parks Vic Info Line**
> **Tel:** 13 19 63

DAVIES HIGH PLAIN AREA

Located 55km north-east of Omeo near NSW border. Access from Benambra-Black Mountain Road or Beloka Road from Benambra or from Tom Groggin (NSW) with 4WD deepwater crossing of the Murray River. Mainly 4WD vehicle, walking and horse access. Remote area, be prepared. Many tracks have seasonal closures. Check with Parks Vic for details.

Dogman Hut camping area

Situated beside the Murray River. Signposted access along Tom Groggin Track, 1.6km north of the Murray River crossing to NSW and Tom Groggin. Deep crossing of Murray River, check crossing first. Murray River crossing is 3km west of the Alpine Way in Kosciuszko National Park in NSW. Off-road camper trailer access via Tom Groggin on the Alpine Way in NSW. Bring drinking water and firewood.
GPS S:36 32.267 E:148 07.972
MR: Map 12 G5

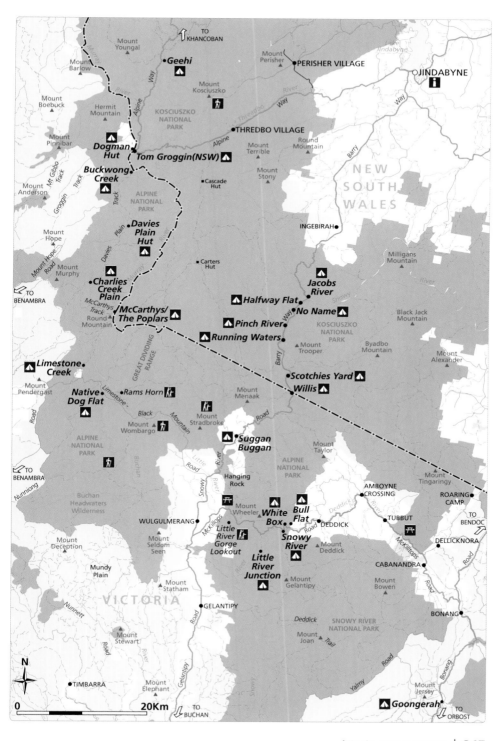

TO
KHANCOBAN

Mount
Youngal ▲

Mount
Barlow ▲

•Geehi

Mount
Perisher ▲
●PERISHER VILLAGE

OJINDABYNE
i

Mount
Boebuck ▲

Hermit
Mountain ▲

Mount
Kosciuszko ▲

Mount
Pinnibar ▲

KOSCIUSZKO
NATIONAL
PARK

●THREDBO VILLAGE

Mount
Terrible ▲

Round
Mountain ▲

NEW
SOUTH
WALES

Mt Gibbo Track

Dogman
Hut

Tom Groggin(NSW)

Mount
Stony ▲

Buckwong
Creek

ALPINE
NATIONAL
PARK

■ Cascade
Hut

Mount
Anderson ▲

Groggin

Davies
Plain Hut

Davies Plain

■ Carters
Hut

INGEBIRAH●

Milligans
Mountain ▲

Mount
Hope ▲

Mount
Murphy ▲

Charlies
Creek
Plain

McCarthys
Track

McCarthys/
The Poplars

Jacobs
River

Halfway Flat

No Name

KOSCIUSZKO
NATIONAL
PARK

Black Jack
Mountain ▲

Mount Hope Road

TO
BENAMBRA

Round
Mountain

Pinch River

Running Waters

Mount
Trooper ▲

Byadbo
Mountain ▲

Mount
Alexander ▲

GREAT DIVIDING RANGE

Limestone.
Creek

Limestone

•Rams Horn

Native
Dog Flat

Mount
Pendergast ▲

Black Mountain

Mount
Menaak ▲

Scotchies Yard

Willis

Mount
Stradbroke ▲

Mount
Wombargo ▲

ALPINE
NATIONAL
PARK

Buchan

Suggan
Buggan

ALPINE
NATIONAL
PARK

Mount
Taylor ▲

Mount
Tingaringy ▲

AMBOYNE
CROSSING●

ROARING
CAMP

TO
BENAMBRA

Buchan
Headwaters
Wilderness

Little
Road

Hanging
Rock

Mount
Wheeler ▲

White
Box

Bull
Flat

DEDDICK

TUBBUT●

TO
BENDOC

DELLICKNORA●

Nunniong

WULGULMERANG●

McKillops Road

Snowy River

Little
River
Gorge
Lookout

Snowy
River

Mount
Deddick ▲

CABANANDRA●

Mount
Deception ▲

Mount
Seldom Seen ▲

Little
River
Junction

Mount
Gelantipy ▲

Mount
Bowen ▲

BONANG●

Mundy
Plain

Mount
Statham ▲

●GELANTIPY

Deddick

Mount
Joan ▲

Trail

SNOWY RIVER
NATIONAL
PARK

VICTORIA

Mount
Stewart ▲

Mount
Elephant ▲

Nunnett

N

●TIMBARRA

Mount
Jersey ▲

TO
ORBOST

Goongerah

0   20Km

TO
BUCHAN

Buckwong Creek camping area

Small campsite beside creek suitable for one or two camps. Located 2.9km south of the Murray River crossing to NSW along Davies Plain Track, and 13.5km north of the access track to Davies Plain CA. Davies Plain Track is signposted on the Vic side of the Murray River crossing. Bring drinking water and firewood.
GPS S:36 34.286 E:148 07.777
MR: Map 12 G5

Davies Plain Hut camping area

Signposted access along Davies Plain Track, 16.4km south of the Murray River crossing to NSW and 15.5km north of the junction of Davies Plain Track and McCarthy Track. A large grassy area in the vicinity of the hut, encircled by snow gums. Horseyards. Bring drinking water.
GPS S:36 39.089 E:148 07.528
MR: Map 12 G5

Davies Plain Hut

Charlies Creek Plain camping area

Located along Davies Plain Track, 13km south of Davies Plain Hut and 2.5km north of the junction of Davies Plain Track and McCarthy Track. Open grassland amid snow gums. Bring drinking water and firewood.
GPS S:36 44.0300 E:148 03.773
MR: Map 12 G6

The Poplars/McCarthys camping area

Located along McCarthys Track, 1.2km east of its junction with Limestone Creek Track. This junction is 8.9km south-east of the Davies Plain Track and McCarthy Track junction and 15km north of the Limestone Creek Track and Black Mountain Road junction. Dispersed campsites beside the Murray River. Bring drinking water and firewood.
GPS S:36 46.579 E:148 06.471
MR: Map 12 G6

Limestone Creek camping area

Signposted access on Limestone Creek Track, 2.4km north of Black Mountain Road and 12.6km south of the junction of Limestone Creek Track and McCarthy Track. Large open area of grassland situated beside Limestone Creek. Bring drinking water and firewod.
GPS S:36 51.315 E:148 03.309
MR: Map 12 F7

Buenba Flat camping area

Located 45km north-east of Benambra near Buenba Creek on Beloka Road. From Benambra proceed in easterly direction along the signposted Limestone Road for 15.9km, then turn left (north) into the signposted Beloka Road. Follow Beloka Road for 22km to where it becomes Buenba Road and continue along Buenba Road for a further 6.9km to a bridge over Buenba Creek. Tracks on left and right before the bridge, and track on right over the bridge lead to dispersed bush campsites. Use of portable chemical toilet is encouraged here.
GPS S:36 42.028 E:147 55.278
MR: Map 12 F7

4WD & Walk-in bush camping

Numerous 4WD and walk-in only access campsites throughout the park, many in the vicinity of huts. Bush camping, no facilities. Follow Parks Vic Bush Camping regulations. Obtain large scale maps and contact Park Ranger for further details.

FURTHER Information

Parks Vic Info Line
Tel: 13 19 63

COBBERAS - TINGARINGY AREA

Located 450km north-east of Melbourne and 60km north-east of Omeo. Access from south via Gelantipy Road from Buchan. From east via McKillops Road from Bonang, via Barry Way from north (NSW) or Benambra-Black Mountain Road from the west. Remote area, be prepared. Use of gas/fuel stove preferred.

Native Dog Flat camping area

Located 50km east of Benambra beside Buchan River along Black Mountain Road. Access signposted. Separate horse camping area. Water from river, boil or treat first. Bring drinking water and firewood.
GPS S:36 53.748 E:148 05.388
MR: Map 12 G7

Willis camping area

Signposted access 1km south of the NSW/Vic border. Access from the north is via the Barry Way, 75km south of Jindabyne. Access from the south is via Snowy River Road, 90km north of Buchan. Camping near Snowy River. Bring drinking water and firewood. NB: Stay to defined tracks, do not create new tracks.
GPS S:36 53.253 E:148 25.194
MR: Map 12 H7

4WD & Walk-in bush camping

Numerous 4WD and walk-in only access campsites throughout the park, many in the vicinity of huts. Bush camping, no facilities. Follow Parks Vic Bush Camping regulations. Obtain large scale maps and contact Park Ranger for further details.

FURTHER Information

Parks Vic Info Line
Tel: 13 19 63

Willis camping area

OMEO REGION

Ferny Flat camping area

Signposted access along Kellys Road, 26km north of Omeo. From Omeo proceed in a northerly direction along the Omeo Highway towards Mitta Mitta for 7.1km, then turn right (north) into road signposted Omeo Valley. Follow this road for a further 18.9km to the signposted access, where a number of tracks lead to bush campsites beside the Mitta Mitta River. Self-sufficient campers. Bring drinking water and firewood.
GPS S:36 53.599 E:147 37.885
MR: Map 12 D7

Anglers Rest camping area

Located 29km north of Omeo near Cobungra River along the Omeo Highway. Bring drinking water and firewood.
MR: Map 12 C8

Joker Flat camping area

Located 38km north of Omeo near Mitta Mitta River along the Omeo Highway. Bring drinking water and firewood.
MR: Map 12 C7

Ah Sye's camping area

Located 30km north of Benambra. Signposted access along the Benambra-Corryong Road south of Exhibition Creek. Large open area, well grassed with some shade. Bring drinking water and firewood.
GPS S:36 43.876 E:147 43.945
MR: Map 12 E6

Gibbo River bush camping area

Located 26km north of Benambra beside the Gibbo River. Access track is unsignposted. No facilities, self-sufficient campers. Very large open area beside the river. Bring drinking water and firewood.
GPS S:36 45.410 E:147 41.942
MR: Map 12 E6

FURTHER Information

> **Parks Vic Info Line**
> **Tel:** 13 19 63
> **Parks Vic Omeo**
> **Tel:** 03 5159 1660

HIGH COUNTRY

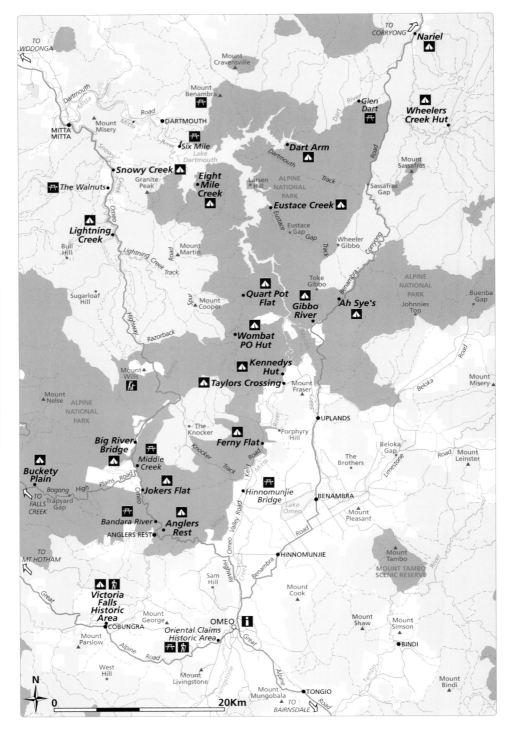

TO WODONGA

TO CORRYONG

Nariel

Mount Cravensville

Dartmouth

Mitta

Mitta

Dartmouth Road

MITTA MITTA

Mount Misery

DARTMOUTH

Mount Benambra

River

Glen Dart

Wheelers Creek Hut

Six Mile

Lake Dartmouth

Dart Arm

Dartmouth

River

Road

Mount Sassafras

Snowy Creek

Eight Mile Creek

Granite Peak

Larsen Hill

ALPINE NATIONAL PARK

Track

Sassafras Gap

The Walnuts

Eustace Creek

Eustace

Gap

Eustace Gap

Wheeler Gibbo

Corryong

Lightning Creek

Bull Hill

Lightning Creek Track

Mount Martin

Road

Benambra

ALPINE NATIONAL PARK

Buenba Gap

Sugarloaf Hill

Spur

Highway

Mount Cooper

Razorback

Quart Pot Flat

Toke Gibbo

Gibbo River

Ah Sye's

Johnnies Top

Wombat PO Hut

River

Mount Wills

Kennedys Hut

Taylors Crossing

Mount Fraser

Beloka

Mount Misery

Mount Nelse

ALPINE NATIONAL PARK

The Knocker

Creek

UPLANDS

Mount Leinster

Road

Big River Bridge

Middle Creek

Knocker Track

Ferny Flat

Porphyry Hill

Kelly Road

The Brothers

Beloka Gap

Road

Buckety Plain

Bogong

High

Plains Road

Omeo

Jokers Flat

Mitta

Hinnomunjie Bridge

BENAMBRA

Limestone

TO FALLS CREEK

Trapyard Gap

Bandara River

ANGLERS REST

Anglers Rest

Lake Omeo

Mount Pleasant

TO MT HOTHAM

Omeo Valley Road

HINNOMUNJIE

Benambra Road

Mount Tambo

MOUNT TAMBO SCENIC RESERVE

River

Great

Sam Hill

Highway

Creek

Mount Cook

Victoria Falls Historic Area

COBUNGRA

Mount George

OMEO

Oriental Claims Historic Area

Great

Mount Shaw

Mount Simson

BINDI

Mount Parslow

Alpine Road

West Hill

Mount Livingstone

Livingstone

Mount Mungobala

Alpine Road

TONGIO

TO BAIRNSDALE

Tambo River

Mount Bindi

N

0   20Km

LAKE DARTMOUTH AREA

Located 50km north of Omeo near Mitta Mitta. Access from Omeo Highway in west or Benambra-Corryong Road from east. Mainly 4WD vehicle, some tracks have seasonal closures. Remote area, be prepared. Check with Parks Vic for details.

Taylors Crossing camping area

4WD access from the west via Four Mile Creek Track off Kellys Road. From Ferny Flat CA proceed in a northerly direction 7.5km to junction and keep right on signposted Wombat Track. At a further 1.8km arrive at junction with signposted Four Mile Creek Track. Turn right into Four Mile Creek Track and follow for 5km to the camping area on the western bank of the Mitta Mitta River. Carry in gear over bollards to campsites. Conventional vehicle access is possible to the eastern bank of river via Table Lands Road, which is signposted 11km north of Benambra along the Corryong Road. Then carry in gear via suspension bridge to camping area. Toilets are located in the day use area on the eastern side of the river. Bring drinking water and firewood. Gas/fuel stove preferred.
GPS S:36 49.576 E:147 39.581
MR: Map 12 D7

Taylors Crossing Riverside camping area

Dispersed bush camping on the eastern banks of the Mitta Mitta River, 400m south of the day use area. Access is via Table Lands Road, 11km north of Benambra along the Corryong Road. Toilets are located in the day use area. Bring drinking water and firewood. Gas/fuel stove preferred.
GPS S:36 49.874 E:147 39.554
MR: Map 12 D7

Kennedys Hut camping area

Located on JP Gap Track, 500m north of its junction with Four Mile Creek Track. JP Gap Track is signposted 4.1km along Four Mile Creek Track from its junction with Kellys Road. See Taylors Crossing CA access details. Camping in hut vicinity. Bring drinking water and firewood.
GPS S:36 48.975 E:147 39.478
MR: Map 12 D6

Wombat PO Hut camping area

Located north of the junction of Wombat Creek Track and Four Mile Creek Track. Four Mile Creek Track is accessed from Kellys Road (see Taylors Crossing CA). Turn north onto Four Mile Creek Track and follow this for 8.4km to the junction with Wombat Creek Track. From Mitta Mitta proceed south along the Omeo Highway, then at 11.9km turn left (east) into the signposted Hollaways Log Road. Follow this for 10.2km then turn right (south) onto the signposted Razorback Spur Tk and follow this 21.8km to turn into the signposted Wombat Ck Tk through a seasonal closure gate. After 5.4km the track drops steeply to Wombat Creek and at a total of 8.8km from the turn-off the track meets with signposted Four Mile Creek Track. Bring drinking water and firewood.
GPS S:36 46.323 E:147 35.685
MR: Map 12 D6

Quartpot Flat camping area

Located 45km south-east of Mitta Mitta near Mt Cooper. Access via Limestone Gap Track. Limestone Gap Track is signposted off Razorback Spur Track, 16.4km from its junction with Hollaways Log Road. Bring drinking water and firewood.
MR: Map 12 D6

4WD & Walk-in bush camping

Numerous 4WD and walk-in only access campsites throughout the park, many in the vicinity of huts. Bush camping - no facilities. Follow Parks Vic Bush Camping regulations. Obtain large scale maps and contact Park Ranger for further details.

FURTHER Information

Parks Vic Info Line
Tel: 13 19 63

---

188 Avondale Gardens Reserve

This scenic reserve is located south of the Murray Valley Highway and is the site where Mrs Peg Bird established an exotic garden in the 1950s when her and her husband moved to the area to farm. Encountering ongoing adverse farming conditions in the area, the Birds sold Avondale in 1962 to the Forests Commission. The original homestead and buildings have been removed, however the beautiful garden remains and small plaques identify the plants. Access to the reserve is via the signposted Avondale Road off the highway at the locality of Shelley, 6.5km east of Koetong.

Avondale Gardens camping area

From the Murray Valley Highway take signposted Avondale Road south for 9.9km to the road signposted to Avondale Gardens. Turn left (east) and follow this road for 1.3km and then turn at the signposted access to Avondale Reserve, which leads 400m to the gardens. Unsealed access roads. A picnic area is located at the northern end of the gardens. Camping is possible in the orchard at the southern end of the gardens. Bring drinking water. NB: Fires only in fireplaces provided, which are in the picnic area at the northern end. Gas/ fuel stove preferred.

GPS S:36 14.356 E:147 31.497

MR: Map 12 D2

FURTHER Information

> **DSE Customer Service Centre**
> **Tel:** 13 61 86
> **Corryong Tourist**
> **Information Centre**
> **Tel:** 02 6076 2277

189 Biggara Valley

Located beside the Murray River south east of Corryong. Access via Upper Murray Road off the Corryong-Khancoban Road. Popular fishing area.

Indi Bridge Reserve camping area

Camping and picnic area located beside the Murray River. Signposted access along Upper Murray Road, 4km south of Towong Upper. Bring drinking water and firewood.

MR: Map 12 F3

Bunroy Junction camping area

Located beside Murray River along Bunroy Creek Track, which is accessed off Bunroy Road off Upper Murray Road, 4km south of the access to Indi Bridge Reserve. Bring drinking water and firewood. Located on edge of Alpine National Park.

MR: Map 12 F3

Hairpin Bend camping area

Located beside Murray River south of Bunroy Junction CA along Indi River Track, off Bunroy Creek Track. Bring drinking water and firewood. Located on edge of Alpine National Park.

MR: Map 12 F3

FURTHER Information

> **Corryong Tourist**
> **Information Centre**
> **Tel:** 02 6076 2277

Located 22km south-west of Bright beside the Buckland River. Gold fever found its way to the remote valley in the early 1850s, however later that decade fierce racial riots broke out between European and Chinese miners, creating mayhem in the once tranquil valley. Access is along the signposted Buckland Valley Road, off the Great Alpine Road at the large round-about at Porepunkah. The unsealed Buckland Valley Road can be rough and pot holed at times.

Maguire Point camping area

Signposted access along Buckland Valley Road, 18.3km south of the Great Alpine Way. Large grassed area beside river. Bring drinking water.
GPS S:36 50.574 E:146 51.020
MR: Map 10 9 K8

Buckland Valley bush camping areas

Camping is permitted between Buckland Valley Road and west of Buckland River, except on areas of private land. Access tracks along Buckland Valley Road lead

to bush campsites beside the river with the first track at 19.8km south of Great Alpine Way (this is 1.5km south of Maguire Point CA) and the last track is at 36.8km south of Great Alpine Way (17km south of the first access track) and 800m north of the Alpine National Park boundary. Self-sufficient campers. Use of portable chemical toilets encouraged. Bring drinking water and firewood.
First access track – **GPS** S:36 51.205 E:146 51.518
Last access track – **GPS** S:36 57.812 E:146 55.905
MR: Map 9 L8 and Map 10 L1

FURTHER Information

> **DSE Customer Service Centre**
> **Tel:** 13 61 86
> **DSE Ovens**
> **Tel:** 03 5731 1222

Located 35km south of Myrtleford beside the Buffalo River. Access is via the unsealed Abbeyards Road which is signposted off the Buffalo River Road, 32km south of Myrtleford. The river is popular for trout and blackfish fishing. The region is also popular for four-wheel drive touring and provides one of the easier access routes into Wonnangatta Valley.

Blades, Tea-Tree, Manna Gum, Abbeyards and McIver picnic and camping areas

Signposted access along Abbeyards Road. Bring drinking water and firewood. Blades: 2.8km south of Buffalo River Road. Tea-Tree: 2.2km south of Blades. Manna Gum: 1.2km south of Tea-Tree.

Abbeyards: 12.8km south of Manna Gum. McIver: 2.1km south of Abbeyards.
McIver – **GPS** S:36 55.699 E:146 43.107
MR: Map 9 J8/K8 and Map 10 K1

FURTHER Information

> **DSE Customer Service Centre**
> **Tel:** 13 61 86
> **DSE Ovens**
> **Tel:** 03 5731 1222

HIGH COUNTRY

Located 120km east of Wodonga and north-west of Corryong. The camping areas are located in the east of the park and are best accessed via the Cudgewa North Road, which is accessed off the Cudgewa-Tintaldra Road, 11.9km south-west of the C546 (Murray River Road) at Tintaldra and 15km north-east of the B400 (Murray Valley Highway via Cudgewa). Explore one of the parks marked walking tracks, take in the views to the Snowy Mountains from a lookout, visit Bluff Falls or go four-wheel drive touring.

Bluff Creek camping area

From Cudgewa-Tintaldra Road take the signposted Cudgewa North Road and follow this north-west for 5.3km to the signposted Bluff Falls Road. Bluff Falls Road leads 3.7km to the camping area. There are five sites here: sites 1, 2 and 5 are suitable for camper trailers or a small van; sites 3 and 4 are suitable for tent based camping or a small campervan. These sites are fuel stove only sites, no fires. The camping area is well grassed and has good shade. Bring firewood.
GPS S:36 07.340 E:147 46.656
MR: Map 12 E2

Bluff Creek camping area

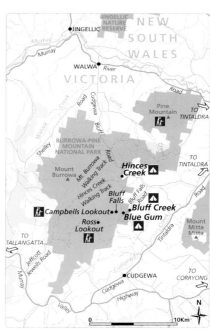

Blue Gum camping area

From Bluff Creek CA continue along Bluff Falls Road for 700m to the signposted access track which leads in 100m to the small camping area with three sites. All-wheel drive vehicle recommended as there are a couple of rocky creek crossings to access the camping area. Bring firewood.
GPS S:36 07.479 E:147 46.180
MR: Map 12 E2

HIGH COUNTRY

Hinces Creek camping area

Located on Hinces Creek Track which is signposted off Cudgewa North Road, 3.3km north-west of Bluff Falls Road. Then 600m to the camping area with two small sites beside Hinces Creek. Well grassed and shaded. Bring drinking water and firewood.

GPS S:36 05.145 E:147 46.058
MR: Map 12 E2

FURTHER Information

> **Parks Vic Info Line**
> **Tel:** 13 19 63

193 Buttercup Creek Reserve

Located 24km east of Mansfield. Conventional vehicle and caravan access via Carter's Road off the Mansfield-Mount Buller Road, 13km east of Merrijig. Access also via Buttercup Road, 13km east of Mansfield. Check road conditions for this route. Five sites beside Buttercup Creek. Good base to explore surrounding areas. Activities include bushwalking, fishing, mountain bike riding and four-wheel drive touring.

Buttercup Creek camping areas – sites 1 to 5

Each site is signposted along Buttercup Road. Site number 1 is 11.2km north-east of the Mansfield-Mount Buller Road along Buttercup Road, and site number 5 is 700m west of Carters Road. Facilities may vary at sites. Toilets located at sites 2, 3 and 4. Each site is a cleared, grassy area beside the creek. Bring drinking water and firewood.

Site 1 – **GPS** S:37 04.880 E:146 19.293
Site 2 – **GPS** S:37 04.831 E:146 19.601
Site 3 – **GPS** S:37 04.130 E:146 20.340
Site 4 – **GPS** S:37 04.094 E:146 20.444
Site 5 – **GPS** S:37 03.926 E:146 21.325
MR: Map 10 H2

FURTHER Information

> **DSE Customer Service Centre**
> **Tel:** 13 61 86

Chiltern-Mt Pilot National Park comprises of a number of sections. The section surrounding the township of Chiltern is accessible via Chiltern off the Hume Highway; and the other section is south of Chiltern. This is accessible via the Chiltern-Beechworth Road. The park is home to the Woolshed Falls, most spectacular after rain, and the Mt Pilot Range. Take in the views from Mt Pilot Lookout, tour along the 25km long Chiltern Tourist Drive, or visit the Yeddonba Aboriginal Cultural Site and the old mining sites. Other activities include bushwalking, cycling, bird and nature watching, prospecting and photography.

Reedy Creek camping area

Dispersed bush camping along Woolshed Road. Woolshed Road is accessed off the Beechworth-Chiltern Road, 7km north of Beechworth and south-east of Eldorado via Main Street. Numerous access tracks lead off Woolshed Road to bush campsites beside the creek. Tracks start at 2.6km east of Eldorado and 5km west of Woolshed Falls. No facilities, self-sufficient campers. Bring drinking water and firewood.
Track at western end
– **GPS** S:36 19.152 E:146 32.563
Track at eastern end
– **GPS** S:36 18.793 E:146 35.618
MR: Map 9 J4

FURTHER Information

> **Parks Vic Info Line**
> **Tel:** 13 19 63

The village of Dargo is located 50km north-west of Bairnsdale and is reached via the bitumen Lindenow-Dargo road from Bairnsdale. Access from the north is via the gravel Dargo High Plains Road from The Great Alpine Road at Mount St Bernard. The surrounding areas of Dargo are popular four-wheel drive touring areas.

Orrs Creek campsite

Signposted access along the Dargo-Bairnsdale Road 7.1km south of Dargo. Small site on the western side of road. Bring drinking water and firewood.
GPS S:37 29.651 E:147 12.081
MR: Map 13 B3

Meyers Flat campsite

Signposted access along the Dargo-Bairnsdale Road, 12.6km south of Dargo and 5.5km south of Orrs Creek CS and 18.6km north of the signposted Freestone Ck Road. Large grassed stretch of land between the road and river.
GPS S:37 30.995 E:147 13.902
MR: Map 13 B3

HIGH COUNTRY

Black Snake Creek camping area

Located 21km west of Dargo beside Wonnangatta River. From Dargo proceed south towards Bairnsdale and at 5.9km take signposted Short Cut Road, which leads 2.2km to a T-intersection. Turn right here, this is Crooked River Road (Wonnangatta Road). Follow this for 12.9km to the access track to camping area. Bring drinking water and firewood. NB: this area is adjacent to Alpine National Park, be aware of your pet.
GPS S:37 26.796 E:147 08.404
MR: Map 13 B3

DARGO HIGH PLAINS

25 Mile Creek camping area

Small site beside creek on Ritchie Road, 10km west of Dargo High Plains Road. Ritchie Road is signposted off Dargo High Plains Road, 45km north of Dargo. Dry weather access only. Bring drinking water and firewood.
MR: Map 13 B1

30 Mile Creek camping area

Small site beside creek on Ritchie Road, 12km west of 25 Mile Creek CA. Dry weather access only. Bring drinking water and firewood.
MR: Map 13 A1

UPPER DARGO ROAD

Upper Dargo Road leaves the Dargo High Plains Road 5.7km north of Dargo. This is a narrow, winding road and caution is required, especially if towing.

Two Mile Creek camping area

Located 2km along Upper Dargo Road, near Two Mile Creek. Bring drinking water and firewood.
GPS S:37 24.533 E:147 15.473
MR: Map 13 B3

Italian Flat camping area

Signposted access 2.9km along Upper Dargo Road. Bring drinking water and firewood.
GPS S:37 24.523 E:147 15.914
MR: Map 13 B3

Black Flat camping area

Signposted access 10.9km along Upper Dargo Road. Bring drinking water and firewood.
GPS S:37 21.861 E:147 17.575
MR: Map 13 B2

Italian Flat camping area

Jimmy Iversons camping area

Signposted access 4.2km along Upper Dargo Road. Steepish clay based access track. Bring drinking water and firewood.
GPS S:37 23.941 E:147 16.277
MR: Map 13 B3

Ollies Jump-Up camping area

Signposted access 6.8km along Upper Dargo Road. Bring drinking water and firewood.
GPS S:37 23.134 E:147 16.608
MR: Map 13 B3

Collins Flat camping area

Signposted access 15.8km along Upper Dargo Road. Bring drinking water and firewood.
GPS S:37 20.356 E:147 17.830
MR: Map 13 B2

FURTHER Information

> **DSE Dargo**
> **Tel:** 03 5140 1243

196 Dogs Grave

This monument to the relationship between man and his 'best friend' is located south-west of Omeo and signposted along Birregun Road. From The Great Alpine Road take Cassilis Road south of Omeo and proceed south for 7km to the signposted Upper Livingstone Road, which leads 7km to the signposted Birregun Road.

Dogs Grave camping area

Signposted access 6km along Birregun Road from Upper Livingstone Road. A small sheltered site. Bring drinking water and firewood.
GPS S:37 14.024 E:147 22.860
MR: Map 13 C1

FURTHER Information

> **DSE Swifts Creek**
> **Tel:** 03 5159 5100

197 Grant Historic Area

Grant Historic Area is accessed via McMillan Road. This road is signposted off the Dargo High Plains Road, 16.8km north of Dargo. This area was once a thriving gold mining town during the late 1800s. Walk the heritage trail to the Jolly Sailor Mine, visit the old cemetery and the water-filled tunnel of the Jeweller Shop Mine.

Grant camping area

Located 5.6km north-west of Dargo High Plains Road. Access signposted along McMillan Track. Located at site of the old township of Grant. Bring drinking water and firewood.
GPS S:37 20.637 E:147 09.340
MR: Map 13 B2

Talbotville camping areas

Dispersed camping at Talbotville beside Crooked River, 16km along McMillan Track from Dargo High Plains Road. Steep unsealed access track is suitable for conventional vehicles in dry weather and for off-road camper trailers with 4WD tow vehicle. Large grassed riverflats on the east and western banks of the river. Water from river, boil or treat first. Bring firewood.
GPS S:37 20.028 E:147 04.038
MR: Map 13 A2

Talbotville camping area

4WD & Walk-in bush camping

Numerous 4WD and walk-in only access campsites throughout the area, notably beside Crooked River. Bush camping, no facilities. Follow Parks Vic Bush Camping regulations. Obtain large scale maps and contact Park Ranger for further details.

FURTHER Information

> **Parks Vic Info Line**
> **Tel:** 13 19 63

198 Haunted Stream

Located 25km south of Swifts Creek. Access from Swifts Creek is via the road to Cassilis, then taking the Brookville Road to Angora Range Road. From this junction access can be made by continuing on Brookville Road which becomes Dorothy Cutting and then take Boomerang Spur Track (steep clay based track) or take Angora Range Road then Dawson City Track. Angora Range Road can also be accessed off the Great Alpine Road at Wattle Circle 10km south of Ensay, or alternatively take Haunted Stream Track off the Great Alpine Road 6km south of Wattle Circle. This area is a popular 4WD and trail bike touring area. Haunted Stream is a tributary of the Tambo River, and gold was discovered in the area in the late 1850s.

Haunted Stream bush camping area

Dispersed bush camping beside Haunted Stream and at old township sites of Stirling, Dogtown and Dawson City, accessed along Haunted Stream Track. Tracks in the area have seasonal closures.
Dawson City – **GPS** S:37 23.248 E:147 37.070
Dog Town – **GPS** S:37 25.951 E:147 43.269
MR: Map 13 D3-E3

FURTHER Information

> **DSE Customer Service Centre**
> **Tel:** 13 61 86

199 Howqua Hills Historic Area

Howqua Hills Historic Area is located 35km south-east of Mansfield. Access via signposted Howqua Track off Mansfield-Mount Buller Road, 18.7km east of Mansfield. The unsealed Howqua Track is narrow and winding in places and can be rough at times, and is not recommended for caravans. Historic gold mining area. Explore relics from this era including the brick chimney of the Great Rand Mine, water race and tunnel. Visit Fry's Hut on Fry's Flat. Popular camping and four-wheel drive touring area. There are numerous campsites beside the Howqua River.

Blackbird Flat camping area

Signposted access along Howqua Track, 16.2km south of Mansfield-Mount Buller Road, then in 200m to scattered bush campsites among trees by the river. Bring drinking water and firewood.
GPS S:37 11.674 E:146 20.715
MR: Map 10 H2

Sheepyard Flat camping area

Signposted access along Howqua Track, 200m east of Blackbird Flat. Large area on both sides of the track beside the river with some shady trees. Very popular. Bring drinking water and firewood.
GPS S:37 11.621 E:146 20.796
MR: Map 10 H3

Davons camping area

Signposted access along Howqua Track, 600m east of Sheepyard Flat. Well shaded area beside the river. Bring drinking water and firewood. Horseyards.
GPS S:37 11.350 E:146 20.979
MR: Map 10 H3

Pickerings Flat camping area

Signposted access along Howqua Track, 400m east of Davons. Very large area stretched along the river. Private hut (locked). Bring drinking water and firewood.
GPS S:37 11.223 E:146 21.194
MR: Map 10 J3

HIGH COUNTRY

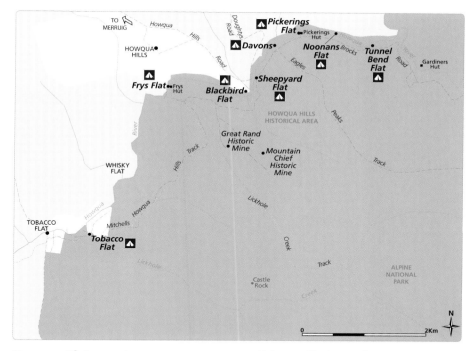

Noonans Flat camping area

Signposted access along Howqua Track, 700m east of Pickerings Flat. Then in 100m to camping area set above the river. Private hut (locked). Seasonal closure applies to access track. Bring drinking water and firewood.
GPS S:37 11.220 E:146 21.651
MR: Map 10 J3

Tunnel Bend Flat camping area

Signposted access along Howqua Track, 400m east of Noonans Flat. Large open area beside the river with some shady trees. Bring drinking water and firewood.
GPS S:37 11.255 E:146 22.136
MR: Map 10 J3

Tobacco Flat camping area

Access via Sheepyard Flat. Proceed through Sheepyard Flat for 2km to junction then turn left into track signposted Tobacco Flat. Follow this for 1.6km to the signposted access track. Dispersed bush camping on open flat beside river. Seasonal closure applies to access track. Bring drinking water and firewood.
GPS S:37 13.050 E:146 18.961
MR: Map 10 H3

Frys Flat camping area

Access through Sheepyard Flat CA.
Proceed through camping area in
southerly direction for 2km to junction.
Turn right here and travel for 400m
to very large, grassed camping area in
the vicinity of the hut (NB: no camping
or overnighting in the hut) beside the
river. Seasonal closure applies to access
track. Horseyards. Bring drinking water
and firewood.
GPS S:37 11.739 E:146 19.798
MR: Map 10 H3

Frys Hut

200 Lake Dartmouth

**Located 20km west of Mitta Mitta. Access via Benambra-Corryong Road or
from Omeo Highway. All other areas 4WD vehicle access. The lake is surrounded
by Alpine National Park, with all campsites located within the park. Popular
fishing venue.**

Eustace Creek camping area

Located 55km north of Benambra beside
lake near Eustaces Gap Creek. Access
via Eustace Gap Road, which leaves the
Benambra-Corryong road at Sassafras
Gap. 4WD vehicle recommended. Boat
access also possible.
MR: Map 12 D5

Eight Mile Creek camping area

Boat access only. Located at Eight
Mile Creek on south-western reaches
of Lake Dartmouth.
MR: Map 12 D5

Dart Arm camping area

Boat access only. Located on southern
banks of Dart Arm, at the eastern reaches
of Lake Dartmouth.
MR: Map 12 D5

FURTHER Information

> **Goulburn-Murray Water
> (Dartmouth Dam)**
> **Tel:** 02 6072 4411
> **Parks Vic Info Line**
> **Tel:** 13 19 63

Forestry areas to the south, east and north of Mansfield. These forests provide excellent recreational opportunities such as mountain biking, horse riding, fishing as well as four-wheel drive and trail bike touring.

Grannys Flat camping reserve

Access signposted 7.8km east of Jamieson along the Jamieson-Licola Road, then in 800m to grassy camping area with shady trees. Steep access track, suitable for camper trailer with 4WD tow vehicle. Seasonal road closure applies. Bring drinking water and firewood.
GPS S:37 17.416 E:146 12.896
MR: Map 10 H3

Grannys Flat camping reserve

Wrens Flat camping reserve

From Jamieson follow the Jamieson-Licola Road for 32km to the signposted Mt Sunday Road/Wrens Flat. Take Mt Sunday Road and follow this for 11.6km to the camping area beside the road (this is 300m south of the Mt Sunday Rd and Mitchells Ck track junction). Bring drinking water and firewood.
GPS S:37 20.576 E:146 22.336
MR: Map 10 H3

Running Creek Reserve camping area

Accessed via Howqua River Road, which is signposted off the Jamieson-Mansfield Road, 13km north of Jamieson and 23km south of Mansfield. Follow Howqua River Road in an easterly direction for 7.8km to the signposted access to the large, well-shaded camping area beside the river. Access road is unsealed and narrow, suitable for conventional vehicles in dry weather and for small caravans with a 4WD tow vehicle. Bring drinking water and firewood.
GPS S:37 14.206 E:146 13.873
MR: Map 10 H3

HIGH COUNTRY

Blue Range Reserve camping area

Grassed sites on northern bank of Blue Range Creek. Located 4.3km along Blue Range Road, which is signposted off the Mansfield-Tolmie Road, 10km north of Mansfield and 16km west of Tolmie.

Facilities are located in the adjacent picnic area. Water from creek, boil or treat first. Bring drinking water and firewood.
GPS S:36 56.107 E:146 05.711
MR: Map 10 G1

FURTHER Information

> **DSE Customer Service Centre**
> **Tel:** 13 61 86

202 Mitta Mitta Area

The delightful village of Mitta Mitta is located on the Omeo Highway, 94km north of Omeo and 54km south of the Murray Valley Highway. The village is the eastern access point to Lake Dartmouth.

Snowy Creek camping area

South of Mitta Mitta beside Snowy Creek. From the Omeo Highway, 12km south of Mitta Mitta, take the signposted Hollaways Log Road and follow this east for 600m. Caravan access in dry weather only.
GPS S:36 35.845 E:147 26.297
MR: Map 12 C5

Lightning Creek camping area

Located south of Mitta Mitta beside Lightning Creek. Signposted access along the Omeo Highway 22km south of Mitta Mitta. Well-shaded site.
GPS S:36 39.669 E:147 25.983
MR: Map 12 C5

FURTHER Information

> **DSE Mitta Mitta**
> **Tel:** 02 6072 3410

Snowy Creek camping area

Located 35km south of Myrtleford. Access via Mt Buffalo Road off Great Alpine Road at Porepunkah. Superb alpine scenery. Snow sports in winter. Bushwalking, fishing and adventure activities in summer.

Lake Catani campground

Located beside Lake Catani. Open November to April. Access via Mt Buffalo Tourist Road. 59 campsites. Laundry facilities. Fires only in communal fireplaces. Bring own firewood. Use of gas/fuel stove preferred.
MR: Map 9 K7

Rocky Creek Campground

Remote walk-in campsite along Rocky Creek Track, which is a 13km (4 hour return) walk. Maximum camper numbers apply. Carry drinking water. Use of gas/fuel stove preferred.
MR: Map 9 K7

Mount McLeod camping area

Remote walk-in campsites along Mount McLeod Track which is a 16km (6 hour return) walk. This is a very remote area of the park and walkers must be proficient navigators. Camping is along the Saltlick Plain. Campers must observe Parks Vic bush camping regulations. Toilet is located at the southern end of plain. Maximum camper numbers apply. Carry drinking water. Gas/fuel stove only.
MR: Map 9 K7

FURTHER Information

Parks Vic Info Line
Tel: 13 19 63. Bookings essential for Melbourne Cup and Labour Day long weekends, Easter, Christmas and January school holidays.
Bookings: Parks Vic Mt Buffalo Entrance Station
Tel: 03 5756 2328 or online at www.parkstay.vic.gov.au
Camping fees: From $15.50 per site/night for 2 people. Remote walk-in campsites from $4.60 per person/night.
NB: maximum stay of 2 nights for remote walk-in campsites.

HIGH COUNTRY

COLLECTING firewood in National Parks

If you plan on camping in a national park and having a small campfire you may find that in some national parks and reserves that you are not permitted to collect wood for your fire from within the park. Either collect firewood outside the park, bring wood from home or use a gas/fuel stove or BBQ.

Located 70km east of Wodonga near Lake Hume. Access is via the village of Granya on the Murray River Road (C546), 15km north of the Murray Valley Highway. Murray River Road leaves the Murray Valley Highway 10km east of Tallangatta. The park provides bushwalking, mountain biking and four-wheel drive touring. Visitors can enjoy views from Mt Granya and walk to Granya Falls.

Cottontree picnic and camping area

From the village of Granya take the signposted Webb Lane and follow this for 1.5km to the signposted access to the camping area. A grassed, open site with some shade. The campsite is located in close proximity of a private farm house. Bring drinking water.

GPS S:36 06.891 E:147 18.314
MR: Map 12 B2

FURTHER Information

Parks Vic Info Line
Tel: 13 19 63

The park is located adjacent to the Murray River, 70km east of Wodonga near Lake Hume. Access to the south of the park is along the Murray Valley Highway and to the north of the park along Murray River Road. Dry weather access only. Good views from summit of Mt Lawson. Spring wildflowers. Four-wheel drive touring, bushwalking and mountain biking.

Koetong Creek camping area

Located in the south of the park near Koetong Creek. From the Murray Valley Highway take the road signposted Mt Lawson State Park, this is 6.5km west of the Koetong pub. Travel north for 300m then continue north along the signposted Firebrace Track for a further 2.4km. Then turn right (north) into the signposted Mt Lawson Road and follow this for 4.6km to the signposted access track to the camping areas. This track then leads 900m to campsite no 1 (no facilities) and a further 200m to campsite no 2 with facilities. Conventional vehicle access is possible in the dry only, all-wheel-drive vehicle is recommended, especially if towing a camper trailer. Bring drinking water and firewood.

Campsite no 1 – **GPS** S:36 05.881 E:147 26.985
Campsite no 2 – **GPS** S:36 05.867 E:147 26.815
MR: Map 12 C2

Koetong Creek camping area — campsite no 1

Kurrajongs camping area

Located in the north of the park opposite Lake Hume. Signposted access along Murray River Road, 21km east of the Murray River Road (C546) and the Talgarno Road (C542) junction. Then in 200m to small camping area with dispersed camping. Bring drinking water and firewood. Gas/fuel stove preferred.

GPS S:35 57.344 E:147 25.193
MR: Map 12 C1

FURTHER Information

Parks Vic Info Line
Tel: 13 19 63

HIGH COUNTRY

Mt Samaria State Park is located 14km north of Mansfield. Access from the south is via Blue Range Road, which is signposted off the Mansfield-Tolmie Road 10km north of Mansfield and 16km west of Tolmie. Access from the north is via Mt Samaria Road, which is signposted off the Swanpool-Tatong Road, 5km east of Swanpool on the Midland Highway. Take in the views from Mt Samaria Summit and Rocky Point Lookout. Visit Back Creek and Wild Dog Creek Falls and the Spring Creek Sawmill ruins. The park has numerous walking trails. Seasonal road closures apply during winter. Total fire ban exists throughout the park during summer; bring a gas/fuel stove.

Samaria Well camping area

Located in north of the park on the eastern side of the Samaria Wells. Access is 400m along Browns Road, which is accessed off Mt Samaria Road at the park's entrance. Grassed area with some shade. NB: Toilet is located on hill above the camping area towards the day use area, a footpath leaves Browns Road north of the creek. Bring drinking water.
GPS S:36 49.473 E:146 03.791
MR: Map 9 G8

Wild Dog Creek Falls camping area

Walk-in 850m from car park. Car park is signposted along Mt Samaria Road, 8km south of the park entrance and a second car park is signposted a further 1.8km along Mt Samaria Road. Campsite set among stately blue gums. Bring drinking water. Gas/fuel stove preferred.
Car park – **GPS** S:36 51.495 E:146 04.130 and
GPS S:36 51.929 E:146 04.702
MR: Map 9 G8

Spring Creek Sawmill camping area

Signposted access 1.1km south of the second car park for Wild Dog Creek Falls CA. Attractive camping area surrounded by tall shady trees. Located close to old sawmill ruins. Bring drinking water.
GPS S:36 52.272 E:146 05.083
MR: Map 9 G8

Spring Creek Sawmill camping area

Camphora camping area

Walk-in 100m from car park. Access to car park is signposted along Mt Samaria Road, 2km south of Spring Creek Sawmill CA, then in 100m to the car park. This access track is located 11.6km north of Blue Range Reserve CA in Mansfield State Forest, see page 267. Bring drinking water. Gas/fuel stove preferred.
Car park – **GPS** S:36 53.078 E:146 05.246
MR: Map 9 G8

FURTHER Information

Parks Vic Info Line
Tel: 13 19 63

207 Mount Stirling Area

Located 40km east of Mansfield. Access via Mt Buller Road. Conventional vehicle access to some areas, others require a four-wheel drive vehicle. The Circuit Road (seasonal closure applies) provides access to many points of interest in the area. Popular area for skiing, bushwalking, horse riding and four-wheel drive touring.

Mt Stirling summit

Craigs Hut camping area

Located 20km east of Telephone Box Junction with signposted access from Circuit Road. Walk-in 1.2km from Circuit Road car park or 4WD vehicle access via Clear Hills Track off Circuit Road. Camp only in designated sites, no camping within the hut vicinity. The hut was originally built for The Man From Snowy River movie. Bring drinking water. Gas/fuel stove preferred.
GPS S:37 06.589 E:146 31.915
MR: Map 10 J2

Razorback Hut camping area

Access track is along Circuit Road, north of Telephone Box Junction and west of

Craig's Hut turn off, and is just 30m east of the signposted No 3 Rd. Then in 600m to large camping area in the vicinity of the hut. Bring drinking water and firewood. Horseyards.
GPS S:37 06.230 E:146 27.853
MR: Map 10 I2

Carters Road camping area

Located 500m along Carters Road, which is off the Mansfield-Mt Buller Road, 13km east of Merrijig. Bring drinking water and firewood.
GPS S:37 06.195 E:146 22.017
MR: Map 10 I2

FURTHER Information

> **DSE Customer Service Centre**
> **Tel:** 13 61 86

GRANYA TO TOWONG

These river reserves are located between the towns of Granya and Towong beside the Murray River. Access roads are signposted off Murray River Road. Activities include camping, fishing, canoeing and swimming.

Burrowye Reserve camping area

Signposted access 25km west of Walwa on the Murray River Road. This is 34km east of the Murray River Road and Talgarno Road (C542) junction. Dispersed bush camping beside the river. An open grassed area with some shade. Self-sufficient campers. Bring drinking water and firewood.
GPS S:35 59.283 E:147 31.650
MR: Map 12 D1

Jingellic Reserve

Signposted access along Murray River Road, 700m east of the Jingellic Road. Then in 400m to small bush campsite on bend in the river. Natural boat launch from river beach. Self-sufficient campers. Bring drinking water and firewood.
GPS S:35 55.780 E:147 42.545
MR: Map 12 E1

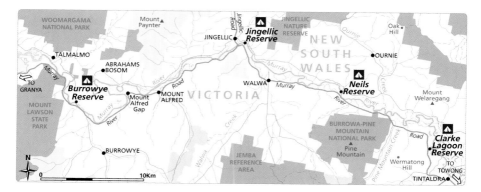

Neil's Reserve camping area

Signposted access along Murray River Road, 7km east of Walwa. Then in 900m to grassed area beside the river with good shade. One site with table, otherwise bush camping. Bring drinking water and firewood.
GPS S:35 58.481 E:147 48.752
MR: Map 12 E1

Clarke Lagoon Reserve camping area

Signposted access along Murray River Road, 11.4km south-east of Neil's Reserve and 4.3km north of Tintaldra. Then in 200m to grassed sites beside the river, some sites with good shade. NB: this area is beside a wildlife refuge, please ensure pets are kept under control. Bring drinking water and firewood.
GPS S:36 01.499 E:147 54.607
MR: Map 12 F1

FURTHER Information

> **Parks Vic Info Line**
> **Tel:** 13 19 63

Nariel Creek Recreation Reserve is located 10km south of Corryong and accessed along the Corryong-Benambra Road, which leaves the Murray Valley Highway 7km west of Corryong. This large reserve is situated on the banks of Corryong Creek, and is a good base whilst exploring the attractions of the surrounding region.

Nariel Creek Recreation Reserve

Signposted access along the Cooryong-Benambra Road, 3km south of the Murray Valley Highway. Large, grassed area beside creek. Bring drinking water and firewood.
GPS S:36 14.529 E:147 49.884
MR: Map 12 E4

FURTHER Information

Corryong Visitor Information Centre
Tel: 02 6076 2277
Camping fees: From $5.00 per site/night. Fees collected daily.

Nug Nug Reserve is beside the Buffalo River, 15km south of Myrtleford. From Myrtleford take the Buffalo River Road for 13km, then take the signposted Nug Nug Road and the reserve is located 1.3km along this road.

Nug Nug camping reserve

Located along Nug Nug Road which is signposted off the Buffalo River Road south of Myrtleford. Tennis courts. Bring drinking water and firewood. Dogs must be kept on a lead at all times.
GPS S:36 39.688 E:146 42.308
MR: Map 9 K7

FURTHER Information

Nug Nug Management Committee
Tel: 03 9786 1672 or 03 9798 6549
Camping fees: From $3.50 per adult/night and $0.50 per child/night. Power additional $3.00 per site/night. Fees collected daily.

These forests, located in the mountains east of Swifts Creek, are a popular four-wheel drive touring and walking destination. Visit the Washington Winch (18.6km along Nunniong Road) where interpretive boards explain how the winch and the spar trees were used to snig logs out of the valley below, or visit Moscow Villa hut and learn about local bushman Bill Ah Chow who built the hut in the early 1940s. Nunniong State Forest is located 35km east of Swifts Creek. Access is via Nunniong Road, which is signposted 4.7km along Bindi Road or the Tambo Valley Golf Club road, which is signposted off the Omeo Highway, 8km north of Swifts Creek.

Moscow Villa Hut camping area

Signposted 3.4km along Bentley Plain Road, which is signposted off Nunniong Road, 2.4km east of the Washington Winch. Camping in vicinity of hut. Bring drinking water.
GPS S:37 13.574 E:147 55.326
MR: Map 13 F1

Bentleys Plain Reserve camping area

Signposted 200m east of Moscow Villa Hut along Bentley Plain Road. Scenic location on edge of plain. Bring drinking water and firewood.
GPS S:37 13.685 E:147 55.406
MR: Map 13 F2

HIGH COUNTRY

Nunniong Plains bush camping areas

Dispersed bush camping on the plains beside Timbarra River. Access the plains via Nunniong Plains Track, which is signposted off Nunniong Road, 14km north of Bentley Plain Road. Self-sufficient campers. Bring drinking water and firewood.
MR: Map 13 F1

FURTHER Information

> **DSE Swifts Creek**
> **Tel:** 03 5159 5100

Bentleys Plain Reserve camping area

212 Omeo Area

The historic village of Omeo is located along the Great Alpine Road east of Mt Hotham and 119km north of Bairnsdale. The region has many relics of its mining past.

Big River Bridge camping area

Located in Mt Wills Historic Area beside the Mitta Mitta River. Signposted access on the Omeo Highway, 63km south of Mitta Mitta and 45km north of Omeo. Grassed area amongst black sallies.
GPS S:36 53.584 E:147 27.824
MR: Map 13 C6

Gibbo River camping areas

Located 34km north of Omeo along the Corryong-Benambra Road, north of Exhibition Creek Bridge and north of Alpine National Park. Numerous tracks leave the main road in a westerly direction to bush campsites beside the river (these are located in state forest). Bring drinking water and firewood. Fishing and canoeing.
MR: Map 13 E4

Victoria River Track bush camping area

Bush campsite beside large dam. Access track is 8km along Victoria River Track.

Victoria River Track is signposted off the Great Alpine Road, 24km west of Omeo. This is a seasonal closure track and passes through private property. Leave all gates as found and stay on the main track. Suitable for off-road trailers with four-wheel drive tow vehicle.
GPS S:37 06.009 E:147 18.419
MR: Map 13 C1

FURTHER Information

> **Parks Vic Info Line**
> **Tel:** 13 19 63
> **Parks Vic Omeo**
> **Tel:** 03 5159 1660

213 Pendergast State Forest

Located 65km south of Corryong. Access via Wheeler Creek Logging Road off Benambra-Corryong Road. Conventional vehicle access to main areas. Other roads may require 4WD. Popular 4WD touring area.

O'Hagens camping area

Acessed via Wheeler Creek Logging Road, which is signposted along the Benambra-Corryong Road, 67km north of Benambra. Located east of the Benambra-Corryong Road and west of Wheelers Creek Hut.
MR: Map 12 F4

Wheelers Creek Hut camping area

Signposted access along the Benambra-Corryong Road, 67km north of Benambra. Located 22km east of the Benambra-Corryong Road along Wheeler Creek Logging Road. Near hut.
MR: Map 12 F4

Bush camping areas

Numerous bush campsites along Dunstans Logging Road. Some near old logging huts. Conventional vehicle access to some sites, others require 4WD. No facilities. Dogs OK on lead. Contact ranger for details.

FURTHER Information

> **DSE Corryong**
> **Tel:** 02 6076 3100

Pigs Point Reserve

This reserve is situated on the western bank of the Mitta Mitta River. Water-based activities such as swimming, fishing and canoeing are popular along this stretch of river. Access is signposted along the Omeo Highway, 8km south of the Murray Valley Highway.

Pigs Point Reserve camping area

Signposted access 7.8km south of the Murray Valley Highway and 155km north of Omeo along the Omeo Highway. Large, open grassed area beside the river with some shade. Natural boat launch. Bring drinking water and firewood.
GPS S:36 16.801 E:147 14.230
MR: Map 12 B3

FURTHER Information

> **Parks Vic Info Line**
> **Tel:** 13 19 63

---

215 Stanley State Forest

Located 32km south of Wodonga and 4km south of Yackandandah. Access the signposted Bells Flat Road from Yackandandah. Visit the old township site of Yackandandah Junction. Travel along the Yackandandah Forest Drive, a circuit drive from Yackandandah of 14km. Dispersed camping areas beside Yackandandah Creek.

Stanley Forest camping areas

From Yackandandah take the road signposted Bells Flat Road/Forest Drive. Follow this for 3.8km where the road becomes Yack Gate Road, then a further 600m arrive at the first campsite. From the first campsite the Forest Drive continues south to No 1 Link Road, which then proceeds in a north-easterly direction to meet with Moyler Road/Kirby Flat Road then onto Back Creek Road, which leads back into Yackandandah. There are six campsites signposted along the Forest Drive. Campsites no 1 to 4 are accessible by conventional vehicles; access to campsite no 5 is recommended for all-wheel drive vehicle as there is a creek crossing to access the campsite; and campsite no 6 is by four-wheel drive only. NB: Toilets are located close to sites 1 and 2. Bring drinking water and firewood.
Campsite 1 – **GPS** S:36 20.217 E:146 48.513
Campsite 6 – **GPS** S:36 20.533 E:146 49.379
MR: Map 9 K5

FURTHER Information

> **DSE Customer Service Centre**
> **Tel:** 136 186
> **DSE Beechworth**
> **Tel:** 03 5720 8190

HIGH COUNTRY

Stanley State Forest

Staceys Bridge Reserve is located at Nariel, beside Wheeler Creek. Access is signposted along the Corryong-Benambra Road, 46km south of Corryong and 80km north of Benambra.

Staceys Bridge camping area

Signposted access along the Corryong-Benambra Road, 46km south of Corryong at Nariel. Bring drinking water and firewood.
GPS S:36 26.602 E:147 49.825
MR: Map 12 E4

FURTHER Information

Corryong Visitor Information Centre
Tel: 02 6076 2277

Located in state forest north-east of Mansfield and south-east of Benalla. Access is via Tatong-Tolmie Road, which is signposted at both towns. From the south Tolmie is 26km north-east of Mansfield and from the north Tatong is 26km south-east of Benalla. This area offers vehicle touring with historic sites such as the Kelly Tree to visit, fish, horse ride, trail bike or mountain bike ride through the scenic forests and ranges.

Toombullup East School Site camping area

Signposted access along the Tatong-Tolmie Road, 6.3km north of Tolmie. Open area located beside the road, best suited for an overnight stop. Bring drinking water and firewood.
GPS S:36 53.284 E:146 14.126
MR: Map 9 H8

Stringybark Creek camping reserve

Access road signposted along Tatong-Tolmie Road, 4km north of Toombullup East School Site CA. Then in 400m to very large area. Some sites well-shaded; others in the open. Walk to the Kelly Tree. Bring drinking water and firewood.
GPS S:36 52.375 E:146 12.084
MR: Map 9 H8

Jones camping reserve

Situated beside Hollands Creek along Jones Road, off the Tatong-Tolmie Road, 11km north-west of Stringybark Creek access road and 7.5km south of Tatong. Jones Road is 500m south of Fords Bridge. Then travel 2.2km south along Jones Road to the large, well-grassed and well-maintained picturesque camping area. Some shaded sites. Jones Road is very narrow in some sections and is not suitable for caravans. Seasonal road closure to camping reserve, closed June 15 to November 2 (dates may change from year to year). Horseyards. Bring drinking water and firewood.
GPS S:36 50.783 E:146 08.644
MR: Map 9 G8

FURTHER Information

DSE Mansfield
Tel: 03 5733 1200

Jones camping reserve

Snakes Reserve camping area

Signposted access 1.7km south of Picnic Point Reserve and 2.6km north of Knockwood Camping Reserve along the Mansfield-Woods Point Road. Large, well-grassed area with good shade. Bring drinking water and firewood.
GPS S:37 24.994 E:146 14.390
MR: Map 10 H4

Knockwood Reserve camping area

Signposted access 2.6km south of Snakes Reserve and 22.2km north of Scotts Reserve and 24.2km north of Woods Point General Store. Very large grassed area. Some sites with good tree shelter. Bring drinking water and firewood.
GPS S:37 26.083 E:146 13.777
MR: Map 10 H4

FURTHER Information

Vic Info Line
Tel: 13 19 63
Camping fees: Doctors Creek and LR Skipworth Reserves: From $5.00 per tent/night. Fees collected daily by volunteer.

HIGH COUNTRY

Victoria Falls Historic Area is the site of the state's first hydro-electric-power scheme. Walk to the falls and view ruins from the scheme. Signposted access is along the Great Alpine Road, 22km west of Omeo.

Victoria Falls Historic Area camping area

Signposted access off the Great Alpine Way, 22km west of Omeo. Bring drinking water and firewood.
GPS S:37 05.634 E:147 25.510
MR: Map 13 C1

FURTHER Information

> **Parks Vic Info Line**
> **Tel:** 13 19 63

The rural city of Wangaratta encompasses a region that is known for its gold rush history, its ties to Ned Kelly and its fabulous gourmet food and wines. The city is situated between the Ovens and King Rivers, which have a number of riverside camping reserves.

Pioneer Bridges

Located south-east of Wangaratta beside the Ovens River. From the Great Alpine Road east of Everton take the signposted Markwood-Everton Road/ Markwood 5. This is 9.3km south-east of the Wangaratta-Beechworth Road. Follow this road south for 1.5km to bridge over the Ovens River and on south side of bridge is a track on left which leads into the reserve. This reserve is beside the road and the river and has a large sandy beach. Best suited for an overnight stop. Bring drinking water and firewood.
GPS S:36 26.503 E:146 31.534
MR: Map 9 I5

Edi Cutting camping area

Located south of Wangaratta beside the King River. From Wangaratta take the Wangaratta-Whitfield Road south towards Whitfield for 36km to track signposted Edi Cutting. This is 14km north of Whitfield. This access is 600m south of the signposted Edi-Cheshunt Road. Access track leads in 100m to grassed camping area beside the river. Bring drinking water and firewood.
GPS S:36 39.372 E:146 25.284
MR: Map 9 I7

HIGH COUNTRY

Ovens Billabongs

Located south-east of Wangaratta. From town take the signposted Faithfull Street and follow in a south-easterly direction for 4.5km to a track signposted Ovens Billabongs, which leads 100m to a bush camping area beside the river and the Hume Freeway. This is site is best for an overnight stop. Self sufficient campers. Bring drinking water and firewood.
GPS S:36 22.797 E:146 21.904
MR: Map 9 I5

River Road Reserve

Located south-east of Wangaratta beside the Ovens River. From the Great Alpine Road east of Tarrawingee, take the signposted River Road. This is 12km from Wangaratta and 800m south-east of the Wangaratta-Beechworth Road. Follow River Road south for 2.1km to the signposted access to the reserve. This is just over the bridge over Ovens River. Track leads in 200m to bush campsites beside the river. Bring drinking water and firewood.
GPS S:36 24.846 E:146 27.384
MR: Map 9 I5

Frosts Reserve camping area

Located north of Wangaratta beside the Ovens River. From Wangaratta take Wangaratta-Yarrawonga road north for 17km to road signposted River Access. This is Frost Crossing Track and is 3.5km north of the signposted road to Boweya. Follow Frost Crossing Track for 1km, then turn left into the signposted Frosts Track which leads 900m to the river and a T-intersection. At the intersection the track on right leads to a number of good bush camping areas, including Gravel Point and Hills Bend. Self-sufficient campers. Bring drinking water and firewood.
Gravel Point – **GPS** S:36 13.569 E: 146 16.067
Hills Bend – **GPS** S:36 13.927 E:146 16.197
MR: Map 9 H4

FURTHER Information

> ### Wangaratta Visitor Information Centre
> **Tel:** 1800 801 065. Open daily (except Christmas day) 9am to 5pm.
> **Web:** www.visitwangaratta.com.au

HIGH COUNTRY

The historic village of Woods Point lies in a remote valley 90km south of Mansfield. Gold was first found in the region in 1861 and was mined until the late 1920s when the last goldmine, the Morning Star, closed. The region is still a popular area for fossickers as well as with four-wheel drivers, trail bike riders, fisherfolk and walkers. Access to Woods Point from Mansfield is via Jamieson along the Mansfield-Woods Point Road. Access from the south is via Matlock, which is 75km east of Marysville.

Scotts Reserve camping area

Signposted access 2km north-west of Woods Point General Store along the Mansfield-Woods Point Road. Open area on bend in the river. Good shade.
GPS S:37 33.565 E:146 14.406
MR: Map 10 H5

Comet Flat camping reserve

Signposted 3km south-east of Woods Point. Take signposted road opposite the Woods Point hotel. Well shaded, open area, however can be wet and muddy after rain. 4WD vehicle recommended as access track has two creek crossings. Bring drinking water and firewood.
GPS S:37 34.643 E:146 16.032
MR: Map 10 H5

FURTHER Information

Woods Point General Store
Tel: 03 5777 8220

Panning for gold near Dargo

Roadside Rest Areas

REST AREA/TOWN	LOCATION	TOILET	TABLE	FIREPLACE	SHELTER	WATER	MAP
HUME FREEWAY (M31) – MELBOURNE TO WODONGA							
Great Divide RA	59km N of Melbourne/48km S of Seymour	✓	✓	✓	✓	✓	10 A4
SEYMOUR							10 B2
Grass Trees RA	12km NE of Seymour/90km SW of Benalla	✓	✓	✓	✓	✓	10 B1
Balmattum RA	59km NE of Seymour/41km SW of Benalla	✓	✓	✓	✓	✓	9 E7
BENALLA		✓	✓	✓			9 G6
Mokoan RA	13km NE of Benalla/27km SW of Wangaratta	✓	✓	✓	✓	✓	9 G6
Wangaratta Service Centre	26km NE of Benalla/13km S of Wangaratta	✓	✓		✓		9 H5
WANGARATTA							9 H5
Ironbark RA	40km NE of Wangaratta/29km SW of Wodonga	✓	✓	✓	✓	✓	9 J3
WODONGA/ALBURY							9 L3
PRINCES HIGHWAY (A1) – MELBOURNE TO SA BORDER							
Avalon RA	52km SW of Melbourne/22km NE of Geelong	✓	✓			✓	8 J1
GEELONG							8 I2
WINCHELSEA							8 G2
COLAC							8 D3
Pirron Yallock West RA	13km W of Colac/32km E of Camperdown		✓		✓		8 D3
Floating Islands Lagoon Nature Reserve	17km W of Colac/28km E of Camperdown		✓				8 C3
CAMPERDOWN							8 B2
Ash Wednesday Memorial RA	42km W of Camperdown/25km NE of Warrnambool		✓				4 K7
WARRNAMBOOL							4 J7
Fitzroy River, west of Tyrendarra	45km W of Warrnambool/25km NE of Portland					✓	4 F6
PORTLAND							4 E7
HEYWOOD							4 E5
Glenelg River RA	37km NW of Heywood/31km E of Vic/SA Border		✓	✓		✓	4 D4
Vic/SA Border RA	68km NW of Heywood/18km E of Mt Gambier	✓	✓	✓	✓	✓	4 B3

PRINCES HIGHWAY (A1) – MELBOURNE TO NSW BORDER

REST AREA/TOWN	LOCATION	TOILET	TABLE	FIREPLACE	SHELTER	WATER	MAP
Gumbuya RA	78km E of Melbourne/42km W of Yarragon	✓	✓	✓	✓	✓	11 E1
YARRAGON							11 G2
MOE							11 H2
MORWELL							11 I2
Traralgon West RA	8km E of Morwell/5km W of Traralgon	✓	✓		✓	✓	11 I2
TRARALGON							11 J2
Blind Joe Creek RA	21km E of Traralgon/2km W of Rosedale	✓	✓	✓	✓	✓	11 K1
ROSEDALE							11 K1
La Trobe River RA	1km E of Rosedale/25km W of Sale		✓	✓	✓	✓	11 K1
SALE							13 A7
STRATFORD							13 A6
Providence Ponds RA	16km E of Stratford/35km W Bairnsdale	✓	✓	✓	✓		13 B6
BAIRNSDALE							13 D5
Howitt Park	1km E of Bairnsdale/34km W of Lakes Entrance	✓	✓	✓	✓	✓	13 D5
Nicholson Park	9km E of Bairnsdale/26km W of Lakes Entrance	✓	✓	✓	✓	✓	13 E5
LAKES ENTRANCE							13 F6
Hospital Creek RA	33km NE of Lakes Entrance/33km W of Orbost		✓	✓	✓		13 G5
Newmerella RA	61km NE of Lakes Entrance/5km W Orbost	✓	✓	✓	✓	✓	13 H5
ORBOST							13 I5
Murrungower RA	18km E of Orbost/58km W of Cann River	✓	✓	✓	✓		13 I5
Bemm River Scenic Reserve	45km E of Orbost/30km W of Cann River	✓	✓				13 K4
Brightlight Saddle RA	58km E of Orbost/17km W of Cann River		✓		✓		13 K4
CANN RIVER							13 L4
Cann River East RA	4km E of Cann River/58km S of Vic/NSW Border		✓				14 A4
Thurra River RA	12km E of Cann River/50km S of Vic/NSW Border	✓	✓	✓	✓	✓	14 B4
Lomond Hill RA	15km E of Cann River/47km S of Vic/NSW Border		✓		✓		14 B4
Governors Bend RA	24km E of Cann River/38km S of Vic/NSW Border		✓		✓		14 C4
Vic/NSW Border RA	62km E of Cann River at border/48km S of Eden		✓	✓	✓		14 D3

REST AREAS

REST AREA/TOWN	LOCATION	TOILET	TABLE	FIREPLACE	SHELTER	WATER	MAP
HENTY HIGHWAY (A200) PORTLAND TO HORSHAM							
Branxholme RA	62km N of Portland/25km S of Hamilton	✓	✓				4 F3
HAMILTON							4 H3
Cavendish RA	26km N of Hamilton/1km N of Cavendish/106km S of Horsham	✓	✓	✓	✓		4 H1
HORSHAM							3 I4
HENTY HIGHWAY (A200) PORTLAND TO HORSHAM							
Meredith Pioneer Park RA	43km NW of Geelong/43km S of Ballarat	✓	✓	✓	✓	✓	7 G7
Clarendon RA	63km NW of Geelong/ 23km S of Ballarat		✓		✓		7 G6
BALLARAT							7 F6
O'Keefe's Dam RA	14km N of Ballarat/2km S of Creswick		✓		✓		7 F5
CRESWICK							7 F5
DAYLESFORD							7 H4
Jessie Kennedy RA	34km N Daylesford/6km S Castlemaine		✓		✓	✓	7 H3
CASTLEMAINE							7 H2
Ravenswood RA	21km N of Castlemaine/17km S of Bendigo		✓		✓		7 H1
BENDIGO		✓	✓	✓	✓		6 H8
Huntly RA	12km N of Bendigo/35km S of Elmore	✓	✓	✓	✓	✓	6 I7
ELMORE							6 J6
Stanhope RA	30km E of Elmore/6km W of Stanhope				✓		6 L6
STANHOPE							6 L6
Mooroopna RA	35km E of Stanhope/4km W of Shepparton	✓	✓	✓	✓		9 A5
SHEPPARTON							9 C5
Nalinga RA	32km SE of Shepparton/34km NW of Benalla		✓		✓		9 E5
Benalla North RA/Casey Weir	56km SE of Shepparton/11km NW of Benalla		✓		✓		9 F5
BENALLA							9 G6
Lima East Creek RA	22km S of Benalla/42km N of Mansfield		✓	✓	✓		9 G8
Lake Nillahcootie RA	43km S of Benalla/27km N of Mansfield	✓	✓	✓			9 G8
MANSFIELD							10 G2

REST AREAS

SOUTH GIPPSLAND HIGHWAY (M420 & A440) DANDENONG TO SALE

REST AREA/TOWN	LOCATION	TOILET	TABLE	FIREPLACE	SHELTER	WATER	MAP
Swamp Tower Reserve	22km W of Cranbourne/2km W of Koo-wee-rup	✓			✓		11 D2
Yallock Creek RA	2km E of Koo-wee-rup/61km NW of Leongatha	✓			✓		11 D2
LEONGATHA							11 G4
Foster North Scenic Lookout RA	33km SE of Leongatha/3km W of Foster	✓					11 H5
FORSTER							11 H5
Franklin River Reserve	10km E of Foster/45km SW of Yarram	✓	✓	✓	✓		11 H5
Agnes River RA	17km E Foster/38km SW of Yarram	✓			✓		11 I5
Nine Mile Creek RA	28km E of Foster/27km SW of Yarram	✓			✓		11 J5
John Crew Memorial Picnic Area	45km E of Foster/10km S of Yarram	✓	✓	✓	✓	✓	11 J4
YARRAM							11 J4
Tarra River RA	1km NE of Yarram/71km S of Sale	✓			✓		11 J4
SALE							13 A7

WESTERN HIGHWAY (A8) – BALLARAT TO SA BORDER

REST AREA/TOWN	LOCATION	TOILET	TABLE	FIREPLACE	SHELTER	WATER	MAP
Trawalla West RA	43km W of Ballarat/4km E of Beaufort	✓			✓		7 D5
BEAUFORT							7 C5
Beaufort West RA	5km W of Beaufort/16km E of Buangor	✓	✓		✓		7 C4
BUANGOR							7 B4
Mt Langi Ghiran RA	5km W of Buangor/19km E of Ararat	✓			✓		7 B4
ARARAT							7 A4
Great Western RA	18km N of Ararat/13km S of Stawell	✓			✓		3 L7
STAWELL							3 L6
Canadian Gully Bushland Reserve	8km NW of Stawell/55km SE of Horsham	✓			✓		3 K6
Dadswells Bridge South RA	22km NW of Stawell/43km SE of Horsham	✓			✓		3 K5
Green Lake RA	52km NW of Stawell/13km SE of Horsham	✓	✓		✓		3 I4
Burnt Creek RA	58km NW of Stawell/7km SE of Horsham	✓			✓		3 I4
HORSHAM							3 I4
Wail RA	26km NW of Horsham/10km SE of Dimboola	✓			✓		3 H2

REST AREAS

REST AREA/TOWN	LOCATION	TOILET	TABLE	FIREPLACE	SHELTER	WATER	MAP
WESTERN HIGHWAY (A8) – BALLARAT TO SA BORDER							
DIMBOOLA							3 H2
Wimmera River RA	6km W of Dimboola/32km E of Nhill	✓	✓		✓	✓	3 G1
Native Waterhole RA	22km W of Dimboola/16km E of Nhill				✓		✓	3 G1
NHILL							3 F1
Camerons Reserve RA	17km W of Nhill/24km E of Kaniva				✓		✓	3 E1
KANIVA							3 C1
Mooree Reserve	25km W of Kaniva at border/19km E of Bordertown	✓	✓		✓	✓	3 B1
HENTY HIGHWAY (B200) HORSHAM TO SUNRAYSIA HIGHWAY							
WARRACKNABEAL							2 J8
Brim RA	20km N of Warracknabeal/40km S of Hopetoun	✓	✓	✓	✓	✓	2 J7
HOPETOUN							2 J5
Hopetoun RA	1km N of Hopetoun/25km SW of Sunraysia Highway			✓		✓		2 J5
Lascelles West RA	12km NE of Hopetoun/14km SW of Sunraysia Highway			✓		✓		2 K4
STURT HIGHWAY(A20) – MILDURA TO SA BORDER							
Airport View RA	12km W of Mildura/47km E of Cullulleraine			✓		✓		1 H2
Merrinee North RA	35km W of Mildura/24km E of Cullulleraine			✓		✓		1 G2
CULLULLERAINE							1 E2
Rest Area	32km W of Cullulleraine/26km E of Vic/SA Border			✓		✓		1 C2
Vic/SA Border RA	58km W of Cullulleraine at border/27km E of Renmark			✓		✓		1 B2
GOULBURN VALLEY HIGHWAY (A39) – SEYMOUR TO MURRAY VALLEY HIGHWAY							
Calder Woodburn Memorial RA	64km N of Seymour/18km S of Shepparton			✓		✓		9 C6
SHEPPARTON							9 C5
Wunghnu RA	26km N of Shepparton/6km S of Numurkah	✓	✓	✓	✓	✓	9 D3
NUMURKAH							9 D3
MURRAY VALLEY H/WAY							9 E2

REST AREAS

REST AREA/TOWN	LOCATION	TOILET	TABLE	FIREPLACE	SHELTER	WATER	MAP
CALDER HIGHWAY (A79) – BENDIGO TO MILDURA							
Ryans Creek RA	63km NW of Bendigo/12km SE of Wedderburn	✓	✓	✓			6 E6
WEDDERBURN							6 E5
Skinners Flat Reservoir RA, located 1km east of highway	Turn off highway 5km NW of Wedderburn/26km SE Charlton	✓			✓		6 E5
CHARLTON							6 C4
Teddywaddy RA	9k N of Chartlon/22km SE of Wycheproof	✓	✓	✓			6 C4
WYCHEPROOF							6 C3
Torneys Tank Reserve/ Culgoa South RA	39km NW of Wycheproof/36k SE of Sea Lake	✓			✓		6 B1
SEA LAKE							5 A7
Lake Tyrrell RA	7km N of Sea Lake/81km SE of Ouyen	✓	✓	✓			2 L3
OUYEN							1 I8
Rest Area	22km N of Ouyen/12km S of Hattah/79km S of Mildrua	✓			✓		1 I7
Rest Area	37km N of Ouyen/3km N of Hattah/64km S of Mildura	✓	✓	✓			1 I6
MILDURA							1 I2
MALLEE HIGHWAY (B12)– TOOLEYBUC TO SA BORDER							
Piangil North RA	1km SW of Tooleybuc/3km N of Piangil	✓			✓		5 D4
PIANGIL							5 C4
Piangil West RA	11k W of Piangil/31km E of Manangatang	✓			✓		5 B4
MANANGATANG							5 A4
OUYEN							1 I8
Walpeup RA	30km W of Ouyen/21km E of Underbool	✓	✓		✓		1 H8
UNDERBOOL							1 F8
Danyo RA	53km W of Underbool/6km E of Murrayville	✓			✓		2 D1
MURRAYVILLE							2 C1
HAMILTON HIGHWAY (B140) – GEELONG TO HAMILTON							
Leigh River	28km W of Geelong/1km E of Inverleigh	✓	✓	✓			8 G1
INVERLEIGH							8 G1
LISMORE							7 C8
DERRINALLUM							7 C8
MORTLAKE							4 L5
HAMILTON							4 H3

REST AREAS

REST AREA/TOWN	LOCATION	TOILET	TABLE	FIREPLACE	SHELTER	WATER	MAP
SUNRAYSIA HIGHWAY (B220) – BALLARAT TO OUYEN							
Lexton South RA	43km NW of Ballarat/27km S of Avoca	✓			✓		7 D4
AVOCA							7 D2
No 2 Creek RA	3km N of Avoca/ 61km S of St Arnaud	✓			✓		7 D2
Tanwood South RA	10km N of Avoca/54km S of St Arnaud	✓			✓		7 D2
Stuart Mill South RA	34km N Avoca/30km S of St Arnaud	✓			✓		6 C8
ST ARNAUD							6 C7
DONALD							6 A5
Lake Watchem, located 1km west of highway	33km N of Donald/19km S of Birchip	✓	✓		✓		6 A4
BIRCHIP							6 A2
Kinnabulla RA	24km NW of Birchip/105km SE of Ouyen	✓					2 L6
Tempy RA	96km NW of Birchip/33km S Ouyen	✓			✓		2 J2
OUYEN							1 I8
MURRAY VALLEY HIGHWAY (B400) – ROBINVALE TO CORRYONG							
BOUNDARY BEND							5 C2
Boundary Bend East RA	45km E of Robinvale/1km E of Boundary Bend/89km N of Swan Hill	✓	✓	✓	✓		5 C2
Piangil North RA	45km S Boundary Bend/45km N of Swan Hill	✓			✓		5 D4
Wood Wood RA	51km S of Boundary Bend/49km N of Swan Hill	✓	✓		✓		5 D4
SWAN HILL							5 E6
Lake Boga	17km SE of Swan Hill/41km NW of Kerang	✓	✓	✓	✓	✓	5 E7
Lake Charm RA	39km SE of Swan Hill/19km NW of Kerang	✓	✓	✓	✓	✓	5 F8
Ibis Rookery RA	50km SE of Swan Hill/8km NW of Kerang	✓	✓	✓	✓		5 F8
KERANG							6 G1
COHUNA							6 H1
Major Mitchells Campsite RA	8km SE of Cohuna/57km NE of Echuca	✓			✓		6 I2
Wharparilla Flora Reserve RA	61km SE of Cohuna/4km NW of Echuca	✓			✓		6 K3
ECHUCA							6 K4

REST AREA/TOWN	LOCATION	TOILET	TABLE	FIREPLACE	SHELTER	WATER	MAP
MURRAY VALLEY HIGHWAY (B400) – ROBINVALE TO CORRYONG							
Rest Area	19km E of Echuca at Tongala turn off/93km W of Cobram		✓	✓	✓		6 L4
Goulburn River RA	39km E of Echuca/73km W of Cobram		✓	✓	✓		9 B3
COBRAM							9 E2
Bourke Bend RA	19km SE of Cobram/17km NW of Yarrawonga		✓		✓		9 F2
Yarrawonga West RA	33km E of Cobram/3km W of Yarrawonga		✓		✓		9 G2
YARRAWONGA							9 G2
Bundalong RA	15km E of Yarrawonga/34km W of Rutherglen		✓		✓		9 H2
RUTHERGLEN							9 I3
Indigo Creek RA	15km E of Rutherglen/29km W of Wodonga		✓	✓	✓		9 J3
WODONGA							9 L3
Ebden Reserve RA	14km E of Wodonga/25km W of Tallangatta	✓	✓	✓	✓	✓	12 A2
Ludlows Reserve RA	17km E of Wodonga/22km W of Tallangatta	✓	✓	✓	✓		12 A2
TALLANGATTA							12 B2
Tallangatta Creek	13km E of Tallangatta/69km W of Corryong		✓	✓			12 C2
CORRYONG							12 F2

REST AREAS

Victoria Key Map

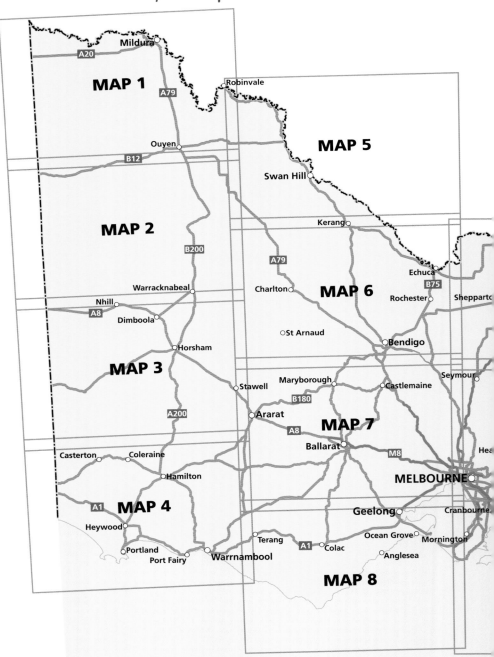

MAP 1

A20 Mildura

A79

Robinvale

MAP 5

Ouyen

B12

Swan Hill

MAP 2

B200

Kerang

A79

Echuca

B75

Charlton

MAP 6

Rochester

Shepparto

Warracknabeal

Nhill

A8

Dimboola

St Arnaud

Bendigo

Horsham

MAP 3

Stawell

Maryborough

Castlemaine

Seymour

Ararat

B180

MAP 7

A200

A8

Casterton

Coleraine

Ballarat

M8

Hea

Hamilton

MELBOURNE

A1

MAP 4

Geelong

Cranbourne

Heywood

Terang

A1

Colac

Ocean Grove

Mornington

Portland

Port Fairy

Warrnambool

Anglesea

MAP 8

TOURING MAPS LEGEND

MELBOURNE○	Town Major	———	Freeway		National Park/Reserve
Geelong○	Town Medium	———	Principal Road		State Forest
Torquay○	Town Minor	———	Secondary Road		Recreation Reserve
Portsea •	Locality	———	Minor Road		Orchard/Plantation
Mount Gellibrand ▲	Mountain Peak	- - - - -	Vehicular Track		Perrenial Waterbody
Gow Hill •	Physical Feature	·········	Walking Track		Non-Perrenial Waterbody
Cobb Highway	Road Name	-·-·-·-	State Border		Land Subject to Inundation
20	National Route Number	———	Railway		Built Up Area
A79	State Route Number	———	Dam Wall		
		———	Cliff		
		·········	Major River		
		·········	Minor River		

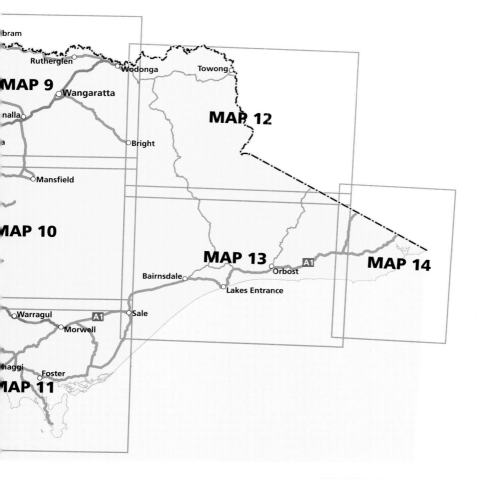

Camping GUIDE TO **VICTORIA** | **VICTORIA KEY MAP**

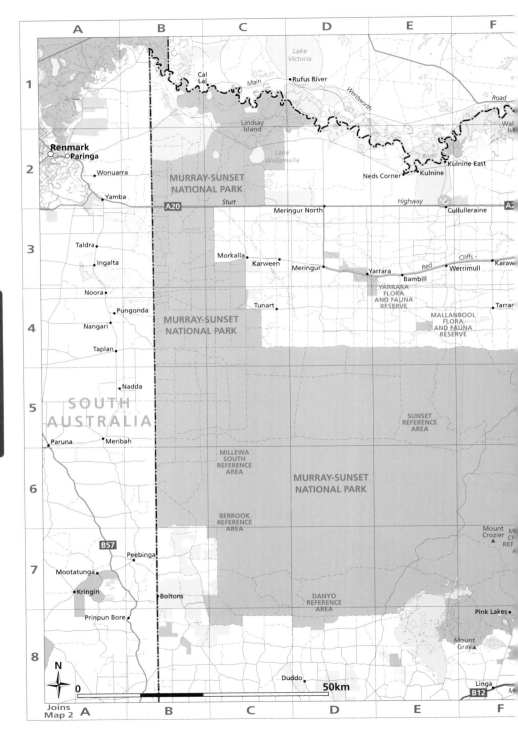

MAP 1 | *Camping* GUIDE TO **VICTORIA**

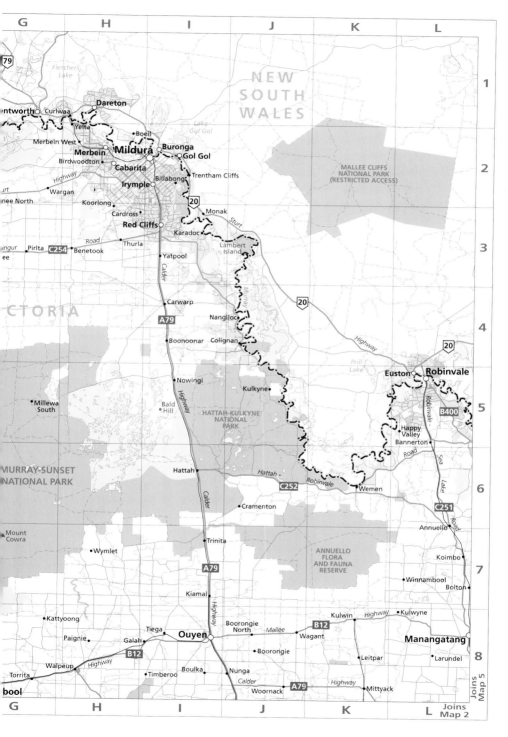

79

Fletchers
Lake

NEW
SOUTH
WALES

ntworth○ Curlwaa   **Dareton**

Yelta   •Boeil

Merbein West   •Buronga

Merbein   Mildura○   •Gol Gol

Birdwoodton   **Cabarita**

Highway   •Billabong   •Trentham Cliffs

Irymple○

Wargan

nee North

Koorlong•   20

Cardross•   •Monak

Red Cliffs○   •Karadoc   Lambert
                              Island

ngur Pirlta **C254** •Benetook   Thurla

ee   •Yatpool

Road

Calder

MALLEE CLIFFS
NATIONAL PARK
(RESTRICTED ACCESS)

Sturt

Murray

•Carwarp

CTORIA   20

A79   •Nangiloc

•Boonoonar   •Colignan

Highway   Prill
Lake

•Nowingi

•Millewa
South   Bald
                 Hill   •Kulkyne

HATTAH-KULKYNE
NATIONAL
PARK

Euston○ **Robinvale**

Robinvale

20

B400

Happy
Valley
•Bannerton

Road

MURRAY-SUNSET
NATIONAL PARK

•Hattah   Hattah-   River

Calder   **C252**   Robinvale   •Wemen

Sea

Lake

•Cramenton

•Mount
Cowra   ANNUELLO
                               FLORA
•Wymlet   AND FAUNA
                               RESERVE

C251

Road

•Annuello

•Koimbo

•Trinita

•Winnambool
              •Bolton

•Kiamal

•Kattyoong   Boorongie Mallee Kulwin Highway •Kulwyne
                   North
•Tiega   Galah• **Ouyen**○ •   •Wagant   **Manangatang**
Paignie•   **B12**
             •Boorongie   •Leitpar   •Larundel
Walpeup Highway   •Mittyack
B12

Torrita•   •Timberoo Boulka• •Nunga
bool   Calder **A79**
                         Woornack   Highway

Joins
Map 5

Joins
Map 2

Camping GUIDE TO **VICTORIA** | **MAP 1**

A   B   C   D   E   F

1

Duddo

Mulcra

Linga
Mallee
Unde
Boinka

Panitya
Mallee
Murrayville   Tutye
B12   Cowangie
Danyo   Highway

Pinnaroo

2

WYPERFELD
NATIONAL
PARK

BROOM
REFER
AR

3

SCORPION
SPRINGS
CONSERVATION
PARK

RUDDS ROO
REFERENCE A

4

BIG
DESERT
WILDERNESS

WYPERFELD
NATIONAL
PARK

NGARKAT
CONSERVATION
PARK

VI

5

Mount
Shaugh

RED BLUFF
NATURE
CONSERVATION
RESERVE

TELOPEA DOWNS
REFERENCE AREA

6

SOUTH
AUSTRALIA

KARRANGOOK FLORA
AND FAUNA RESERVE

7

Perer

Baker
Netherby   Lo
W

Mount
Edgerley

Telopea Downs

Yanac   Lorquor

Broughton

Yanac
South   Woorak
West   Niniw

C225   Propodollah

8

Woora

Cholla   Yarrock   Sandsmere   Boyeo

Bordertown   Dinyarrak   Yearinga   Diapur   Tarranginnie   Nhill

A   B   C   D   E   F

MAP 2 | Camping GUIDE TO VICTORIA

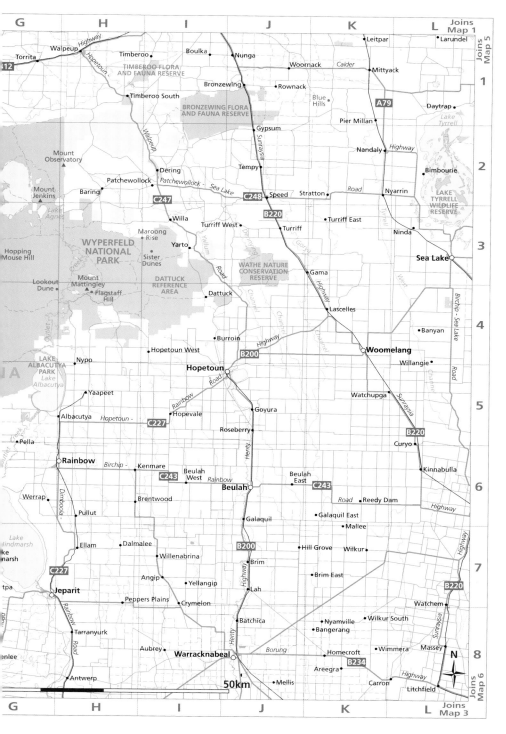

G H I J K L

Torrita
B12
Walpeup
Hopetoun Highway
Timberoo • Boulka • Nunga
Woornack Calder Mittyack
Leitpar • Larundel

TIMBEROO FLORA AND FAUNA RESERVE

Bronzewing • Rownack
Blue Hills
A79
Daytrap

1

• Timberoo South

BRONZEWING FLORA AND FAUNA RESERVE

Pier Millan

Lake Tyrrell

Mount Observatory

Gypsum

Walpeup

Nandaly
Highway
Bimbourie

2

Mount Jenkins
Baring
Patchewollock
Dering
Patchewollock - Sea Lake
C247
Tempy
C248
Speed Stratton
Road
Nyarrin

LAKE TYRRELL WILDLIFE RESERVE

Lake Agnes

Willa
Turriff West •
B220
Turriff
Turriff East •
Ninda

Maroong Rise
Yarto
Sister Dunes

WYPERFELD NATIONAL PARK

WATHE NATURE CONSERVATION RESERVE

Gama

Sea Lake

3

Hopping Mouse Hill

DATTUCK REFERENCE AREA

Lookout Dune
Mount Mattingley
Flagstaff Hill
Dattuck

Lascelles

Banyan

4

• Burroin

Channel

NA
LAKE ALBACUTYA PARK
Nypo
Hopetoun West

B200
Hopetoun
Highway
Woomelang

Willangie •

Lake Albacutya

Yaapeet

Rainbow
Hopevale
Goyura

Watchupga

Surnasia
B220

5

Albacutya
Hopetoun -
C227
Roseberry •

Curyo

Pella

Rainbow
Birchip -
Kenmare
C243
Beulah West
Rainbow
Beulah
Beulah East
C243
Kinnabulla

6

Werrap
Pullut
Brentwood
Reedy Dam
Road
Highway

Dimboola -

Lake Hindmarsh
Ellam
Dalmalee
Willenabrina
Galaquil
Galaquil East •
• Mallee

7

ke marsh

Angip
Yellangip
B200
Brim
Hill Grove • Wilkur

C227
tpa
Jeparit
Peppers Plains
Lah
Brim East •

Tarranyurk
Crymelon

Watchem

enlee
Aubrey
Batchica
Nyamville
Wilkur South
Wimmera
Massey

Warracknabeal
Borung
Bangerang
Homecroft
B234

N

8

Antwerp
50km
Areegra
Carron
Highway
Litchfield

Mellis •

G H I J K L

TOURING MAPS

Camping GUIDE TO VICTORIA | **MAP 2**

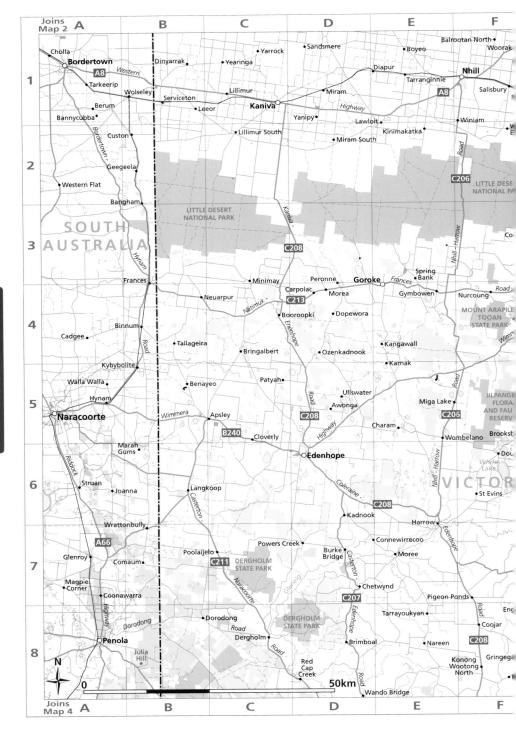

TOURING MAPS

| | A | B | C | D | E | F |

Cholla

Bordertown
A8 Western
Tarkeerip
Wolseley

Berum

Bannycubba

Custon

Geegeela

Western Flat

Bangham

Dinyarrak
Yearinga
Yarrock
Sandsmere
Boyeo
Balrootan North
Woorak

Diapur
Tarranginnie
Nhill
A8 Salisbury

Wolseley
Serviceton
Lillimur
Kaniva
Miram
Highway

Leeor
Yanipy
Lawloit
Winiam

Lillimur South
Miram South
Kinimakatka

C206
LITTLE DESE
NATIONAL PA

SOUTH
AUSTRALIA

LITTLE DESERT
NATIONAL PARK

Hynam

C208

Frances

Minimuk
Peronne
Goroke Frances
Spring
Bank

Carpolac
Morea
C213
Gymbowen
Nurcoung
Road

Neuarpur
Booroopki
Dopewora
MOUNT ARAPIL
TOOAN
STATE PARK

Cadgee

Binnum

Tallageira
Bringalbert
Ozenkadnook
Kangawall
Karnak

Kybybolite

Walla Walla

Hynam

Naracoorte

Benayeo
Patyah
Ullswater
J
Miga Lake
C206
JILPANGI
FLORA
AND FAU
RESERV

Wimmera
Apsley
Awonga
C208
Charam

B240
Cloverly
Highway
Wombelano
Brookst

Edenhope
White
Lake
Dou

Marah
Gums
Joanna
Langkoop
Coleraine
VICTOR

Struan
C208
St Evins

Wrattonbully

A66
Kadnook
Harrow

Glenroy
Comaum
Poolaijelo
Powers Creek
Burke
Bridge
Moree
Connewirrecoo

C211
DERGHOLM
STATE PARK
Moree

Magpie
Corner
Coonawarra
Chetwynd
Pigeon Ponds

Naracoorte
Glenelg
C207
Road

Dorodong
Tarrayoukyan
Coojar
Eng

Penola
Dorodong
Road
Dergholm
DERGHOLM
STATE PARK
Brimboal
Nareen
C208
Gringega

Julia
Hill
Red
Cap
Creek
Konong
Wootong
North

N
0
50km
Wando Bridge

| | A | B | C | D | E | F |

MAP 3 | Camping GUIDE TO **VICTORIA**

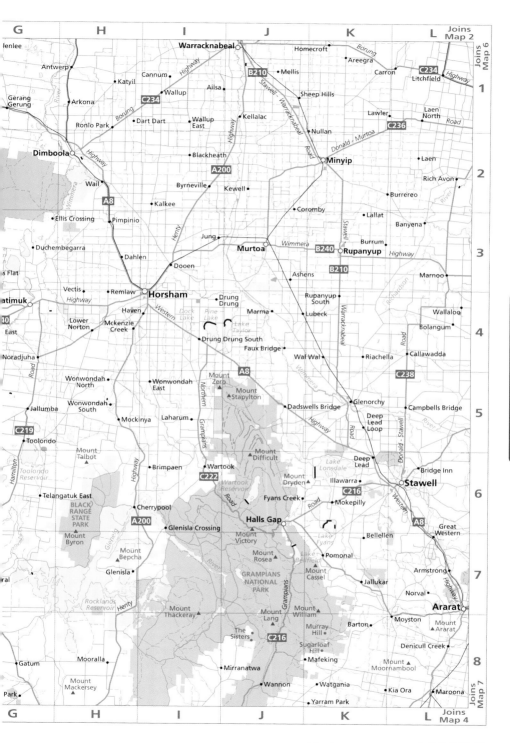

G H I J K L

1

2

3

4

5

6

7

8

enlee

Antwerp

Gerang
Gerung

Katyil

Cannum

Wallup

Ailsa

Warracknabeal

B210

Mellis

Homecroft

Areegra

Borung

Carron

C234

Litchfield

Highway

Arkona

C234

Dart Dart

Wallup
East

Kellalac

Sheep Hills

Lawler

Laen
North

Road

Ronlo Park

Nullan

C236

Dimboola

Blackheath

Minyip

Donald - Murtoa

Road

Laen

Wail

A200

Byrneville

Kewell

Rich Avon

A8

Kalkee

Coromby

Burrereo

atimuk

Ellis Crossing

Pimpinio

Lallat

Banyena

Duchembegarra

Dahlen

Jung

Murtoa

Wimmera

B240

Rupanyup

Burrum

Highway

s Flat

Dooen

Ashens

B210

Marnoo

Vectis

Remlaw

Horsham

Highway

Drung
Drung

Marma

Rupanyup
South

Lubeck

Wallaloo

East

Lower
Norton

Haven

Mckenzie
Creek

Western

Dock
Lake

Pine
Lake

Lake
Taylor

Bolangum

Noradjuha

Drung Drung South

Faux Bridge

Wal Wal

Riachella

Callawadda

Jallumba

Wonwondah
North

Wonwondah
East

Mount
Zero

A8

Mount
Stapylton

Dadswells Bridge

Glenorchy

C238

Campbells Bridge

Wonwondah
South

Mockinya

Laharum

Northern

Grampians

Highway

Deep
Lead
Loop

C219

Toolondo

Mount
Talbot

Mount
Difficult

Mount
Dryden

Lake
Lonsdale

Illawarra

C216

Deep
Lead

Bridge Inn

Stawell

Telangatuk East

BLACK
RANGE
STATE
PARK

Cherrypool

Wartook

Wartook
Reservoir

Road

Fyans Creek

Mokepilly

Western

A8

Great
Western

Mount
Byron

A200

Glenisla Crossing

Halls Gap

Mount
Victory

Lake
Fyans

Bellellen

Mount
Bepcha

Glenisla

Mount
Rosea

Lake
Bellfield

Pomonal

Mount
Cassel

Jallukar

Armstrong

Highway

GRAMPIANS
NATIONAL
PARK

Norval

Rocklands
Reservoir

Henty

Mount
Thackeray

Mount
Lang

Mount
William

Grampians

Murray
Hill

Barton

Moyston

Ararat

Mount
Ararat

Gatum

Mooralla

The
Sisters

C216

Sugarloaf
Hill

Mafeking

Denicull Creek

Mount
Mackersey

Mirranatwa

Wannon

Watgania

Mount
Moornambool

Kia Ora

Maroona

Park

Yarram Park

G H I J K L

Southern Ocean

Discovery Bay

VICTORIA

SOUTH AUSTRALIA

N

0   50km

MAP 4 | Camping GUIDE TO **VICTORIA**

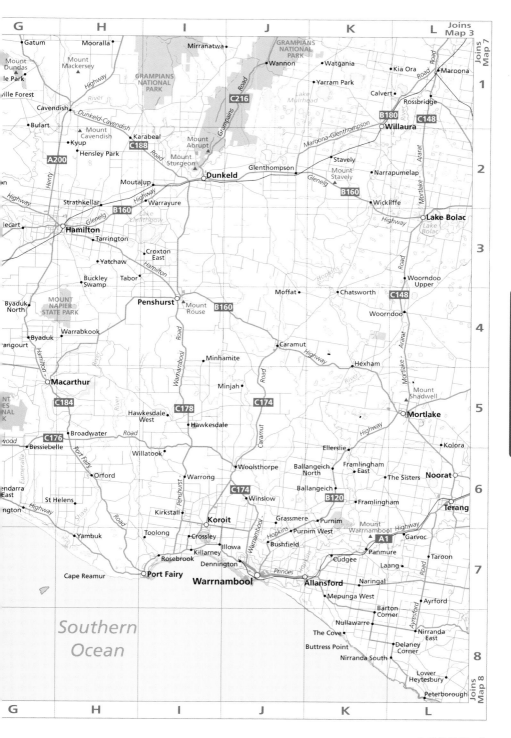

G   H   I   J   K   L

Gatum
Mooralla
Mirranatwa
GRAMPIANS
NATIONAL
PARK
Wannon
Watgania
Kia Ora
Maroona

Mount
Dundas
Mount
Mackersey
Highway
GRAMPIANS
NATIONAL
PARK
Yarram Park
Calvert
Rossbridge

le Park
River
Lake
Muirhead
B180
C148

ville Forest
Cavendish
Dunkeld-Cavendish
C216
Willaura

Bulart
Mount
Cavendish
Karabeal
Maroona-Glenthompson

A200
Kyup
C188
Mount
Abrupt
Stavely

Hensley Park
Mount
Sturgeon
Glenthompson
Mount
Stavely
Narrapumelap

Moutajup
Dunkeld
Glenelg
B160

Strathkellar
Warrayure
Wickliffe

B160
Lake
Linlithgow
Highway
Lake Bolac

lecart
Glenelg
Lake
Bolac

Hamilton
Tarrington

Croxton
East

Buckley
Swamp
Tabor
Hamilton
Hopkins
Woorndoo
Upper

Byaduk
North
MOUNT
NAPIER
STATE PARK
Moffat
Chatsworth
C148

Byaduk
Warrabkook
Penshurst
Mount
Rouse
B160
Woorndoo

angourt
Caramut
Hexham

Hamilton
Warrnambool
Road
Minhamite
Highway
Mount
Shadwell

Macarthur
Minjah

C184
C178
C174
Mortlake

C176
Broadwater
Road
Hawkesdale
West
Ellerslie
Kolora

wood
Bessiebelle
Hawkesdale
Caramut
Ballangeich
North
Framlingham
East
The Sisters
Noorat

Willatook
Woolsthorpe
Ballangeich

Port Fairy
Orford
Warrong
C174
Framlingham
Terang

endarra
East
Penshurst
C174
Winslow
B120

St Helens
Kirkstall
Grassmere
Purnim
Mount
Warrnambool
Highway

ngton
Highway
Koroit
Purnim West
A1
Garvoc

Yambuk
Toolong
Crossley
Hopkins
Bushfield
Panmure
Taroon

Shaw
Killarney
Illowa
Cudgee
Laang

Rosebrook
Dennington
Cape
Curdie

Cape Reamur
Port Fairy
Warrnambool
Princes
Allansford
Naringal

Mepunga West

Southern
Ocean
Nullawarre
Barton
Corner
Ayrford

The Cove
Nirranda
East

Buttress Point
Delaney
Corner

Nirranda South
Peterborough
Lower
Heytesbury

G   H   I   J   K   L

1 2 3 4 5 6 7 8

TOURING MAPS

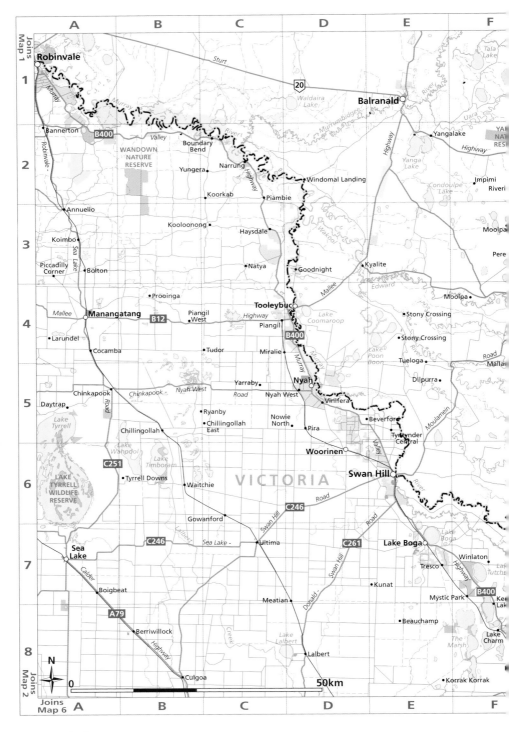

A   B   C   D   E   F

1   Robinvale

Sturt

20

Waldaira
Lake

Balranald

Tala
Lake

Murray

Murray   River   Uara

2   Bannerton   Yangalake   YA
    B400   NAT
           Valley   Boundary   River   Highway   Highway RES
           WANDOWN   Bend   Murrumbidgee
           NATURE   Narrung   Yanga
           RESERVE   Yungera   Windomal Landing   Condoulpe Lake   Impimi
                                                                                  Lake   Riveri
           Koorkab   Piambie

    Annuello   Kooloonong   Haysdale   Moolpa

3   Koimbo   Kyalite   Pere
                                              Natya   Goodnight   Edward
    Piccadilly   Moolpa
    Corner   Bolton   Mallee
                         Prooinga   Stony Crossing

    Mallee   Manangatang   Piangil   Tooleybuc   Lake   Stony Crossing
4   B12   West   Highway   Coomaroop
             Larundel   Piangil   B400   Lake   Tueloga   Road   Malla
                  Cocamba   Tudor   Poon
                                       Miralie   Murray   Boon   Dilpurra
                             Yarraby   Nyah
    Chinkapook   Chinkapook-   Nyah West   Nyah West
5   Daytrap   Road   Vinifera   Moulamein
    Lake   Ryanby   Nowie   Beverford
    Tyrrell   Chillingollah North   Pira
                             East   Tyntynder
             Chillingollah   Central
    Lake   Lake   Woorinen   Valley
    Wahpool   Timboram
6   LAKE   C251   VICTORIA   Swan Hill   River
    TYRRELL   Tyrrell Downs
    WILDLIFE   Waitchie
    RESERVE   River
                                        Swan Hill   Road
                  Gowanford   C246   Road

    Sea   Ultima   C261   Lake Boga   Lake
7   Lake   C246   Sea Lake -   Boga   Winlaton
                                                                        Tresco   Lake
    Boigbeat   Kunat   Tutchl
             A79   Meatian   Mystic Park   Ker
                  Berriwillock   Beauchamp   Lak
                             Highway   Lake   The   Lake
8   Calder   Lalbert   Lalbert   Marsh B400 Charm
    N   Korrak Korrak
    0   Culgoa   50km

TOURING MAPS

MAP 5 | Camping GUIDE TO VICTORIA

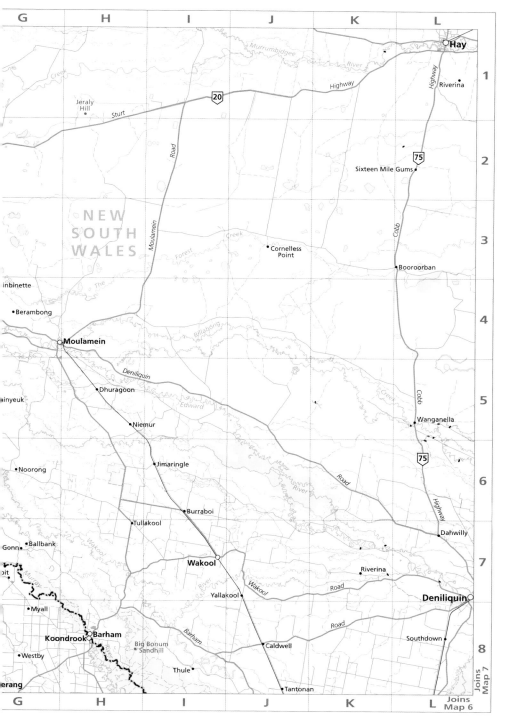

G   H   I   J   K   L

○ **Hay**

Murrumbidgee

River

Highway

Highway

1

Riverina

Jeraly
Hill •

Sturt

[20]

Road

[75]

2

Sixteen Mile Gums •

Cobb

NEW
SOUTH
WALES

Moulamein

Creek

Forest

• Cornelless
Point

3

• Booroorban

inbinette

The

Billabong

4

• Berambong

Cobb

Moulamein ○

Deniliquin

Edward

Creek

Cobb

5

• Dhuragoon

Wanganella •

inyeuk

• Niemur

[75]

River

• Jimaringle

Road

6

• Noorong

• Burraboi

• Tullakool

Road

Dahwilly •

Gonn • • Ballbank

Wakool

7

Wakool ○

Riverina •

Murray

Wakool

Road

Yallakool •

Deniliquin ○

pit

• Myall

River

Road

Barham

Southdown •

Koondrook ○ **Barham**

Big Bonum
Sandhill

• Caldwell

8

• Westby

erang

Thule •

• Tantonan

Joins
Map 7

Joins
Map 6

G   H   I   J   K   L

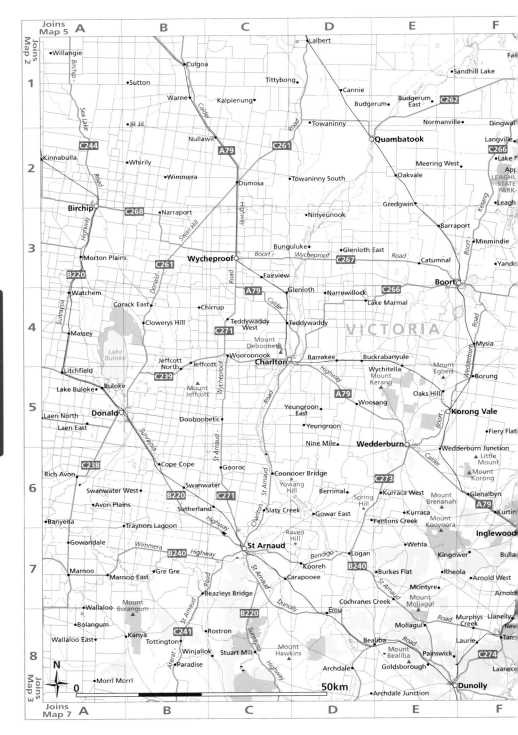

A B C D E F

•Willangie

•Lalbert

•Sandhill Lake

Fai

1

•Sutton

•Culgoa

Tittybong•

•Cannie

Budgerum•

Budgerum East

C262

•Warne

Kalpienung•

•Towaninny

Normanville•

Dingwal

•Jil Jil

Langville•

C266

Nullawil•

C261

Quambatook

Meering West•

•Lake

C244

Kinnabulla•

•Whirily

•Wimmera

Dumosa•

•Towaninny South

•Oakvale

App LEAGHU STATE PARK

2

•Gredgwin

•Leagh

Birchip

C268

•Narraport

•Ninyeunook

•Barraport

•Minmindie

•Morton Plains

Bunguluke•

Glenloth East•

•Catumnal

•Yando

3

B220

Wycheproof

Boort

Wycheproof

C267

Boort

•Watchem

Fairview•

C261

Corack East•

•Chirrup

Glenloth•

Narrewillock•

C266

Lake Marmal

A79

•Massey

•Clowerys Hill

Teddywaddy West•

•Teddywaddy

VICTORIA

•Mysia

4

C271

Wooroonook•

Barrakee•

Buckrabanyule•

•Borung

Litchfield•

Jeffcott North•

Jeffcott•

Charlton

Wychitella

Mount Kerang

Mount Egbert

Lake Buloke• •Buloke

C239

Mount Jeffcott

Oaks Hill•

Korong Vale

5

Laen North•

Donald

Dooboobetic•

Yeungroon East•

•Woosang

•Fiery Flat

Laen East•

•Yeungroon

Wedderburn

Wedderburn Junction•

C238

Rich Avon•

•Cope Cope

Gooroc•

Nine Mile•

Little Mount

Coonooer Bridge•

C273

Mount Korong

6

•Swanwater West

•Swanwater

B220

C271

Yowang Hill

Berrimal•

Kurraca West•

Mount Brenanah

Glenalbyn•

A79

•Avon Plains

Sutherland•

Slaty Creek•

Spring Hill

•Kurraca

Mount Kooyoora

Kurtir

•Banyena

•Traynors Lagoon

Gowar East•

•Fentons Creek

Inglewood

7

•Gowandale

Wimmera

B240

Highway

St Arnaud

Raven Hill

Bendigo•

•Logan

•Wehla

Kingower•

Bulla

•Marnoo

Marnoo East•

•Gre Gre

Beazleys Bridge•

•Kooreh

B240

•Burkes Flat

Rheola•

•Arnold West

Carapooee•

Mcintyre•

Arnold

•Wallaloo

Mount Bolangum

B220

Cochranes Creek•

Mount Moliagul

Murphys Creek

Lianelly

8

•Bolangum

Kanya•

C241

Rostron•

Emu•

Moliagul•

Nev

•Wallaloo East

Tottington•

Winjallok•

Stuart Mill•

Mount Hawkins

Bealiba•

Mount Bealiba

Painswick•

Laurie

Tarn

C274

•Paradise

Archdale•

Goldsborough•

Dunolly

•Morrl Morrl

Archdale Junction•

Laanec

N

0   50km

MAP 6 | Camping GUIDE TO VICTORIA

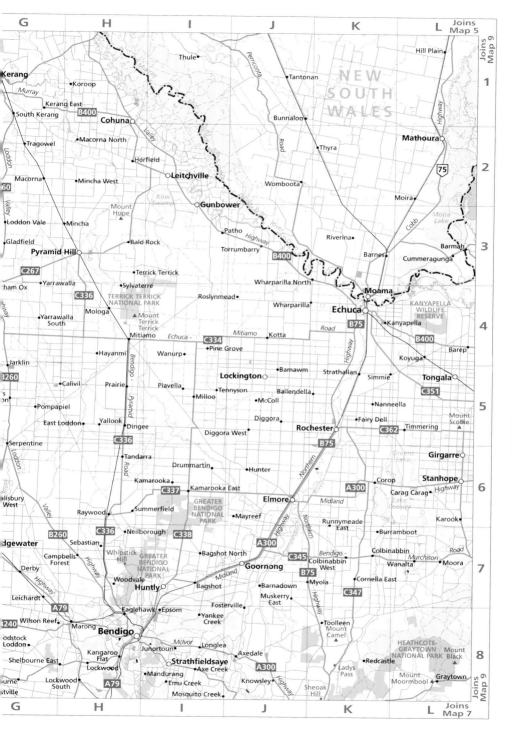

Joins Map 9

NEW SOUTH WALES

Kerang
Koroop
Kerang East
South Kerang
B400
Cohuna
Tragowel
Macorna North
Horfield
Macorna
Mincha West
Leitchville
Loddon Vale
Mincha
Gladfield
Bald Rock
Pyramid Hill
C267
Yarrawalla
ham Ox
Sylvaterre
Terrick Terrick
C336
TERRICK TERRICK NATIONAL PARK
Yarrawalla South
Mologa
Mount Hope
Gunbower
Patho
Torrumbarry
Highway
B400
Wharparilla North
Roslynmead
Wharparilla
Mount Terrick Terrick
Jarklin
Mitiamo
Echuca - Mitiamo Road
C334
Kotta
Hayanmi
Wanurp
Pine Grove
Calivil
Prairie
Piavella
Milloo
Lockington
Bamawm
Strathallan
Simmie
Pompapiel
Yallook
Dingee
Tennyson
McColl
Ballendella
Nanneella
Fairy Dell
Serpentine
C336
Tandarra
Diggora West
Diggora
Rochester
B75
C362
Timmering
Drummartin
Hunter
Kamarooka
Kamarooka East
C337
Elmore
A300
Corop
Carag Carag
B260
dgewater
C336
Neilborough
C338
GREATER BENDIGO NATIONAL PARK
Mayreef
Midland
Runnymeade East
Burramboot
lisbury West
Raywood
Summerfield
Sebastian
Bagshot North
A300
C345
Colbinabbin West
B75
Colbinabbin
Wanalta
Moora
Campbells Forest
Whipstick Hill
GREATER BENDIGO NATIONAL PARK
Goornong
Bendigo
Cornella East
C347
Karook
Derby
Huntly
Bagshot
Barnadown
Myola
Woodvale
Muskerry East
Leichardt
A79
Eaglehawk
Epsom
Fosterville
Yankee Creek
240
Wilson Reef
Marong
odstock Loddon
Mclvor
Longlea
Axedale
A300
Toolleen
Mount Camel
HEATHCOTE-GRAYTOWN NATIONAL PARK
Mount Black
Shelbourne East
Kangaroo Flat
Lockwood
Junortoun
Strathfieldsaye
Axe Creek
Redcastle
burne
Lockwood South
tville
A79
Mandurang
Emu Creek
Mosquito Creek
Knowsley
Ladys Pass
Sheoak Hill
Mount Moormbool
Graytown

Thule
Tantonan
Perricoota
Bunnaloo
Thyra
Koroop
Womboota
Mathoura
75
Moira
Moira Lake
Riverina
Barnes
Barmah
Cummeragunga
Moama
Echuca
B75
Kanyapella
KANYAPELLA WILDLIFE RESERVE
B400
Koyuga
Barep
Tongala
C351

TOURING MAPS

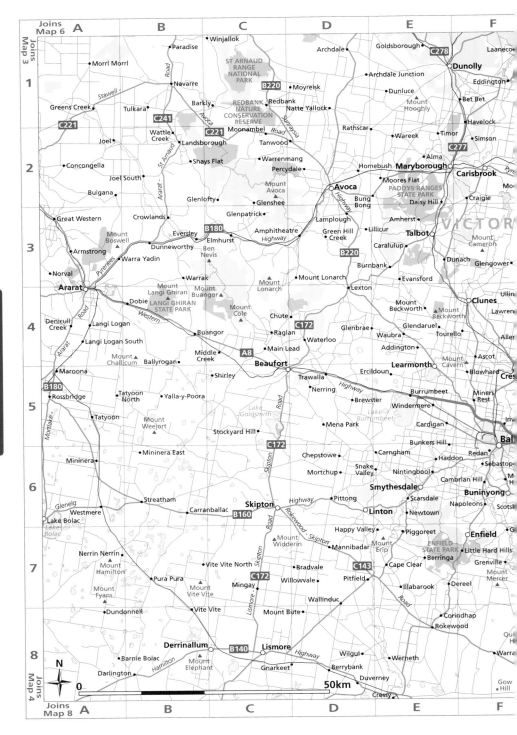

A   B   C   D   E   F

1
2
3
4
5
6
7
8

• Winjallok
• Paradise
• Morrl Morrl
• Navarre
ST ARNAUD RANGE NATIONAL PARK
• Archdale
• Goldsborough
C278
Laaneco
• Dunolly
• Eddington
B220
• Moyreisk
• Archdale Junction
• Dunluce
Mount Hooghly
• Bet Bet
• Barkly
REDBANK NATURE CONSERVATION RESERVE
• Redbank
• Natte Yallock
• Rathscar
• Havelock
• Greens Creek
• Tulkara
C221
Wattle Creek
C221
• Moonambel
Avoca Road
Tanwood
• Wareek
• Timor
Alma
• Simson
C277
• Joel
• Landsborough
• Warrenmang
Percydale
• Homebush
Maryborough
• Carisbrook
Mo
• Concongella
• Shays Flat
Mount Avoca
Moores Flat
PADDYS RANGES STATE PARK
• Joel South
• Bulgana
• Glenlofty
• Glenshee
Avoca
Bung Bong
Daisy Hill
• Craigie
• Great Western
• Crowlands
Glenpatrick
• Lamplough
• Amherst
VICTOR
Mount Boswell
Eversley
B180
• Elmhurst
Amphitheatre Highway
Green Hill Creek
• Lillicur
Talbot
Mount Cameron
• Dunneworthy
Ben Nevis
• Caralulup
Mount Cameron
• Armstrong
• Warra Yadin
B220
• Burnbank
• Dunach
Glengower•
Pyrenees
• Warrak
Mount Lonarch
• Evansford
Ararat
Mount Langi Ghiran
Mount Buangor
Mount Lonarch
• Lexton
Mount Beckworth
Mount Beckworth
Clunes
Ullin
Western
LANGI GHIRAN STATE PARK
Mount Cole
• Chute
C172
• Glenbrae
Glendaruel
• Tourello
Lawren
• Denicull Creek
• Dobie
• Buangor
• Raglan
• Waterloo
• Waubra
• Addington
Aller
• Langi Logan
Middle Creek
A8
• Main Lead
Ercildoun
Learmonth
Mount Cavern
• Ascot
• Langi Logan South
Beaufort
• Trawalla
• Blowhard
Cres
• Maroona
Mount Challicum
• Ballyrogan
• Shirley
Nerring
Highway
• Burrumbeet
Windermere
Miners Rest
B180
• Rossbridge
Tatyoon North
• Yalla-y-Poora
• Brewster
Lake Burrumbeet
• Cardigan
Inv
Bal
• Tatyoon
Mount Weejort
• Stockyard Hill
Lake Goldsmith
• Mena Park
Bunkers Hill
• Mininera East
C172
• Chepstowe
• Carngham
• Haddon
Redan
Sebastop
• Mininera
• Mortchup
Snake Valley
• Nintingbool
Cambrian Hill
M H
• Streatham
• Carranballac
Skipton
B160
Highway
• Pittong
Smythesdale
• Scarsdale
Napoleons
Buninyong
Scotsl
Glenelg
• Westmere
Rokewood - Skipton Road
Linton
• Newtown
• Enfield
G
Lake Bolac
Lake Bolac
• Happy Valley
• Piggoreet
ENFIELD STATE PARK
• Little Hard Hills
• Nerrin Nerrin
Mount Widderin
• Mannibadar
Mount Erip
Cape Clear
• Berringa
• Grenville
Mount Hamilton
• Vite Vite North
• Bradvale
C143
• Pitfield
Mount Mercer
• Pura Pura
Mount Vite Vite
• Mingay
• Willowvale
• Illabarook
• Dereel
Mount Fyans
• Vite Vite
• Wallinduc
Road
• Corindhap
• Rokewood
• Dundonnell
Mount Bute
Qui H
• Derrinallum
B140
Lismore
Highway
• Wilgul
• Werneth
• Warra
N
• Barnie Bolac
Mount Elephant
• Gnarkeet
Berrybank
Duverney
Gow Hill
• Darlington
Hamilton
50km
Cressy

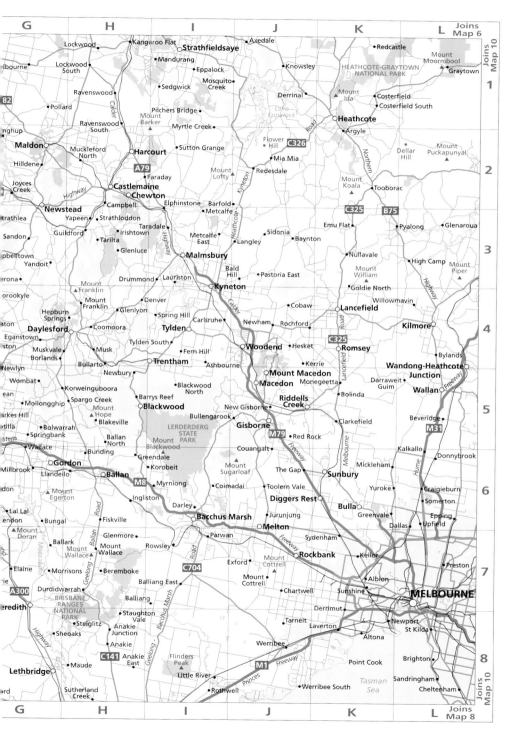

G H I J K L

Lockwood
•Kangaroo Flat •Axedale
Lockwood •Strathfieldsaye •Redcastle •Mount
South •Mandurang •Knowsley Moormbool
Ibourne •Eppalock HEATHCOTE-GRAYTOWN •Graytown
•Mosquito NATIONAL PARK
Ravenswood •Sedgwick Creek •Mount 1
82 •Pilchers Bridge Ida •Costerfield
•Pollard •Derrinal •Costerfield South
Mount
Ravenswood Barker •Argyle
South •Myrtle Creek •Heathcote
Maldon •Sutton Grange Flower C326 •Dellar •Mount
Muckleford •Hill Hill Puckapunyal 2
Hilldene North •Harcourt •Mia Mia
Mount •Redesdale •Mount
Joyces •Faraday Lofty Koala •Tooborac
Creek •Castlemaine •Sidonia
rathlea •Chewton •Barfold •Langley •Baynton C325 B75
•Campbell •Elphinstone •Metcalfe •Emu Flat •Pyalong •Glenaroua
Newstead •Yapeen •Strathloddon •Metcalfe •Nullavale 3
Sandon •Guildford •Taradale East •High Camp •Mount
•Tarilta •Irishtown •Langley •Mount Piper
pbelltown •Glenluce •Malmsbury William
Yandoit •Bald •Pastoria East •Goldie North
erona •Drummond •Lauriston Hill •Willowmavin
Mount •Kyneton •Cobaw •Lancefield
orookyle Franklin •Denver •Kilmore 4
Mount •Newham •Rochford C325
Hepburn Franklin •Glenlyon •Spring Hill •Carlsruhe •Romsey •Bylands
Springs •Coomoora •Tylden •Woodend •Hesket Wandong-Heathcote
Daylesford •Musk •Kerrie Junction
Eganstown •Tylden South •Fern Hill Darraweit •Wallan 5
ston •Muskvale •Trentham •Ashbourne •Mount Macedon •Guim
Newlyn •Borlands •Bullarto •Newbury •Blackwood •Macedon •Monegeetta •Beveridge
Wombat •Korweinguboora North •Riddells Bolinda •Kalkallo M31
ean •Mollongghip •Spargo Creek •Barrys Reef •New Gisborne Creek •Clarkefield •Donnybrook
arkes Hill Mount •Blackwood •Gisborne •Mickleham
tilla •Bolwarrah Hope •Bullengarook M79 •Red Rock •Yuroke •Craigieburn 6
•Springbank •Blakeville LERDERDERG •Couangalt •Somerton
tern •Wallace Ballan STATE •Greendale •The Gap •Sunbury •Epping
•Bunding North Mount PARK •Korobeit •Diggers Rest •Greenvale •Upfield
•Gordon Blackwood Mount •Coimadai •Bulla
Millbrook •Llandeilo •Ballan M8 •Myrniong Sugarloaf •Toolern Vale •Dallas
don •Ingliston •Darley •Bacchus Marsh •Jurunjung •Keilor 7
Lal Lal Mount •Fiskville •Melton •Sydenham •Albion
endon Egerton •Parwan •Rockbank •Sunshine •Preston
Mount •Bungal •Glenmore •Rowsley Mount •Chartwell MELBOURNE
Doran •Ballark •Exford Cottrell •Derrimut •Newport
Elaine •Morrisons Mount •Beremboke Mount •St Kilda
A300 •Durdidwarrah Wallace •Balliang East Cottrell •Tarneit •Altona 8
eredith BRISBANE •Balliang •Laverton •Brighton
RANGES •Staughton •Werribee •Sandringham
NATIONAL Steiglitz Vale •Anakie •Point Cook •Cheltenham
Lethbridge PARK •Sheoaks Junction Tasman
C141 •Anakie •Werribee South Sea Joins
rd •Maude East •Flinders M1 Map 10
•Sutherland Peak
Creek •Little River •Rothwell

G H I J K L

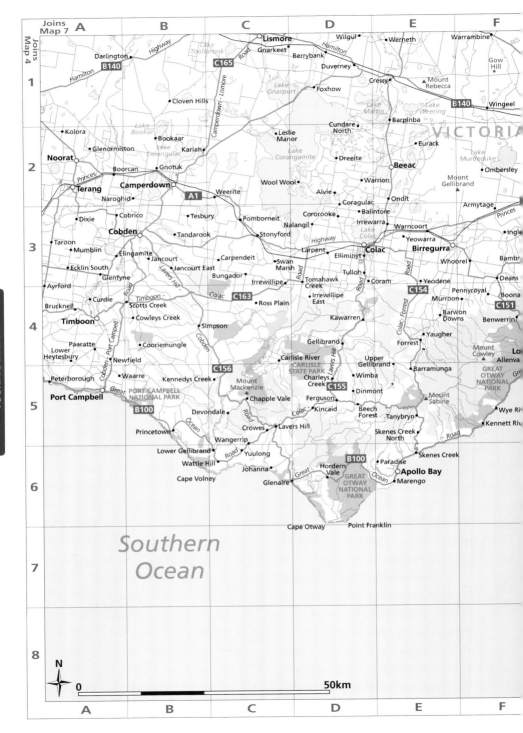

A   B   C   D   E   F

1

2

3

4

5

6

7

8

Lismore

Darlington
Gnarkeet
Berrybank
Wilgul
Werneth
Warrambine

Highway
B140
C165
Duverney
Hamilton
Cressy
Mount Rebecca
Gow Hill

Lake Toolbrook
Cressy
B140
Wingeel

Cloven Hills

Lake Gnarpurt
Foxhow
Lake Martin
Lake Weering

Kolora
Bookaar
Leslie Manor
Cundare North
Barpinba

VICTORIA

Glenormiston
Kariah
Lake Colongulac
Dreeite
Eurack
Lake Murdeduke
Ombersley

Noorat
Boorcan
Gnotuk
Wool Wool
Warrion
Beeac
Mount Gellibrand

Terang
Naroghid
Camperdown
Weerite
Alvie
Coragulac
Ondit
Armytage

Princes
A1
Cobrico
Tesbury
Pomborneit
Cororooke
Balintore
Irrewarra
Warncoort
Princes

Dixie
Tandarook
Stonyford
Nalangil
Lake Colac
Yeowarra
Ingl

Cobden
Highway
Larpent
Elliminyt
Colac
Birregurra

Taroon
Mumblin
Elingamite
Jancourt
Carpendeit
Swan Marsh
Tulloh
Whoorel
Bambr

Ecklin South
Jancourt East
Bungador
Tomahawk Creek
Coram
Yeodene
Deans

Glenfyne
Irrewillipe
Irrewillipe East
C154
Pennyroyal
Murroon
Boona

Ayrford
Curdie
Timboon
Colac
C163
Ross Plain
Kawarren
Barwon Downs
Benwerrin
C151

Brucknell
Scotts Creek
Cowleys Creek
Simpson
Gellibrand
Forrest
Yaugher
Mount Cowley
Lo

Timboon
Cooriemungle
Carlisle River
Upper Gellibrand
Forrest
Allenva

Paaratte
Lower Heytesbury
Newfield
C156
CARLISLE STATE PARK
Charleys Creek
Wimba
Barramunga
GREAT OTWAY NATIONAL PARK
Gre

Peterborough
Waarre
Kennedys Creek
Mount Mackenzie
C155
Dinmont
Mount Sabine
Wye Ri

Port Campbell
B100
PORT CAMPBELL NATIONAL PARK
Chapple Vale
Ferguson
Kincaid
Beech Forest
Tanybryn
Kennett Riv

Devondale
Crowes
Lavers Hill
Skenes Creek North

Princetown
Wangerrip
Yuulong
Skenes Creek

Lower Gellibrand
Wattle Hill
Johanna
Hordern Vale
B100
Paradise

Cape Volney
Glenaire
GREAT OTWAY NATIONAL PARK
Marengo
Apollo Bay

Cape Otway
Point Franklin

Southern Ocean

N

0   50km

A   B   C   D   E   F

MAP 8 | Camping GUIDE TO **VICTORIA**

TOURING MAPS

G   H   I   J   K   L

Lethbridge • Maude

Anakie • East

Flinders ▲ Peak

• Little River   Freeway

Brighton Beach •

Sandringham •

ford

A300

Sutherland Creek

• Teesdale

Lara

M1

• Rothwell

• Werribee South

Cheltenham •

Princes

1

Bannockburn

Gheringhap

Mooraboo

• Corio

Port Phillip Bay

• Mordialloc

Murgheboluc   Batesford

leigh

Mount Pollock ▲

• Gnarwarre

River   Fyansford

Geelong

• Thomson

Clifton Springs

• Ceres

Portarlington

• Indented Head

2

Mount Moriac •

Highway

B100

Drysdale

• Murradoc

St Leonards

Buckley •

Leopold

Wallington

chelsea

Layard •

Moriac

Marcus

Mornington

• Paraparap

Connewarre

Ocean Grove

Queenscliff

Mount Martha •

Bellbrae •

Torquay

Barwon Heads

Observatory Point

• Portsea

3

Surfcoast   Highway

Sorrento

Dromana

M7

• Red Hill

• Wensleydale

GREAT OTWAY NATIONAL PARK

Road

Blairgowrie •

Rosebud

Rye

B100

Anglesea

• Boneo

Shoreham

4

Ocean

Aireys Inlet-Fairhaven

Mornington Peninsula

• Flinders

Cape Schanck •

Bass Strait

5

6

7

8

G   H   I   J   K   L

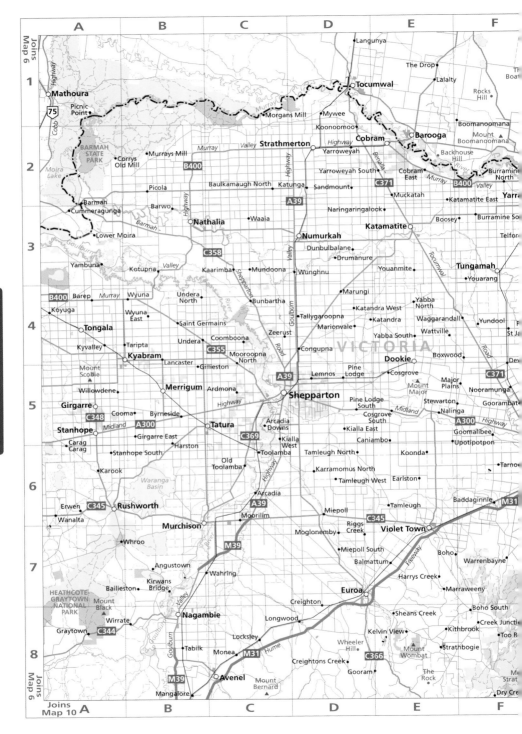

A   B   C   D   E   F

1

2

3

4

TOURING MAPS

5

6

7

8

A   B   C   D   E   F

MAP 9 | *Camping* GUIDE TO **VICTORIA**

Langunya

The Drop • Lalalty

Tocumwal

Mathoura

Picnic Point

Morgans Mill

Mywee

Koonoomoo

Cobram

Strathmerton

Yarroweyah

Baulkamaugh North

Katunga

Sandmount

Yarroweyah South

Muckatah

Naringaringalook

Boosey

Katamatite

Corrys Old Mill

Murrays Mill

Picola

Barwo

Barmah

Cummeragunga

Nathalia

Waaia

Numurkah

Dunbulbalane

Drumanure

Youanmite

Youarang

Tungamah

Lower Moira

Yambuna

Kotupna

Kaarimba

Mundoona

Wunghnu

Marungi

Katandra West

Yabba North

Waggarandall

Yundool

Barep

Wyuna

Undera North

Bunbartha

Katandra

Yabba South

Wattville

Koyuga

Wyuna East

Saint Germains

Coomboona

Zeerust

Congupna

VICTORIA

Boxwood

Tongala

Undera

Marionvale

Kyvalley

Taripta

Kyabram

Lancaster

Gillieston

Mooroopna North

Lemnos

Pine Lodge

Cosgrove

Major Plains

Nooramunga

Willowdene

Merrigum

Ardmona

Shepparton

Pine Lodge South

Mount Major

Stewarton

Gooramba

Girgarre

Cooma

Byrneside

Highway

Cosgrove South

Nalinga

Stanhope

Midland

Girgarre East

Harston

Tatura

Kialla West

Toolamba

Kialla East

Caniambo

Koonda

Goomalibee

Upotipotpon

Carag Carag

Stanhope South

Old Toolamba

Tamleugh North

Tarno

Karook

Waranga Basin

Arcadia

Karramomun North

Tamleugh West

Earlston

Erwen

Rushworth

Moorilim

Miepoll

Tamleugh

Baddaginnie

Wanalta

Murchison

Moglonemby

Riggs Creek

Violet Town

Whroo

Miepoll South

Boho

Warrenbayne

Angustown

Wahring

Balmattum

Harrys Creek

Marraweeny

Kirwans Bridge

Bailieston

Creighton

Euroa

Sheans Creek

Boho South

Creek Junction

HEATHCOTE-GRAYTOWN NATIONAL PARK

Mount Black

Wirrate

Nagambie

Longwood

Kelvin View

Strathbogie

Graytown

Tabilk

Locksley

Monea

Wheeler Hill

Mount Wombat

The Rock

Avenel

Mount Bernard

Creightons Creek

Gooram

Mangalore

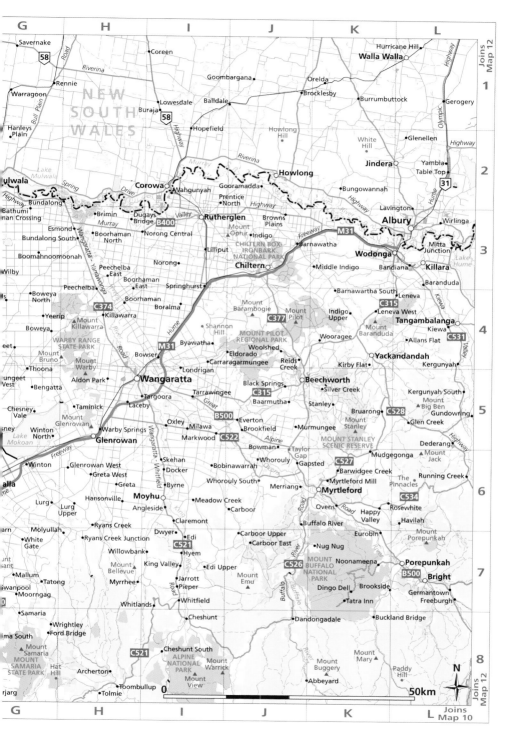

G H I J K L

Savernake

58 Road

Riverina

Warragoon •Rennie

Hanleys •Plain

Coreen•

Goombargana•

Orelda•

Brocklesby•

Lowesdale• Balldale•

Buraja• 58

NEW
SOUTH
WALES

Hopefield•

Howlong
Hill

Murray

Riverina

Howlong•

Hurricane Hill•

Walla Walla○

1

Burrumbuttock•

Gerogery•

White
Hill

Glenellen•

Highway

Jindera○

Olympic

Yambla
Table Top•

31

2

ulwala

Lake
Mulwala

Bundalong• Spring

Bathumi
nan Crossing

Bundalong South•

Esmond•

Boomahnoomoonah•

Wilby•

Corowa○

Brimin•
Dugays
Bridge• B400

Boorhaman
North•

Norong•

Peechelba
East•

Wahgunyah•

Prentice
North

Murray Valley

Rutherglen○

Norong Central•

Lilliput•

Gooramadda•

Highway

Mount
Ophir Indigo•

CHILTERN BOX-
IRONBARK
NATIONAL PARK

Chiltern○

Browns
Plains

Barnawatha•

Bungowannah•

Lavington•

Freeway

M31

Wodonga○

Middle Indigo•

Bandiana

Albury

Wirlinga•

Mitta
Junction•

Killara○

Baranduda

Lake
Hume

3

Wangaratta-Yarrawonga

C374

Boweya
North•

Yeerip•

Boweya•

Mount
Killawarra•

Killawarra•

Peechelba
East•

Boorhaman
East•

Boorhaman•

Boralma•

Springhurst•

Shannon
Hill•

Mount
Barambogie

MOUNT PILOT
REGIONAL PARK

Mount
Pilot• C377

Barnawartha South•

Indigo
Upper•

Wooragee•

Barnawartha South

Leneva•

C315

Leneva West•

Mount
Baranduda

Kiewa•

Allans Flat•

Tangambalanga

C531

Kiewa Valley

4

eet•

Mount
Bruno•

WARBY RANGE
STATE PARK

•Thoona

Mount
Warby•

•Bengatta

Byawatha•

Hume Road

Bowser•

Aldon Park•

Londrigan•

Woolshed•

Eldorado•

Carraragarmungee•

Reids
Creek

Black Springs•

Kirby Flat•

Yackandandah○

Kergunyah•

Kergunyah South•

5

Chesney
Vale•

sney

Lake
Mokoan

Mount
Glenrowan•

Winton
North•

Taminick•

Glenrowan○

Wangaratta○

Targoora•

Laceby•

Tarrawingee•

Great Alpine

Baarmutha•

B500

Beechworth○

Silver Creek•

Stanley•

C315

Murmungee•

Mount
Stanley

Bruarong•

Mount
Big Ben

C528

Glen Creek•

Gundowring•

Dederang•

Mount
Jack

Highway

•Winton

Glenrowan West•

Greta West•

•Greta

Oxley•

Milawa•

Markwood•

Everton•

Brookfield•

C522

Bowman•

Whorouly•

Taylor
Gap

Gapsted•

C527

Mudgegonga•

Barwidgee Creek•

Running Creek•

The
Pinnacles

6

alla

Lurg•

Lurg
Upper•

Hansonville•

Angleside•

Moyhu○

Skehan•

Docker•

Byrne•

Bobinawarrah•

Whorouly South•

Meadow Creek•

Carboor•

Merriang•

Myrtleford○

Myrtleford Mill•

Ovens

Road

Happy
Valley

Rosewhite•

Havilah•

C534

Molyullah•

•White
Gate

Ryans Creek•

Ryans Creek Junction•

Willowbank•

Dwyer•

Claremont•

Edi•

C521

Hyem•

Carboor Upper•

Carboor East•

Nug Nug•

Buffalo River•

Eurobin•

Mount
Porepunkah

7

unt
sant

•Mallum

•Tatong

wanpool

•Moorngag

Mount
Bellevue•

King Valley•

Myrrhee•

Road

Jarrott•

Pieper•

Whitlands•

Edi Upper•

Whitfield•

Mount
Emu

C526

MOUNT
BUFFALO
NATIONAL
PARK

Buffalo River

Noonameena•

Dingo Dell•

Brookside•

Tatra Inn•

Porepunkah○

B500

Bright●

Germantown
Freeburgh•

•Samaria

•Wrightley

ma South •Ford Bridge

Mount
Samaria

MOUNT
SAMARIA
STATE PARK

rjarg

Cheshunt•

C521

Cheshunt South•

Hat
Hill

Archerton•

•Toombullup

•Tolmie

ALPINE
NATIONAL
PARK

Mount
Warrick•

Mount
View

Dandongadale•

Mount
Mary

Mount
Buggery

•Abbeyard

Buckland Bridge•

Mount
Buffalo

Paddy
Hill•

0 50km

N

8

Joins
Map 12

Joins
Map 10

Joins
Map 12

G H I J K L Joins
Map 10

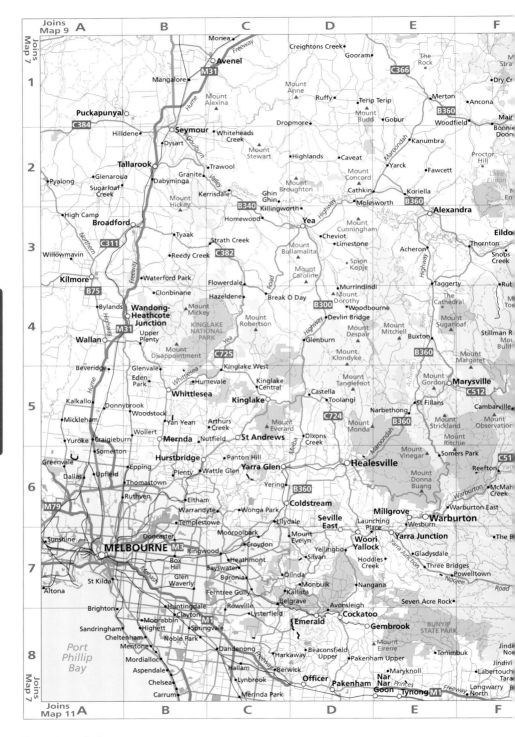

TOURING MAPS

MAP 10 | *Camping* GUIDE TO **VICTORIA**

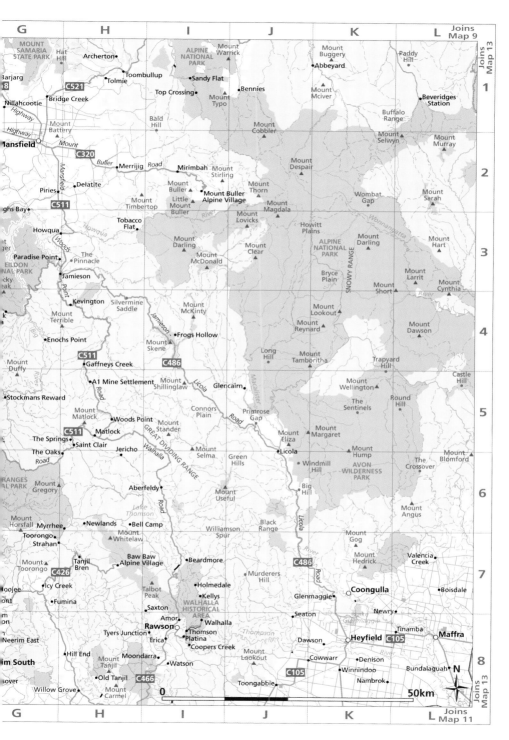

G   H   I   J   K   L

Joins
Map 13

MOUNT SAMARIA STATE PARK
Hat Hill
Archerton•

Barjarg
8

Toombullup
C521   Tolmie•

Nillakootie
Bridge Creek•

ALPINE NATIONAL PARK
Mount Warrick
Mount Buggery
•Abbeyard
Paddy Hill•

Sandy Flat•

•Bennies
Mount Mciver

Beveridges Station•

1

Top Crossing•
Mount Typo

Buffalo Range

Mount Battery
Bald Hill

Mount Cobbler

Mount Selwyn
Mount Murray

Mansfield

C320   Buller   Road
Merrijig•   •Mirimbah
Mount Stirling

Mount Despair

2

Piries•   •Delatite
Mount Buller
Little Mount Buller
Mount Buller Alpine Village

Mount Thorn

Mount Magdala

Wombat Gap

Mount Sarah

C511

•Mount Timbertop

Mount Lovicks

ghs Bay•

Howqua•
Tobacco Flat•

Mount Darling
Mount McDonald

Mount Clear

Howitt Plains

ALPINE NATIONAL PARK

Mount Darling

Mount Hart

3

Paradise Point•
The Pinnacle

SNOWY RANGE

Mount Larrit

Mount Cynthia

EILDON AL PARK
cky eak•

•Jamieson

Bryce Plain

Mount Short

•Kevington
Silvermine Saddle

Mount McKinty

Mount Lookout

Mount Dawson

4

Mount Terrible

•Frogs Hollow
Mount Skene

Mount Reynard

•Enochs Point

Long Hill

Mount Tamboritha

Trapyard Hill

Mount Duffy
C511   •Gaffneys Creek
C486

Licola   Road

Glencairn•

Mount Wellington

Castle Hill

•Stockmans Reward
•A1 Mine Settlement
Mount Shillinglaw

The Sentinels
Round Hill

5

Mount Matlock
•Woods Point
Saint Clair•   •Matlock
Jericho•
Mount Stander

Connors Plain

Primrose Gap

•Licola

Mount Eliza
Mount Margaret

Mount Hump

The Crossover

Mount Blomford

The Springs•
The Oaks
Road

GREAT DIVIDING RANGE   Walhalla

Mount Selma

Green Hills

AVON WILDERNESS PARK

RANGES AL PARK
Mount Gregory

•Aberfeldy

Road

Mount Useful

Big Hill

6

Lake Thomson

Williamson Spur

Black Range

Mount Angus

Mount Horsfall
•Myrrhee
•Newlands
•Bell Camp
Mount Whitelaw

Mount Gog

Toorongo
Strahan•

Baw Baw Alpine Village
•Beardmore

Murderers Hill

Mount Hedrick

Valencia Creek

7

Mount Toorongo
Tanjil Bren
C426

Talbot Peak

Licola River

Road

•Boisdale

oojee
•Icy Creek
•Holmedale

•Kellys

Glenmaggie•
C486

Newry•

•Fumina

Saxton•

WALHALLA HISTORICAL AREA
Amor•

•Seaton

Glenmaggie

Tinamba•
•Maffra

on
on

Neerim East

Rawson
Tyers Junction•
•Erica
Thomson Platina
•Coopers Creek

•Walhalla

Thompson   River

Dawson•

Heyfield C105

8

m South

•Hill End
Mount Tanjil
Moondarra•
•Watson

Mount Lookout

Cowwarr•
•Denison
Bundalaguah•

over

•Old Tanjil
C466

Mount Carmel

Toongabbie•

C105
Winnindoo•
Nambrok•

N

Willow Grove•

0   50km

G   H   I   J   K   L

Joins
Map 13

TOURING MAPS

Camping GUIDE TO **VICTORIA** | **MAP 10**

Port
Phillip
Bay

Mordialloc
Aspendale
Chelsea
Carrum
Seaford
Kananook
Frankston
Leawarra
Langwarrin
Mount Eliza
Baxter
Mornington
Narambi
Moorooduc
Mount Martha
Martha Point
Dromana
Rosebud
Red Hill
Rye
Mornington
Peninsula
Shoreham
Merricks
North
Somers
Bittern
Morradoo
Fairhaven
Hastings
Tyabb
Somerville
Pearcedale
Warneet
East
Scrub
Point

Hallam
Berwick
Lyndhurst
Lynbrook
Carrum
Downs
Merinda Park
Cranbourne
Clyde
Fiveways
Dalmore
Tooradin
Sandy
Point
Tankerton
Cowes
Flinders
Ventnor
Summerland
Newhaven
San
Remo
Cape Woolamai
Cape
Schanck

Officer
Pakenham
Nar Nar
Goon
Tynong
Cardinia
Koo-Wee-Rup
Monomeith
Palmer
Point
Mount
Wellington
Western
Port
Grantville
Corinella
Coronet Bay
Rhyll
Stony
Point
Bass
Glen
Forbes
Woolamai
Anderson
Kilcunda
Dalyston
Wonthaggi
Inverloch
Cape
Paterson

Pakenham Upper
Maryknoll
Garfield North
Jindivi
Labertouch
Tara
Garfield M1
Longwarry Bunyip
Vervale
Cora Lynn
Iona
Drouin
Warn
Bayles
Modella
Ripplebrook
Lang Lang
Athlone
Ellir
South
Westernport
Nyora
Loch
Strzele
Poowong
Ranceby
Jeetho
Bena C425
Korumburra
Krowera
Queensferry
Almurta
Moyarra
Jumbunna
Kongwak
Outtrim
Ellerside
Leongatha
South
B460
Bass
Venus Bay
Tarwin Meadows
L
Tute
CAPE
LIPTRAP
COASTA
PARK
Morgan
Cape

A440
B460
C437
C431
M420

Tasman

Sea

N

0   50km

MAP 11 | Camping GUIDE TO **VICTORIA**

TOURING MAPS

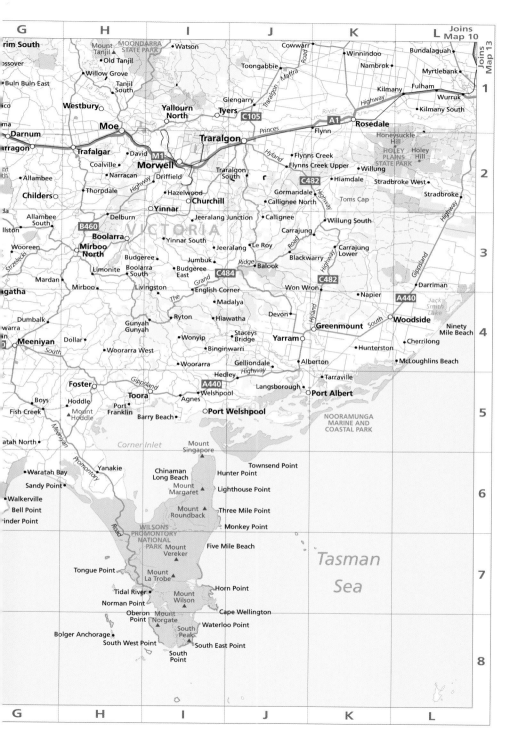

G   H   I   J   K   L

rim South

Mount
Tanjil ▲   MOONDARRA
STATE PARK   •Watson   Cowwarr•   •Winnindoo   Bundalaguah•

ossover   •Old Tanjil   Toongabbie•   Nambrok•   Myrtlebank•

•Buln Buln East   •Willow Grove   Kilmany   Fulham   Wurruk•

ico   Tanjil
South   Glengarry•   Highway   •Kilmany South

ma   Westbury○   Yallourn
North   •Tyers   C105

Darnum   Moe○   Traralgon•   Princes   Flynn   Rosedale○

rragon○   Trafalgar•   •David   Honeysuckle
Hill

nt
th   Coalville•   Morwell○   M1   •Flynns Creek   HOLEY   Holey
Hill

•Allambee   •Narracan   Driffield•   Traralgon
South   •Flynns Creek Upper   •Willung   PLAINS
STATE PARK

Childers○   •Thorpdale   Highway   •Hazelwood   Gormandale•   C482   •Hiamdale   Stradbroke West•

Yinnar○   ○Churchill   •Callignee North   Toms Cap   Stradbroke•

da   Allambee
South•   •Delburn   •Jeeralang Junction   •Callignee   •Willung South

Ilston•   B460   Boolarra○   •Yinnar South   Carrajung

Wooreen•   Mirboo
North○   Budgeree•   •Jeeralang   Le Roy   Carrajung
Lower

Mardan•   Limonite•   Boolarra
South•   Jumbuk•   Budgeree
East   C484   •Balook   Blackwarry•

gatha   Mirboo•   Livingston•   •English Corner   Won Wron•   C482   •Darriman

Dumbalk•   The   •Madalya   •Napier   A440   Jack
Smith
Lake

warra•   Gunyah
Gunyah   •Ryton   •Hiawatha   Devon•   Greenmount   South   ○Woodside

Meeniyan○   Dollar•   •Wonyip   Staceys
Bridge   Yarram○   •Cherrilong   Ninety
Mile Beach

•Woorarra West   •Binginwarri   •Hunterston

•Woorarra   Gelliondale•   •Alberton   •McLoughlins Beach

Foster○   Gippsland   Hedley•   Highway   •Tarraville

Boys   Toora○   Agnes○   A440   Langsborough•   ○Port Albert

Hoddle•   Port
Franklin•   •Welshpool

Fish Creek•   Mount
Hoddle   Barry Beach•   ○Port Welshpool   NOORAMUNGA
MARINE AND
COASTAL PARK

atah North•   Corner Inlet   Mount
Singapore

Waratah Bay•   Yanakie•   Chinaman
Long Beach   Townsend Point

Sandy Point•   Mount
Margaret   Hunter Point

•Walkerville   Lighthouse Point

Bell Point   Mount ▲
Roundback   Three Mile Point

inder Point   WILSONS
PROMONTORY
NATIONAL
PARK   Monkey Point

Mount
Vereker ▲   Five Mile Beach

Tongue Point•   Mount
La Trobe▲   Tasman

Tidal River•   Mount
Wilson▲   Horn Point   Sea

Norman Point•

Oberon
Point   Mount
Norgate   Cape Wellington

Bolger Anchorage•   South
Peak▲   Waterloo Point

South West Point   •South East Point

South
Point

VICTORIA

La Trobe

Strzelecki

Meeniyan

Promontory

Road

Traralgon-Maffra   Road

Princes

Hyland

Hyland

Grand   Ridge   Road

Gippsland

TOURING MAPS

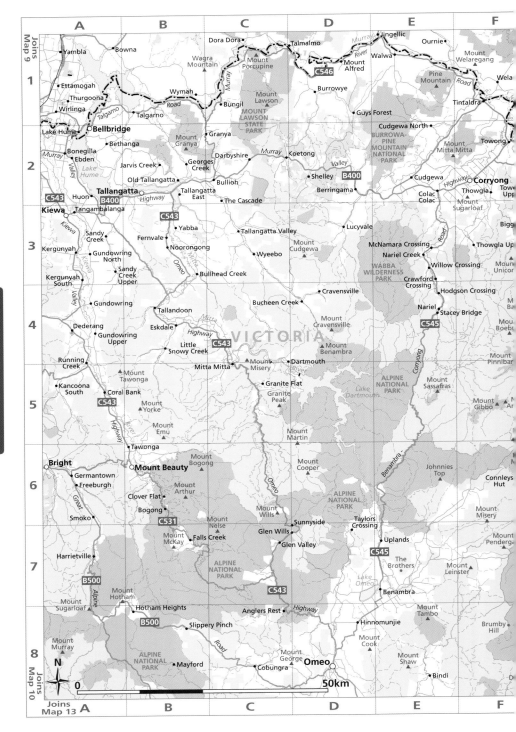

A   B   C   D   E   F

1

Yambla   Bowna   Dora Dora   Talmalmo   Murray   Jingellic   Ournie   Mount Welaregang
Wagra Mountain   Mount Porcupine   C546   Mount Alfred   Walwa   Pine Mountain   Road   Wela
Ettamogah   Wymah   Burrowye   Pine Mountain   Tintaldra
Thurgoona   Road   Bungil   Mount Lawson   Guys Forest
Wirlinga   Talgamo   Talgarno   MOUNT LAWSON STATE PARK   Cudgewa North   Towong

2

Lake Hume   **Bellbridge**   Granya   Murray   Koetong   BURROWA-PINE MOUNTAIN NATIONAL PARK   Mount Mitta Mitta   Towong
Bethanga   Mount Granya   Darbyshire   Valley   **Corryong**   Towong Upp
Bonegilla   Ebden   Jarvis Creek   Georges Creek   Shelley   B400   Cudgewa   Highway
Murray   Lake Hume   Old Tallangatta   Bullioh   Berringama   Colac Colac   Thowgla
Tallangatta   Tallangatta East   Mount Sugarloaf   Bigg
C543   Huon   Highway   The Cascade   Lucyvale   Thowgla Up
Kiewa   Tangambalanga   B400   Yabba   Tallangatta Valley   McNamara Crossing   Mount Unicor

3

Sandy Creek   Fernvale   Noorongong   Wyeebo   Mount Cudgewa   Nariel Creek   Willow Crossing
Kergunyah   Gundowring North   Bullhead Creek   WABBA WILDERNESS PARK   Crawford Crossing   Hodgson Crossing
Sandy Creek Upper   Cravensville   Nariel   Stacey Bridge   M Ba
Kergunyah South   Gundowring   Tallandoon   Bucheen Creek   Mount Cravensville   C545   Mou Boebt

4

Dederang   Eskdale   Little Snowy Creek   C543   VICTORIA   Mount Benambra   Mount Pinnibar
Gundowring Upper   Mitta Mitta   Mount Misery   Dartmouth   ALPINE NATIONAL PARK   Mount Sassafras
Running Creek   Mount Tawonga   Granite Flat   Lake Dartmouth   Mount Gibbo   M Ar
Kancoona South   Coral Bank   Granite Peak
C543   Mount Yorke   Mount Martin

5

Mount Emu   Johnnies Top   Connleys Hut
Bright   Tawonga   Mount Bogong   Mount Cooper   Mount Misery
Germantown   **Mount Beauty**   ALPINE NATIONAL PARK   Mount Pendergra

6

Freeburgh   Clover Flat   Mount Arthur   Mount Wills   Sunnyside   Taylors Crossing   Mount Misery
Smoko   Bogong   C531   Mount Nelse   Glen Wills   Uplands   C545
Falls Creek   Glen Valley   The Brothers   Mount Leinster
Harrietville   Mount McKay   ALPINE NATIONAL PARK   Benambra

7

B500   Mount Hotham   C543   Lake Omeo   Mount Tambo
Mount Sugarloaf   Alpine   Hotham Heights   Anglers Rest   Highway   Hinnomunjie   Brumby Hill
B500   Slippery Pinch   Mount Cook   Mount Shaw

8

Mount Murray   Road   Mount George   **Omeo**   Mount Shaw   Bindi
ALPINE NATIONAL PARK   Mayford   Cobungra

N

0   50km

A   B   C   D   E   F

MAP 12 | *Camping* GUIDE TO **VICTORIA**

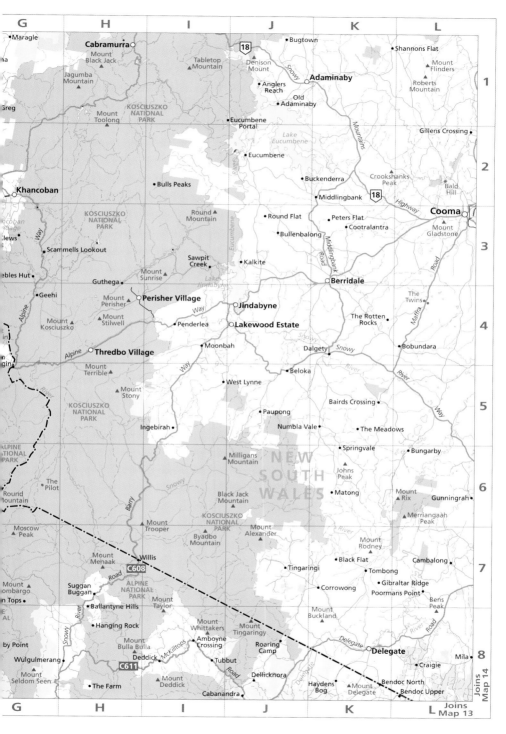

Maragle

Cabramurra ○

Mount Black Jack

Jagumba Mountain

Greg

Mount Toolong

KOSCIUSZKO NATIONAL PARK

Khancoban ○

ncoban age

lews

KOSCIUSZKO NATIONAL PARK

Scammells Lookout

Mount Sunrise

Guthega

ebles Hut

Geehi

Mount Perisher ○ Perisher Village

Mount Stilwell

Penderlea

Mount Kosciuszko

Alpine Way

Thredbo Village ○

Mount Terrible ▲

Mount Stony

in

gin

KOSCIUSZKO NATIONAL PARK

Ingebirah

ALPINE NATIONAL PARK

The Pilot

Round ountain

Moscow Peak ▲

Mount Trooper

KOSCIUSZKO NATIONAL PARK

Byadbo Mountain

Mount Alexander

Barry

Snowy

Mount Menaak ▲

Willis

C608

Mount ombargo

n Tops

Suggan Buggan

ALPINE NATIONAL PARK

Mount Taylor

Ballantyne Hills

Hanging Rock

Mount Bulla Bulla

Deddick

C611

McKillops

Mount Deddick

by Point

Wulgulmarang

Mount Seldom Seen

The Farm

Cabanandra

Bugtown

18

Denison Mount

Tabletop Mountain ▲

Anglers Reach

Adaminaby ○

Old Adaminaby

Eucumbene Portal

Eucumbene

Lake Eucumbene

Bulls Peaks

Round ▲ Mountain

Sawpit Creek

Kalkite

Lake Jindabyne

Jindabyne ○

Lakewood Estate ○

Moonbah

West Lynne

Milligans Mountain ▲

Black Jack Mountain

NEW SOUTH WALES

Mount Whittakers

Amboyne Crossing

Tubbut

Dellicknora

Buckenderra

Middlingbank

Round Flat

Bullenbalong

Berridale ○

Paupong

Numbla Vale

Beloka

Dalgety

Bairds Crossing

Springvale

Johns Peak

Matong

Black Jack Mountain

Mount Buckland

Mount Tingaringy

Roaring Camp

Haydens Bog

18

Peters Flat

Cootralantra

The Rotten Rocks

Snowy River

Bobundara

The Meadows

Bungarby

Mount Rix

Mount Rodney

Black Flat

Tingaringi

Corrowong

Delegate

Mount Delegate ▲

Shannons Flat

Mount Flinders

Roberts Mountain

Gillens Crossing

Crookshanks Peak

Bald Hill

Cooma ○

Mount Gladstone

The Twins

Maffra

Highway

Gunningrah

Merriangaah Peak

Cambalong

Tombong

Gibraltar Ridge

Poormans Point

Bens Peak

Delegate ○

Bendoc North

Bendoc Upper

Craigie

Mila

Middlingbank Road

Snowy River

Way

Delegate River

Road

Joins Map 14

Joins Map 13

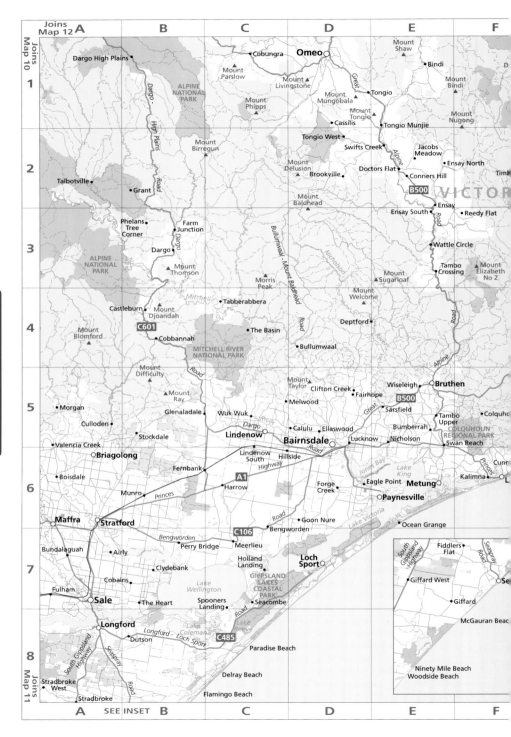

TOURING MAPS

A   B   C   D   E   F

1   2   3   4   5   6   7   8

Dargo High Plains

Cobungra

Omeo

Mount Shaw

Bindi

Mount Parslow

Mount Livingstone

Mount Bindi

Mount Mungobala

Tongio

Mount Nugong

ALPINE NATIONAL PARK

Mount Phipps

Mount Tongio

Tongio Munjie

Cassilis

Tongio West

Swifts Creek

Jacobs Meadow

Ensay North

Mount Birregun

Mount Delusion

Brookville

Doctors Flat

Conners Hill

Tim

Talbotville

Grant

Mount Baldhead

B500

Ensay

VICTOR

Ensay South

Reedy Flat

Phelans Tree Corner

Farm Junction

Wattle Circle

Dargo

ALPINE NATIONAL PARK

Mount Thomson

Morris Peak

Mount Sugarloaf

Tambo Crossing

Mount Elizabeth No 2

Mount Blomford

Castleburn

Mount Djoandah

C601

Cobbannah

Tabberabbera

MITCHELL RIVER NATIONAL PARK

The Basin

Bullumwaal

Mount Welcome

Deptford

Mount Difficulty

Mount Ray

Glenaladale

Wuk Wuk

Mount Taylor

Clifton Creek

Fairhope

Melwood

Wiseleigh

Bruthen

B500

Sarsfield

Morgan

Dargo

Calulu

Eliaswood

Bumberrah

Tambo Upper

Colquho

Culloden

Stockdale

Lindenow

Bairnsdale

Lucknow

Nicholson

COLQUHOUN REGIONAL PARK

Swan Reach

Valencia Creek

Lindenow South

Hillside

Jones Bay

Lake King

Cunn

Briagolong

Fernbank

Highway

Princes

Eagle Point

Metung

Kalimna

L

Boisdale

A1

Harrow

Forge Creek

Paynesville

Munro

Princes

Lake Victoria

Ocean Grange

Maffra

Stratford

Bengworden

C106

Goon Nure

Bengworden

Bundalaguah

Airly

Perry Bridge

Meerlieu

Loch Sport

Clydebank

Holland Landing

GIPPSLAND LAKES COASTAL PARK

Cobains

Lake Wellington

South Gippsland Highway

Fiddlers Flat

Seaspray Road

Fulham

Spooners Landing

Seacombe

Giffard West

Se

Sale

The Heart

Giffard

Longford

Lake Coleman

C485

McGauran Beac

Dutson

Longford - Loch Sport

Paradise Beach

Stradbroke West

Delray Beach

Ninety Mile Beach

Woodside Beach

Stradbroke

Flamingo Beach

A   SEE INSET   B   C   D   E   F

MAP 13 | Camping GUIDE TO VICTORIA

Wulgulmerang
Deddick
C611
Road
Tubbut
McKilltops
Delegate River
Craigie
NEW
SOUTH
WALES

1

Mount
Seldom Seen
Mount
Deddick
C611
Dellicknora
Haydens Bog
Mount
Delegate

Mount
Gelantipy
Cabanandra
Bendoc

SNOWY RIVER
NATIONAL PARK
Mount
Bendoc

Mount
Statham
Gelantipy
River
Mount
Bowen
Bonang
Mount
Tennyson

Glenmore

Butchers Ridge
Tulloch Ard
Mount
Joan
Granite
Mountain

C608

Mount
Jersey
Brown
Mountain
ERRINUNDRA
NATIONAL
PARK
Buldah

W Tree
River
Goongerah
Cobb
Hill

Three
Sisters

2

Murrindal
Mount
McLeod
Mount
Tabby
Mount
Ellery
Errinunda
High
Peak

Mount
inston
Mount
Sardine
C612
Combienbar

Buchan
Mount
Pinnak
Brodribb
Waldron
Mountain

3

Mount
Tara
Mount
Watt
Mount
Jack
Green
Road
Mount
Puggaree
Morris
Peak
Noorinbee

608
Orbost
Sandy Point
Mount
Buck
Bonang
Mount
Murrungowar
Combienbar
Club Terrace
LIND
NATIONAL
PARK
Highway
Cann
River

4

Stringer
Knob
Murrungowar
A1
Mount
Cann

Wairewa
Road
Orbost
Brodribb
River
BRODRIBB
FLORA
RESERVE
Cabbage
Tree Creek
Princes
Bellbird Creek

Waygara
Newmerella
Tabbara
Mount
Raymond
Coast
CROAJINGOLONG
NATIONAL PARK
Furnell

5

ostaree
Highway
Lake
Corringle
Old
CAPE CONRAN
COASTAL PARK
Bemm River
Tamboon

YERS
PARK
EWING MORASS
STATE GAME
RESERVE
Ninety Mile Beach
Marlo
Point
Ricardo
Cape Conran
Pearl Point
Tamboon
South

Bass Strait

6

Tasman Sea

7

0
50km

8

N

G H I J K L

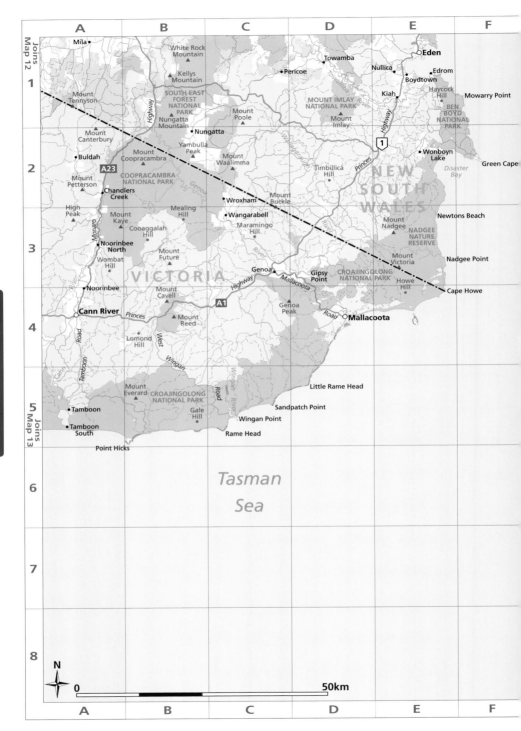

A · Mila

White Rock
Mountain

Towamba

Nullica · Eden

Kellys
Mountain

Pericoe

Edrom

Boydtown

Mount
Tennyson

SOUTH EAST
FOREST
NATIONAL
PARK

Kiah

Haycock
Hill

Mowarry Point

MOUNT IMLAY
NATIONAL PARK

BEN
BOYD
NATIONAL
PARK

Mount
Poole

Mount
Canterbury

Nungatta
Mountain

Mount
Imlay

Nungatta

· Buldah

A23

Mount
Petterson

Mount
Coopracambra

Yambulla
Peak

Mount
Waalimma

Timbillica
Hill

· Wonboyn
Lake

Disaster
Bay

Green Cape

Chandlers
Creek

COOPRACAMBRA
NATIONAL PARK

Genoa

NEW
SOUTH
WALES

High
Peak

Mealing
Hill

Wroxham

Mount
Buckle

Mount
Nadgee

Newtons Beach

Mount
Kaye

Wangarabell

Maramingo
Hill

NADGEE
NATURE
RESERVE

Cooaggalah
Hill

Mount
Victoria

Nadgee Point

Noorinbee
North

Mount
Future

River

VICTORIA

Genoa

Gipsy
Point

CROAJINGOLONG
NATIONAL PARK

Howe
Hill

Wombat
Hill

Mallacoota

Cape Howe

· Noorinbee

Mount
Cavell

Highway

Genoa
Peak

A1

Cann River

Princes

Mount
Reed

Road

Mallacoota

Road

Lomond
Hill

West

Wingan

Mount
Everard

CROAJINGOLONG
NATIONAL PARK

Road

Wingan

River

Little Rame Head

Sandpatch Point

· Tamboon

Gale
Hill

Wingan Point

· Tamboon
South

Rame Head

Point Hicks

Tasman

Sea

N

0   50km

MAP 14 | *Camping* GUIDE TO **VICTORIA**

Parks, Forests, Reserves and Campsites Index

* **Denotes areas with facilities (usually
special access to toilets) for people
with disabilities**

Campsite Index

L

M

Boiling Billy and

The Camping Guide to Victoria is just one of a growing series of outdoor and souvenir guides from Boiling Billy and Sydney co-publishers Woodslane.

Boiling Billy have been publishing guides for the Australian outdoor enthusiast for nearly 15 years, and details of all their titles can be found at www.boilingbilly.com.au. They are now co-publishing with Woodslane, one of Australia's leading book distributors and publishers. To browse through other titles available from Woodslane, visit www.woodslane.com.au. If your local bookshop does not have stock of a Boiling Billy or Woodslane book, they can easily order it for you. In case of difficulty please contact our customer service team on 02 9970 5111 or info@woodslane.com.au.

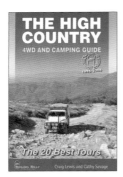

High Country 4WD & Camping Guide 2/e

4WD Tracks of the High Country will lead the reader through twenty of the best four-wheel drive touring destinations in the Victorian and New South Wales High Country. Packed with features, including the region's history, natural features and highlights, this guide is an indispensable travelling companion for those setting out to explore one of this country's most unique areas. Comprehensive route notes will keep you on track from start to finish.

Available now • **$29.95** • **ISBN-13:** 9781876296339

4WD Touring SE NSW & East Gippsland

Features 20 touring routes (in forward and reverse) with both GPS Lat/Long and UTM Grid References. NSW treks include: Pigeon House Mountain, No Name Trail, Monga National Park, Tallaganda Forest Tour, Deua National Park, Hanging Mountain, Tuross River Run, Wadbilliga Trail, Postmans Track, Wolumla Peak, Cow Bail Trail, Exploring the Far South, Blue Waterholes, Back Way to Talbingo. East Gippsland Treks include: The Playgrounds, Jacksons Crossing, Deddick Trail, WB Line and Croajingolong Coast.

Available now • **$24.95** • **ISBN-13:** 9781876296322

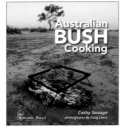

Australian Bush Cooking 3/e

From roasts to rissoles, salads to savouries and dampers to deserts, Australian Bush Cooking will help bring a tempting new twist to your camp cooking whether it's on an open fire, on a gas cooker or in your caravan or camper's kitchen. The easy and tempting recipes have all been planned for simplicity as well as good eating, using basic ingredients that are readily available Australia-wide, and all road tested by the authors in the great outdoors. Now in full colour, most of the recipes are illustrated as are many of the techniques and equipment the authors use whilst out on the road.

Available now • **$34.95** • **ISBN-13:** 9781921203930

Woodslane

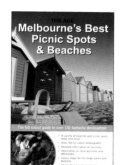

Melbourne's Best Picnic Spots & Beaches

Melbourne has some of the most beautiful parks and coastline in the world. There are many places to spread out a blanket or towel, unpack a hamper and soak up the great Australian outdoors, and in this book you'll find the very best of them. From the inner city to the outer suburbs and key areas beyond, Melbourne's Best Picnic Spots & Beaches includes over 100 great locations from the Dandenong's to Daylesford, and from Mornington to the Bellarine Peninsula. Illustrated with over 150 full-colour photos and detailed full-colour maps.

Available now • **$29.95** • **ISBN-13:** 9781921203237

Also Available

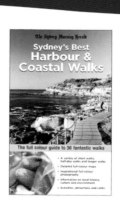

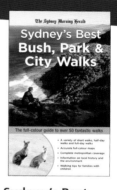

Sydney's Best Picnic Spots, Parks & Reserves

$29.95

ISBN: 9781921203879

Sydney's Best Beaches & Rock Baths

$29.95

ISBN: 9781921203367

Sydney's Best Harbour and Coastal Walks

$29.95

ISBN: 9781921203145

Sydney's Best Bush, Park & City Walks

$29.95

ISBN: 9781921203145

Your thoughts appreciated!

We do hope that you are enjoying using this book, and although we take great care we know that nothing in this world is perfect. Your suggestions for improving on this edition would be much appreciated.

Your name:

Your address or email address:

Your contact phone number:

Are you a resident or visitor to Victoria?

What you most liked about this book:

What you least liked about this book:

Which is your favourite campsite featured in this book?

Which campsite wasn't featured but you think should have been included?

Would you like us to keep you informed of other Boiling Billy books?
If so: are you interested in:

❏ camping

❏ 4WDriving

❏ national parks & reserves

❏ bushwalking

❏ activities in Victoria

❏ activities around Australia

What other books would you like to see from Boiling Billy Publications?

Please send your feedback to: Boiling Billy Publications, Locked Bag 1, Wyndham, NSW 2550.
Email: info@boilingbilly.com.au or go to our website feedback section at www.boillingbilly.com.au